Ecological
Literacy

Also in The Bioneers Series

Ecological Medicine: Healing the Earth, Healing Ourselves.
Edited by Kenny Ausubel with J. P. Harpignies

Nature's Operating Instructions: The True Biotechnologies.
Edited by Kenny Ausubel with J. P. Harpignies

Ecological Literacy

Educating Our Children for a Sustainable World

Edited by Michael K. Stone
and Zenobia Barlow

Foreword by David W. Orr
Preface by Fritjof Capra

Sierra Club Books
San Francisco

The Sierra Club, founded in 1892 by John Muir, has devoted itself to the study and protection of the earth's scenic and ecological resources—mountains, wetlands, woodlands, wild shores and rivers, deserts and plains. The publishing program of the Sierra Club offers books to the public as a nonprofit educational service in the hope that they may enlarge the public's understanding of the Club's basic concerns. The point of view expressed in each book, however, does not necessarily represent that of the Club. The Sierra Club has some sixty chapters throughout the United States. For information about how you may participate in its programs to preserve wilderness and the quality of life, please address inquiries to Sierra Club, 85 Second Street, San Francisco, California 94105, or visit our website at www.sierraclub.org.

Permission to reprint copyrighted or previously published material is acknowledged on pages 269–70.

Published by Sierra Club Books
85 Second Street, San Francisco, CA 94105
www.sierraclub.org/books

Sierra Club Books are published in association
with Counterpoint (www.counterpointpress.com).

SIERRA CLUB, SIERRA CLUB BOOKS, and the Sierra Club design logos
are registered trademarks of the Sierra Club.

Library of Congress Cataloging-in-Publication Data

Ecological literacy : educating our children for a sustainable world / edited by Michael K. Stone and Zenobia Barlow ; foreword by David W. Orr ; preface by Fritjof Capra.
p. cm. — (Bioneers series)
Includes bibliographical references.
ISBN 978-1-57805-153-3 (alk. paper)
1. Ecology—Study and teaching. 2. Environmental education. I. Stone, Michael K. II. Barlow, Zenobia. III. Series.
QH541.2.E238   2005
333.72'071—dc22   2005049908

Book and cover design by Lynne O'Neil
Cover art by Ernst Haeckel; from *Art Forms in Nature* (1899–1904)
Photographs © James Tyler

Printed in the United States of America on acid-free paper that contains a minimum of 30 percent post-consumer recycled fiber

First Edition
14   13   12   11   10
10   9   8   7   6   5

We dedicate this book to our teachers, the teachers in this book, and teachers everywhere whose expertise, commitment, and wisdom inspire in their students wonder and love for the world.

Contents

Part III. Relationship

Part IV. Action

A photo essay, "Ecological Literacy: Learning in Context," with photographs by James Tyler, follows p. 148.

Foreword

David W. Orr

THE MOST IMPORTANT DISCOVERY of the past two centuries is that we are joined in one fragile experiment, vulnerable to happenstance, bad judgment, shortsightedness, greed, and malice. Though divided by nation, tribe, religion, ethnicity, language, culture, and politics, we are comembers of one enterprise stretching back through time beyond memory, but forward no further than our ability to recognize that we are, as Aldo Leopold once put it, plain members and citizens of the biotic community. This awareness carries both an imperative and a possibility. The imperative is simply that we ought to pay full and close attention to the ecological conditions and prerequisites that sustain all life. That we seldom know how human actions affect ecosystems or the biosphere gives us every reason to act with informed precaution. And, because of the scale and momentum of the human presence on earth, it is utter foolishness to assert otherwise.

There is, too, the possibility that in the long gestation of humankind we acquired an affinity for life, earth, forests, water, soils, and place, what E. O. Wilson calls "biophilia." That is more than a defensible hypothesis—it is the best hope for our future that I know. For real hope, as distinguished from wishful thinking, we ought not look first to our technological cleverness or abstractions about progress of one kind or another, but rather to the extent and depth of our affections, which set boundaries to what we do and direct our intelligence to better or worse possibilities. The possibility of affection for our children, place, posterity, and life is in all of us. It is part of our evolutionary heritage. It is embedded in all of our best religious teachings. And it is now a matter of simple self-interest that we come to realize the full extent of the obligations that arise from an alert, thorough, and farsighted affection.

Perhaps biophilia helps to explain the rise of something that is beginning to look a great deal like a worldwide ecological enlightenment. The global transition to wind and solar energy systems has begun in earnest. Sustainable agriculture and forestry are gaining ground. The art and science of energy-efficient building is flourishing. The possibilities for transforming manufacturing and technology to mimic natural systems are revolutionary. The science of ecological healing and restoration has made significant progress. And the most exciting career opportunities that I know add the word "environmental" to fields such as design, planning, medicine, business, law, journalism, education, agriculture, and development. Small nongovernmental organizations such as the Center for Ecoliteracy, the Rocky Mountain Institute, Bioneers, Schumacher College, Ecotrust, the Jane Goodall Institute, and Ocean Arks are influential worldwide. The Internet is opening new possibilities for citizens of the world to cooperate, spread ideas, and hold governments accountable. Still, I think H. G. Wells had it right when he said that we are in a race between education and catastrophe. This race will be decided in all of the places, including classrooms, that foster ecological imagination, critical thinking, awareness of connections, independent thought, and good heart.

For its part, environmental education is becoming well established in nonprofit organizations, public agencies, schools, colleges, and universities. The words "environmental education," however, imply education about the environment, just another course or two, a curricular outbuilding to the big house of formal schooling where the really important things go on. We will have to aim toward a deeper transformation of the substance, process, and scope of education at all levels. The term "ecological literacy" identifies that goal, which is built on the recognition that:

- The disorder of ecosystems reflects a prior disorder of mind, making it a central concern to those institutions that purport to improve minds. In other words, the ecological crisis is in every way a crisis of education.

- The problem, as Wes Jackson once said of agriculture, is one *of* education, not merely *in* education.

- All education is environmental education ... by what is included or excluded we teach the young that they are part of or apart from the natural world.

- The goal is not just mastery of subject matter but making connections between head, hand, heart, and cultivation of the capacity to discern systems—what Gregory Bateson once called "the pattern that connects."

An ecologically literate person would have at least a basic comprehension of ecology, human ecology, and the concepts of sustainability, as well as the wherewithal to solve problems. Taken to its logical conclusion, the goal of making all of our students ecologically literate would restore the idea that education is first and foremost a large conversation with technical aspects, not merely a technical subject. Whatever the state of our pedagogical research, the life of the mind is and will remain a mysterious and serendipitous process only somewhat influenced by formal instruction (sometimes to no good effect). As a large conversation, we would restore to the subject of education the importance that every great philosopher from Plato, through Rousseau, to John Dewey and Alfred North Whitehead has assigned to it. Education, as they knew, had to do with the timeless question of how we are to live. And in our time the great question is how we will live in light of the ecological fact that we are bound together in the community of life, one and indivisible.

Preface:
How Nature Sustains the Web of Life

Fritjof Capra

THE TERM "SUSTAINABLE" has recently been so overused, and so often misused, that it is important to state clearly how we understand it at the Center for Ecoliteracy and how we use it in this book. A sustainable community is usually defined as "one that is able to satisfy its needs and aspirations without diminishing the chances of future generations." This is an important moral exhortation. It reminds us of our responsibility to pass on to our children and grandchildren a world with as many opportunities as the ones we inherited. However, this definition does not tell us anything about how to build a sustainable community. What we need is an operational definition of ecological sustainability.

The key to such an operational definition, and the good news for anyone committed to sustainability, is the realization that we do not need to invent sustainable human communities from scratch. We can learn from societies that have sustained themselves for centuries. We can also model human societies after nature's ecosystems, which *are* sustainable communities of plants, animals, and microorganisms. Since the outstanding characteristic of the biosphere is its inherent ability to sustain life, a sustainable human community must be designed in such a manner that its ways of life, technologies, and social institutions honor, support, and cooperate with nature's inherent ability to sustain life.

A first step in this endeavor must be to understand in some detail how nature sustains the web of life. How have ecosystems organized themselves to sustain the basic life processes over billions of years of evolution? How can they flourish with an abundance of energy and without waste? How does nature manufacture surfaces (in abalone shells) that are harder than our hardest high-tech ceramics and silk threads (spun by spiders) that, ounce for ounce, are five times stronger than steel? And how are these miracle materials produced silently, at ambient temperatures, and without any toxic by-products?

Education for sustainable living—the subject of the present book—is a pedagogy that facilitates this understanding by teaching the basic principles of ecology, and with them a profound respect for living nature, through an experiential, participatory, and multidisciplinary approach.

The systemic understanding of life that is now emerging at the forefront of science is based on three fundamental insights: life's basic pattern of organization is the network; matter cycles continually through the web of life; all ecological cycles are sustained by the continual flow of energy from the sun. These three basic phenomena—the web of life, the cycles of nature, and the flow of energy—are exactly the phenomena that children experience, explore, and understand through direct experiences in the natural world.

Through these experiences, we also become aware of how we ourselves are part of the web of life, and over time the experience of ecology in nature gives us a sense of place. We become aware of how we are embedded in an ecosystem; in a landscape with a particular flora and fauna; in a particular social system and culture.

There are many ways to experience nature and learn from her wisdom. Among the projects supported by the Center for Ecoliteracy and described in this book are stream restoration, watershed exploration, art and poetry, lunch programs built around fresh food, partnerships between farms and schools, and urban environmental justice.

One "classroom" that we have found to be especially appropriate for children is the school garden, which reconnects children to the fundamentals of food—indeed, to the fundamentals of life—while integrating and enriching virtually every activity that takes place at a school. When school gardens are made part of the curriculum, for instance, we learn about food cycles, and we integrate the natural food cycles into our cycles of planting, growing, harvesting, composting, and recycling. Through this practice, we also learn that the garden as a whole is embedded in larger systems that are again living networks with their own cycles. The food cycles intersect with these larger cycles—the water cycle, the cycle of the seasons, and so on—all of which are links in the planetary web of life.

In the garden, we learn that a fertile soil is a living soil containing billions of living organisms in every cubic centimeter. These soil bacteria carry out various chemical transformations that are essential to sustain life on earth. Because of the basic nature of the living soil, we need to preserve the integrity of the great ecological cycles in our practice of gardening and agriculture. This principle is embodied in many traditional farming methods, based on a profound respect for life, which are now being rediscovered in a worldwide renaissance of organic farming. The school garden is the ideal place to teach the merits of organic farming to children.

For children, most importantly, being in the garden is something magical. As one of our teachers put it, "one of the most exciting things about the garden is that we are creating a magical childhood place for children who would not have such a place otherwise, who would not be in touch with the earth and the things that grow. You can teach all you want, but being out there, growing and cooking and eating, that's an ecology that touches their heart and will remain important to them throughout their lives."

Education for sustainable living fosters both an intellectual understanding of ecology and emotional bonds with nature that make it more likely that our children will grow into responsible citizens who truly care about sustaining life, and develop a passion for applying their ecological understanding to the fundamental redesign of our technologies and social institutions, so as to bridge the current gap between human design and the ecologically sustainable systems of nature.

Acknowledgments

WE ARE, FIRST, PROFOUNDLY GRATEFUL to the contributors for allowing us to include their work here, and for their willingness to respond so diligently to our deadlines and requests for revisions in their manuscripts.

We owe much gratitude to Danny Moses, editor-in-chief of Sierra Club Books (SCB), for encouraging us to do this book. Many thanks also to SCB editors Kristi Hein and Diana Landau and to copyeditor Ellen F. Smith, who made the book more graceful and coherent.

We express our abiding appreciation to the Collective Heritage Institute (CHI), in particular our friends Kenny Ausubel and Nina Simons, and their collaborator J. P. Harpignies, for their stewardship of the Bioneers vision. We are grateful to them for inviting us early on to create an Ecoliteracy strand at the annual Bioneers Conference. That opportunity has provided the Center for Ecoliteracy (CEL) with a platform for reporting regularly on work in fostering ecological literacy and a place to exchange ideas with visionary educators from around the world.

We offer our sincere appreciation and affection to Bioneers managing director Ginny McGinn and also to CHI staff members Dylan Clear, Celeste DeMartini, Rey De Lupos, and Kelli Webster.

The ideas in this book emerged from the philanthropic initiatives of the Center for Ecoliteracy, and we offer special thanks to two cherished friends, CEL founding directors Fritjof Capra and Peter Buckley. They have dedicated themselves for more than a decade to realizing the Center's vision of educating our children for a sustainable world.

We acknowledge a rich web of thinkers and activists for their roles in the evolution of the ideas and practices reported in this book. We are especially grateful for the contributions of David W. Orr and Gay Hoagland, who joined our board of directors at its first meeting. We are also grateful to Michael Ableman, Jeannette Armstrong, Wendell Berry, Malcolm Margolin, and Alice Waters.

We created this book in part to honor the many educators whose expertise, wisdom, and risk-taking have shaped our understandings, and whose devotion has kept us motivated. The list is long, and we apologize to anyone whom we have neglected to name. Among those who have greatly influenced us are Sherrin Bennett, Marilyn Briggs, Jeanne Casella, Linda Chittenden, Ed Clark, Esther Cook, Rafaelita Curva, Grant Davis, Ann Evans, Kathie Fisher, Josie Gerst, Marsha Guerrero, John Harter, Ruth Hicks, Maurice Holt, Dana Lanza, Jerry Kay, Karen Kent, Ken Matheson, Nancy May, Pamela Michael, Jacob Moody, Sandy Neumann, Binet Payne, Laurette Rogers, Stephen Rutherford, Leah Smith, Neil Smith, Susie Stewart, Dee Uyeda, Sandy Wallenstein, Constance Washburn, and the faculty members at the exemplary schools in our networks. We are especially grateful to Jan Austin and Juan Carlos Collins, who shared their insights in extended conversations that helped us clarify our thinking as we worked on the book.

We acknowledge the community of Berkeley, its mayor, Tom Bates, the board of the Berkeley Unified School District (BUSD), Superintendent Michele Lawrence, the members of the Child Nutrition Advisory Committee, and all the parents, BUSD staff, community gardeners, and others who have displayed such dogged willingness to step into untested waters, and such commitment to innovation and transformation of our "home town" schools. Our work has been enriched as well by collaboration with administrators and teachers in the school districts of Marin, Mendocino, Sonoma, and Yolo Counties.

This book would not have been completed without the support and contributions of our colleagues at the Center for Ecoliteracy. We thank Janet Brown, Karen Brown, Margo Crabtree, Misa Koketsu, Jim Koulias, Wendy Ledger, Sara Marcellino, Eric Wallinger, Nobuko Yamada, and our photographer, James Tyler.

We also acknowledge our gratitude to the funding partners who have joined the Center for Ecoliteracy in supporting projects and school communities that showed promise for transforming education: Arkay Foundation, The Bay Institute of San Francisco, Berkeley Unified School District, California Department of Education, The California Endowment, California Nutrition Network, Chez Panisse Foundation, Columbia Foundation, Community Food Security Coalition, East Bay Community Foundation, Funders for Sustainable Food Systems, Gellert Foundation, Greenville Foundation, Clarence E. Heller Charitable Trust, Roy A. Hunt Foundation, W. K. Kellogg Foundation, Marin Community Foundation, National Farm to Schools Program, Rose Foundation, Small Planet Fund, Sustainable Agriculture and Food Systems Funders, United States Department of Agriculture, and Bernard E. and Alba Witkin Charitable Trust.

Finally, we bow deeply to our significant others, Patricia Perry and James Tyler, who put up with us when this project's various stresses (self-inflicted or otherwise) left us less than gracious or not fully present. They cheered us on, kept us steady, helped us keep this project in perspective, and buoyed us with their odd but contagious senses of humor, while tending more than their share of the home fires so that we could complete this book. Our gratitude is beyond words.

—M.K.S. and Z.B.

Introduction

Zenobia Barlow and Michael K. Stone

THIS BOOK HARVESTS THE FRUITS of a decade's labor in addressing essential questions: How do we cultivate in children the competencies of heart and mind that they will need to create sustainable communities? How can we design schools as "apprenticeship communities" that model the practice of living sustainably?

Here you will find a selection of perspectives from theorists, activists, and educators who are deeply engaged in answering these questions. We chose these writers for their knowledge and commitment to transforming education in order, as David W. Orr says, "to open young minds to the forgotten connections between people, places, and nature." These stories and essays offer a glimpse of the results at year ten in an ongoing experiment undertaken by the Center for Ecoliteracy (CEL), a public foundation that supports education for sustainability. Many of these essays began as presentations at the annual Bioneers Conference, at which, for many years, the Center has reported on its work.

The Center for Ecoliteracy is located in Berkeley, California. Its offerings include books, teaching guides, professional development seminars, a sustainability leadership academy, keynote presentations, and consulting services. The Center was founded in 1995 by Peter Buckley, a philanthropist with a deep passion and concern for the environment and the education of children; Fritjof Capra, an esteemed physicist, systems thinker, and author; and Zenobia Barlow, then director of an ecological think tank that was founded by Fritjof to address problems in business and education from the perspective of systems thinking.

1

These three founding directors invited David W. Orr and Gay Hoagland to join them to create CEL's board. David, a professor of environmental sciences at Oberlin College, had recently written *Ecological Literacy: Education and the Transition to a Postmodern World*. Gay was then the executive director of the Coalition for Essential Schools in the Bay Area, an innovative group attempting to bring equitable policies and participatory community to high schools.

When the CEL board met for the first time, in the course of an hour's talk it identified most of the elements that still guide the Center's work. Fritjof advocated teaching ecological knowledge and systems thinking—which views phenomena as wholes rather than parts and emphasizes relationships, connectedness, and context. Peter stressed the need to produce tangible outcomes leading to systemic change. Gay pointed out the need for leadership with a clear vision and recognition that change is an organic process occurring within the context of whole schools. David emphasized understanding the physical and biological patterns and cultural wisdom of particular places. Zenobia spoke for including a reverence for life and nurturing networks of relationships to carry a shared vision to fruition.

The Center's birth at this place and time can also be traced to two factors. First, its geographical base is at a confluence of the terrestrial, marine, and freshwater ecosystems of the San Francisco Bay/Delta—providing vibrant contexts for immersing children in the natural world. Second, the San Francisco Bay Area had recently become a fertile ground in which a "systemic school reform" movement was blossoming. Educators were discovering that children's ability to learn and, to a large degree, *what* they learn are greatly affected by the culture of the school: the networks of relationships, the quality of shared leadership, and the decision-making processes that influence both the children's academic achievement and their well-being. These reformers recognized that achievement depends as much on the vitality and health of the whole culture of the school as on the selection of textbooks, certification of curricula, or prescription of subject matter.

The school reform movement resonated with our desire to apply what Fritjof Capra, eco-philosopher Joanna Macy, author and consultant to business and education Meg Wheatley, and others were saying about leadership and systems change. For example, in his essay, "Speaking Nature's Language" (in Part I in this book), Fritjof describes a needed shift from structures to processes. Proponents of systemic school reform were calling for just such a shift—from hierarchical decision-making to shared leadership; from seeing teachers as experts to seeing them as facilitators.

The Center began by exploring ways in which a systems approach could provide fertile ground for teaching ecological understanding. Early efforts focused on districtwide experiments in schools and dialogues with leaders in school reform.

Nature sustains life by creating networks. We understood that to solve problems in enduring ways, people addressing different parts of the problem would benefit from being brought together in networks of support and conversation to establish conditions from which innovation can emerge. Rather than simply funding isolated projects, CEL began early on to convene networks of its grantees. This encouraged the exchange of resources, inspired creativity, and provided a context for teaching ecological knowledge and systems thinking to teams of educators.

Our working hypothesis said that applying key concepts of systems thinking will lead to sustainable change in education. To test this, we scouted for schools that (1) functioned as whole communities; (2) expressed the spirit of systemic school reform; (3) were committed to teaching ecological knowledge through project-based learning linked to particular places (CEL took care to include school sites in urban, suburban, and rural communities); and (4) desired to integrate their curriculum through school gardens, habitat restoration, or work with energy, shelter, or environmental justice programs.

Our first grantee schools—several of which are described in this book—included Martin Luther King Middle School in Berkeley, site of The Edible Schoolyard founded by restaurateur and food systems activist Alice Waters; Brookside School in suburban Marin County, site of the Freshwater Shrimp Project; César Chavez School in San Francisco, an innovator in school gardens and community involvement; and Laytonville, a whole school district in rural Mendocino County dedicated to environmental place-based education.

Sustained institutional change in public education can take a decade or more, yet the environments in which change happens are fluid and dynamic. Superintendents move to new districts every three to five years, on average. Parents shift their attention as their children mature and move through the grades. We soon realized that to be effective change agents we would need to shift nimbly among the different levels of scale in the system—from individual schools to districts and then to the communities and regions in which schools are embedded. One or another level can break down or experience obstacles: a school district may face financial challenges; key leaders can retire; state or federal education policy may go through a sea change. But, just as dynamic balance is maintained in living systems, networks of relationships give stability and resiliency to social systems in the midst of continual change.

As a philanthropic organization, we have watched for opportunities to develop strategic alliances—and unexpected alliances have sometimes developed through the networks we have nurtured; for example:

- The food service director for an urban high school and the director of the organic farm at nearby Santa Rosa Junior College (SRJC) first met in a carpool to a CEL network gathering. The upshot of their meeting was the creation of an innovative solution to the school district's need for affordable organic produce: contract farming, in which students at the SRJC program in agroecology grow crops specifically for sale to the school food service, to the benefit of both.

- Through a strategic alliance with The Bay Institute of San Francisco, the Freshwater Shrimp Project at Brookside School morphed into Students and Teachers Restoring a Watershed (STRAW)—a cluster of more than thirty schools, a hundred educators, and businesses, government agencies, and NGOs, all restoring miles of creek bed on agricultural land. And while writing a profile of STRAW for *Whole Earth* magazine in 2001, educator and editor Michael K. Stone learned of CEL's work; he joined the staff in 2004 as senior editor and served as coeditor of this book.

- Our collaboration with Alice Waters, the Chez Panisse Foundation, and The Edible Schoolyard at Martin Luther King Middle School inspired a Food Systems Project, which led to the creation of a Food Service Directors' Roundtable, a Fertile Crescent Network of CEL grantees and their partners and allies in a six-county agricultural region around the Bay Area, and eventually to a Rethinking School Lunch project.

As we immersed ourselves in the life of communities and ecosystems, important strategies began to emerge. Through our collaboration with STRAW, we became acutely aware of a nationwide phenomenon: family farms on the urban edge were going out of business for want of a market. We also knew that city kids around San Francisco Bay were going to school hungry. A map of regional problems that we were using in presentations at that time highlighted the problem of urban fringe farms at risk in rural western Marin County. On the same map, we had also identified problems we regularly encountered in the densely urban areas of San Francisco and the East Bay: malnutrition, solid waste generated by students throwing away their lunches, underachievement, and vandalism. Seeing all these together on the map, we recognized them not as isolated problems, but parts of one overarching problem of *disconnection*: of rural communities from urban life, of food from people's understanding of its origins, of health from the environment—and of problems from the patterns that perpetuate them.

As we began to recognize other disconnections, David W. Orr introduced us to Wendell Berry's essay "Solving for Pattern" (in Part I). Berry had brilliantly analyzed and put into words a problem-solving methodology that we had already begun to intuit and to adopt as our own. *Solving for pattern* became one of CEL's important guide stars (see "Sustainability—A New Item on the Lunch Menu" in Part IV).

Another key strategy emerged through collaborations with organizations that share CEL's mission. The impact of CEL's work has been magnified many times by partnerships with individuals, private foundations, academic institutions, and government and nongovernmental organizations at the local, state, and national level; we name many of these with gratitude in the Acknowledgments.

In the course of our work, it has become clear that there is no one-size-fits-all "sustainability curriculum"; thus, the projects described in this book often don't yield explicit step-by step directions for replicating them in other settings. We have discovered that successful programs don't necessarily replicate, but rather *migrate*, as educators, parents, and community activists are inspired by them to seek solutions that solve for pattern in their own situations. For instance, as Marilyn Briggs reports in her essay "Rethinking School Lunch" (in Part IV), CEL's approach of building networks and providing resources inspires the migration of program strategies. For readers inspired by the stories told here, the Resources section of this book provides detailed information on the organizations, books, and articles.

The wisdom of indigenous people, one invaluable foundation for CEL's work, has also inspired the organization of this book. The book's four parts represent four perspectives on attaining sustainability, drawn from the En'owkin process of the Okanagan people of British Columbia.

Jeannette Armstrong, an Okanagan wisdom keeper and a longtime colleague and friend, introduced this understanding to CEL. As Jeannette explains in her essay "En'owkin" (which opens Part I), when the Okanagan community faces a decision, each of its members is responsible for articulating the vital concerns of one of four societal perspectives—"Youth," "Elders," "Mothers," and "Fathers." In this way, the process ensures that the decision takes into consideration the needs of the whole community, which is understood to include the natural world.

The En'owkin practice and terminology are grounded in a centuries-old culture and belief system unfamiliar to nonnative people; for example, terms such as "Elders" and "Mothers" are English renderings of much more complex concepts. So we asked Jeannette to help us translate these Okanagan terms into language and practices more familiar in the settings where we work. In this translation, which Jeannette terms "The Four Societies Process," the Okanagan "societies"—Youth, Elders, Mothers, and Fathers—are expressed as perspectives that we call respectively "Vision," "Tradition/Place," "Relationship," and "Action."

- *Vision*, represented by the writings in Part I, takes long views into consideration. Concerned more with what is possible than with the practical aspects of how to get there, Vision focuses on a sustainable future through new ideas, innovations, and creative possibilities.

- *Tradition / Place*, found in Part II, is the perspective concerned with preserving traditional ways of life that are threatened by so-called progress and development. This perspective weighs each decision for its compatibility with the community's history and values and its potential impact on the land. "Land" here includes not only nonhuman "relatives" living there but a "vast and ancient body of intricately connected patterns, operating in perfect unison" (see "En'owkin").

- The *Relationship* perspective, represented in Part III, considers a decision's impact on other people, reminding us that the community's health depends on each of its members' being adequately fed, sheltered, secure, and justly treated. Viewing the world from this perspective means caring that all people are known by others, recognized for their contributions to the community, and included in the decisions that affect them.

- From the *Action* perspective, which characterizes the writings in Part IV, results matter, and decisions result from strategies that assess costs, obstacles, and the community's resources.

When the concerns of *all* perspectives are heard, the community is better able to arrive at a whole-system solution. For example, while someone with the Vision perspective may ask what the long-term results of a solution should look like, a person with the Action perspective is more likely to say, "What do we do first? What do we do after that? Who's going to pay for it?"

"Revolution Step-by-Step: On Building a Climate for Change" in Part III provides an example. Alice Waters, seeing King School from the Vision perspective, presents a beautiful, inspiring, and absolutely essential image of integrated gardening and cooking curricula for every school in the country. Meanwhile, King's principal, Neil Smith, looking at the school from the Action perspective, sees a broken-down asphalt lot in an urban middle school and asks an equally necessary question: "How can I convince people that we could turn this lot into a garden?" The ultimate success of The Edible Schoolyard depended on both Alice's envisioning and Neil's active problem solving.

We have chosen to organize the book around these four perspectives for several reasons. First, we want to honor Jeannette Armstrong and the Okanagan people and acknowledge how much they have shaped CEL's perception of education for sustainable communities. Second, we acknowledge this decision-making approach as a beautifully realized and useful representation of wholeness. Further, the recognition that a community has not really examined an issue until it has considered all four perspectives—and that its efforts will probably founder unless it addresses the concerns of all four—is one of the simplest, and simultaneously deepest, strategies we can imagine. Finally, grouping the essays into these perspectives underscores for readers the effectiveness of these perspectives as a tool for recognizing how people approach problems differently and why different people sometimes can't seem to communicate.

These perspectives are, of course, constructs, conceptual tools to help us remember to think in whole-systems terms. And they also provide an inspiring vision of the diversity and interdependence that keep whole systems healthy and resilient and that make possible sustainable societies.

A commitment to engaging whole systems, symbolized by the book's organization, has guided the Center for Ecoliteracy's work for the past decade, as we have identified processes by which ecosystems sustain life and by which communities of schools sustain learning, and as we have encouraged the migration of the innovative solutions that arise when those processes are combined. These efforts have led to some of the most satisfying work we have ever done. We offer this book in the hope that what we have learned will inspire people around the world who share our commitment to education for sustainability that engages teachers and students in processes that are relevant, fertile, stimulating, and alive.

Vision

En'owkin: Decision-Making as if Sustainability Mattered

Jeannette C. Armstrong

Jeannette Armstrong's influence on the Center for Ecoliteracy actually began a few years before CEL's founding, when she led a think-tank dialogue on "Native Thinking and Social Transformation" that Zenobia Barlow had convened between native and nonnative activists and thinkers. Armstrong is an Okanagan Indian, born on the Penticton Indian Reserve in British Columbia, where she has lived most of her life. Barlow recalls:

> *In the way that she introduced herself and engaged other people to deepen and shift the way that they communicated, I knew that she was viewing the world in a powerful way that I wanted to learn more about.*
>
> *When she introduced herself, she talked about her heritage and what she was responsible for, and challenged everyone to say authentically who they were. "Don't tell me what books you've written or what your accomplishments are," she said. "Tell me who your grandparents were"—because it was through her grandparents, the names they had given her, and the meaning of those names, that she understood her responsibilities for taking care of other people and all life forms. She wanted to know where we'd come from, who our elders were, what we had inherited, and what our responsibilities were. She changed the dynamic of that meeting. Many of the participants, famous people and established writers who had known each other for a long time, introduced themselves to one another as if for the first time and began to communicate with each other in a much deeper way.*

The following year, Barlow and Armstrong collaborated to convene a gathering of forty leading thinkers and activists for a four-day adaptation of an Okana-

11

gan ceremonial council, facilitated by Native American leaders, based on the
En'owkin decision-making process that Armstrong describes here. She called this
adaptation "The Four Societies Process"; it divided the participants into "societies"
representing the perspectives of vision, tradition/land (or place), relationship, and
action. (These perspectives have continued to inform CEL's decision-making and understanding of community dynamics, and inspired the organization of this book.) Since
1992, Armstrong and Barlow, along with Armstrong's husband, Marlowe Sam,
and CEL staff, have annually conducted Four Societies Processes to introduce this
process, which is steeped in sustainability principles, to educators, school teams, and
projects supported by the Center. Armstrong has acted as an advisor to CEL, providing insight into evolving educational strategies and a conceptual framework from
the perspective of a community that has sustained itself on the same land and resource
base for millennia.

Armstrong is executive director of the En'owkin Centre in Penticton (see
"Okanagan Education for Sustainable Living" in Part II). Her many books include
the novels Whispering in Shadows (2000) and Slash (1985), as well as Breath-
tracks: A Collection of Poetry (1991) and The Native Creative Process (1986),
on which she collaborated with renowned architect Douglas Cardinal. She also
coedited We Get Our Living Like Milk from the Land (1994). She was appointed
as one of seven indigenous judges to the First Nations Court of Justice called by the
Chiefs of Ontario, and she has spoken at universities around the world and has been
a keynote speaker at the Bioneers Conference and the World Council of Churches.
She received Ecotrust's 2003 Buffett Award for Indigenous Leadership. She serves
currently on the Canadian Council for UNESCO.

TO THE OKANAGAN PEOPLE, as to all peoples practicing bioregional self-sufficient economies, the realization that the total community must
be engaged in order to attain sustainability comes as a result of surviving together for thousands of years. The practical aspects of willing teamwork within
a whole-community system clearly emerged from having to cooperate in order to survive. However, to me, the word "cooperation" is insufficient to describe the organic nature by which community members continue, well be-

yond necessity, to cultivate the principles basic to caretaking for one another and for other life forms.

To me the principles of the process seem simple, because they are so deeply embedded in me. I cannot see how community could operate other than within them. Through articulating them for others, though, I have come to discern the complexity and depth of their significance. It is also important to note what we can expect to result from practicing these life principles:

First, we can expect each person to fully appreciate that each *individual*, while singularly gifted, actualizes his or her full human potential only as a result of physical, emotional, intellectual, and spiritual well-being, and that those four aspects of existence are always contingent on external things.

Second, each person is one element of a transgenerational organism known as a *family*. Through this organism flows the powerful lifeblood of cultural transference designed to secure the highest probability of well-being for each generation.

Third, the family system is the foundation of a long-term living network called *community*. In its various configurations this network spreads its life force over centuries and across physical space, acquiring the collective knowledge needed to secure the well-being of all.

Finally, a community is the living process that interacts with the vast and ancient body of intricately connected patterns, operating in perfect unison, called *the land*. The land sustains all life and must be protected from depletion in order to ensure its health and ability to provide sustenance across generations. Much of our belief system, which celebrates life, is demonstrated in how "sharing with community" extends to our "relatives on the land"—the plants, fish, birds, and animals who share their lives with ours.

This idea of community, as understood by my ancestors, encompassed a complex holistic view of interconnectedness that demands our responsibility to everything we are connected to. Our traditional decision-making, grounded in this view, involves a specific process called "En'owkin." The word comes from the high language of the Okanagan people and has its origin in a philosophy perfected to nurture voluntary cooperation. The three syllables that make up the Okanagan word invoke an image of liquid being absorbed drop by single drop through the head (mind)—coming to understanding through a gentle integrative process.

The Okanagan people traditionally used this process when a choice confronted the community. I'm not saying that the process is still practiced in an intact form, but elements of it remain and have been carried forward, because we are still only two generations away from colonization. We use that process continuously in an informal way in our community, and at certain times we can engage it in a formal way.

When the community is faced with a decision, an elder asks the people to engage in En'owkin, requesting that each person contribute information about the subject at hand. What follows is not so much a debate as a process of clarification, incorporating bits of information from as many people as possible—no matter how irrelevant, trivial, or controversial these bits might seem—for in En'owkin, nothing is discarded or prejudged.

The process is deliberately designed not to seek resolution in the first stage. Instead, it seeks concrete information, inquiring how the decision might affect people and other things in both the long and short terms. Although persons with good analytical skills or special knowledge and spokespersons for individuals or families are usually given the opportunity to speak, anyone is welcome to speak, but only to add new information or insight.

The next stage of the process challenges the group to suggest possible resolutions, while remaining mindful of each of the concerns put forward by others. The challenge usually takes the form of questions put to the "elders," the "mothers," the "fathers," and the "youth."

Here, the term "elders" (or "land speakers") refers to those who are like-minded in protecting traditions and our connection to the land. The community seeks the elders' spiritual insight as a guiding force. "Elder" does not necessarily mean chronologically old. I was designated as an elder when I was a young woman, and was fortunate to be trained and brought up as a land speaker in my community. I was trained by elders to think about and speak about the land. I don't think of myself as an expert, but no matter what issue is being decided, it's my responsibility to stand up and ask how the decision is going to impact the land. How is it going to affect our food? How is it going to affect our water? If the land is affected, what will be the impact on my children, my grandchildren, and my great-grandchildren?

"Mothers" refers to those who are like-minded in their concern about the daily well-being of the family and of relationships within the community. The responsibility of mothers (who can be men) is to consider how a decision will impact various groups within the community: children, elders, mothers, working people, and so on. The community seeks from the mothers sound advice on policy and on workable systems based on human relations.

"Fathers" refers to those who are like-minded in their concern about the things necessary for security, sustenance, and shelter. Usually the community seeks practical strategy, logistics, and action from the fathers (who can be women). When the fathers stand up to answer those questions, they also give their views about what actions are necessary and how much these actions are going to cost. These speakers are given the responsibility of always reminding our people that actions are going to have consequences down the road.

"Youth" refers to those who are like-minded in their tremendous creative energy, as they yearn for change that will bring a better future. They are the visionaries in our community—the creative people, the artists and thinkers and performers. We always need to make room for newness because we need to be creative when we come up against something that we can't resolve or that we haven't faced before. Youth's responsibility is to apply their creative and artistic prowess to coming up with innovations, new approaches, and new ways to look at things.

En'owkin does not require a rigid meeting format. Rather, it is imperative that each person plays his or her strongest natural role. Speakers usually identify the role they've assumed by saying, for example, "I speak as a mother," before outlining the perspective that they understand that the mothers are being asked to contribute. Each role is valued as indispensable to the community. Stated and unstated ground rules of the process challenge each person to creatively include in his or her own thinking the concerns of all the others.

The point of the process is not for persons to persuade the community that they are right, as in a debate. Rather, the point is to bring each individual to understand as fully as possible the reasons for opinions opposite to his or hers. Each person is responsible for seeing the views, concerns, and reasons of others, because it is in each person's best interests that the decision addresses all the community's needs.

While the process does not mean that everyone agrees—for that is seldom possible—it does result in everyone's being fully informed while deciding what will take place and what each person will concede or contribute. The action finally chosen will be the best possible action, taking into consideration both the short-term concrete social needs and the long-term psychological and spiritual needs of the community. The elders describe this process as group mind at its best. The word they use means something like "our completeness."

It seems to me that the En'owkin process is even more useful in diverse groups, because there is a greater possibility of differing opinions. To my understanding, democracy in its current form, "majority rule," has embedded in it an adversarial approach. It sets up an oppression of the minority, a construct in which there's always going to be conflict. But in our tradition the minority voice is the *most important* voice to consider, because it is most likely to tell us what is going wrong, what we're not looking after, doing, or acting responsibly toward.

Modern *Robert's Rules of Order* decision-making, in carrying out the will of the majority, often creates great disparity and injustice for the minority, which in turn leads to division, polarity, and ongoing dissension. This type of process is in fact a way to guarantee the continuous hostility and division that give rise to aggressive actions that can destabilize the whole community and create uncertainty, distrust, and prejudice. Real democracy is not about power in numbers; it is about collaboration as an organizational system. Real democracy includes the right of the minority to a remedy, one that is unhampered by the tyranny of a complacent or aggressive majority.

I have noticed that when we include the perspective of the land and of human relationships in our decisions, people in the community change. Material things and all the worrying about matters such as money start to lose their power. When people realize that the community is there to sustain them, they have the most secure feeling in the world. The fear starts to leave, and they are imbued with hope. That's the kind of work that I'm involved in at the En'owkin Centre, building community in our region, and not just among indigenous people.

Our elders have said that unless we can "Okanaganize" the other folks around us, we're all in danger! Although it can seem to be an overwhelming task, I've seen that some of the things that seem everyday and obvious to us also make sense to more and more of the people I meet. We've brought into our community new friends who are now part of our En'owkin family and part of my extended community, and they have become caretakers with us of our land. They belong and become our aunties and uncles. We can depend on them and they on us. There is such an overwhelming hunger for that kind of belonging. There are more and more people who understand how we need to be with each other in order to be the way we need to be on the land. Imagine a future in which the human has attained its fullest potential. Imagine a world in which the good of each human being and each species is considered in every decision made.

Speaking Nature's Language:
Principles for Sustainability

Fritjof Capra

If anyone has learned to speak nature's language, it is Fritjof Capra. A founding director of the Center for Ecoliteracy and currently chair of its board, he has distinguished himself over the past forty years as a scientist, systems theorist, and explorer of the philosophical and social ramifications of contemporary science.

Introducing him to an overflow audience at a Bioneers Conference plenary, Kenny Ausubel said, "One of Fritjof Capra's greatest gifts is his ability to digest enormous amounts of information from highly complex, wide-ranging fields of inquiry. Not only does he explain them elegantly and clearly, but he distills their essence and sees their implications. Because he's a credentialed scientist who did his time with particle accelerators all over Europe and the United States, Fritjof never overstates his case or lapses into wishful thinking."

After receiving his Ph.D. in theoretical physics from the University of Vienna in 1966, Capra did research in particle physics at the University of Paris, the University of California at Santa Cruz, the Stanford Linear Accelerator Center, Imperial College of the University of London, and the Lawrence Berkeley Laboratory at the University of California. He also taught at UC Santa Cruz, UC Berkeley, and San Francisco State University.

He is the author of five international bestsellers: The Tao of Physics *(1975),* The Turning Point *(1982),* Uncommon Wisdom *(1988),* The Web of Life *(1996), and* The Hidden Connections *(2002). He coauthored* Green Politics *(1984),* Belonging to the Universe *(1991), and* EcoManagement *(1993), and coedited* Steering Business Toward Sustainability *(1995).*

He is on the faculty of Schumacher College, an international center for ecolog-

*ical studies in England, frequently gives management seminars for top executives,
and lectures widely to lay and professional audiences in Europe, Asia, and North
and South America. He is an enormously popular speaker, addressing audiences of
thousands, switching easily between German, French, English, Italian, and Spanish. The Center for Ecoliteracy's single greatest source of inquiries is people from as
far away as Brazil and India who find the CEL website by linking from Capra's.*

    *This essay distills thinking that has inspired the Center for Ecoliteracy and served
as its intellectual touchstone for a decade.*

AS I DISCUSSED IN THE PREFACE to this book, we can design sustainable societies by modeling them after nature's ecosystems. To understand
ecosystems' principles of organization, which have evolved over billions of
years, we need to learn the basic principles of ecology—the language of nature, if you will. The most useful framework for understanding ecology today
is the theory of living systems, which is still emerging and whose roots include
organismic biology, gestalt psychology, general system theory, and complexity
theory (or nonlinear dynamics). For more discussion of the theory of living systems and its implications, please see my book *The Hidden Connections*.

    What is a living system? When we walk out into nature, living systems
are what we see. First, *every living organism*, from the smallest bacterium to all
the varieties of plants and animals, including humans, is a living system. Second, *the parts of living systems* are themselves living systems. A leaf is a living
system. A muscle is a living system. Every cell in our bodies is a living system. Third, *communities of organisms*, including both ecosystems and human
social systems such as families, schools, and other human communities, are living systems.

    Thinking in terms of complex systems is now at the very forefront of sci-
ence. It is also very like the ancient thinking that enabled traditional peoples
to sustain themselves for thousands of years. But although the modern version of this intellectual tradition is almost a hundred years old, it has still not
taken hold in our mainstream culture. I've thought quite a lot about why people
find systems thinking so difficult and have concluded that there are two main
reasons. One is that living systems are nonlinear—they're networks—while

our whole scientific tradition is based on linear thinking—chains of cause and effect.

In linear thinking, when something works, more of the same will always be better. For instance, a "healthy" economy will show strong, indefinite economic growth. But successful living systems are highly nonlinear. They don't maximize their variables; they optimize them. When something is good, more of the same will not necessarily be better, because things go in cycles, not along straight lines. The point is not to be efficient, but to be sustainable. Quality, not quantity, counts.

We also find systems thinking difficult because we live in a culture that is materialist in both its values and its fundamental worldview. For example, most biologists will tell you that the essence of life lies in the macromolecules—the DNA, proteins, enzymes, and other material structures in living cells. Systems theory tells us that knowledge of these molecules is, of course, very important, but the essence of life does not lie in the molecules. It lies in the patterns and processes through which those molecules interact. You can't take a photograph of the web of life because it is nonmaterial—a network of relationships.

Perceptual Shifts

Because living systems are nonlinear and rooted in patterns of relationships, understanding the principles of ecology requires a new way of seeing the world and of thinking—in terms of *relationships, connectedness, and context*—that goes against the grain of traditional Western science and education. Such "contextual" or "systemic" thinking involves several shifts of perception:

From the parts to the whole. Living systems are integrated wholes whose properties cannot be reduced to those of their smaller parts. Their "systemic" properties are properties of the whole that none of the parts has.

From objects to relationships. An ecosystem is not just a collection of species, but is a community. Communities, whether ecosystems or human systems, are characterized by sets, or networks, of relationships. In the systems view, the "objects" of study are networks of relationships, embedded in larger networks. In practice, organizations designed according to this ecological principle are more likely than other organizations to feature relationship-based processes such as cooperation and decision-making by consensus.

From objective knowledge to contextual knowledge. The shift of focus from the parts to the whole implies a shift from analytical thinking to contextual thinking. The properties of the parts are not intrinsic, but can be understood only within the context of the whole. Since explaining things in terms of their contexts means explaining them in terms of their environments, all systems thinking is environmental thinking.

From quantity to quality. Understanding relationships is not easy, especially for those of us educated within a scientific framework, because Western science has always maintained that only the things that can be measured and quantified can be expressed in scientific models. It's often been implied that phenomena that can be measured and quantified are more important—and maybe even that what cannot be measured and quantified doesn't exist at all. Relationships and context, however, cannot be put on a scale or measured with a ruler.

From structure to process. Systems develop and evolve. Thus the understanding of living structures is inextricably linked to understanding renewal, change, and transformation.

From contents to patterns. When we draw maps of relationships, we discover certain configurations of relationships that appear again and again. We call these configurations "patterns." Instead of focusing on what a living system is made of, we study its patterns.

Here we discover a tension between two approaches to the study of nature that has characterized Western science and philosophy throughout the ages. One approach begins with the question: What is it made of? Traditionally, this has been called the study of matter. The other approach begins with the question: What is the pattern? And this, since Greek times, has been called the study of form.

In the West, most of the time, the study of matter has dominated in science. But late in the twentieth century, the study of form came to the fore again, with the emergence of systems thinking. Chaos and complexity theory are essentially theories of patterns. The so-called strange attractors of chaos theory are visual patterns that represent the dynamics of a certain chaotic system. The fractals of fractal geometry are visual patterns. In fact, the whole new mathematics of complexity is essentially the mathematics of patterns.

Some Implications for Education

Because the study of patterns requires visualizing and mapping, every time that the study of pattern has been in the forefront, artists have contributed significantly to the advancement of science. In Western science the two most famous examples are Leonardo da Vinci, whose whole scientific work during the Renaissance could be seen as a study of patterns, and the eighteenth-century German poet Goethe, who made significant contributions to biology through his study of patterns.

This opens the door for educators' integrating the arts into the curriculum. Whether we talk about literature and poetry, the visual arts, music, or the performing arts, there's hardly anything more effective than art for developing and refining a child's natural ability to recognize and express patterns.

Because all living systems share sets of common properties and principles of organization, systems thinking can be applied to integrate heretofore fragmented academic disciplines. Biologists, psychologists, economists, anthropologists, and other specialists all deal with living systems. Because they share a set of common principles, these disciplines can share a common framework.

We can also apply the shifts to human communities, where these principles could be called principles of community. Of course there are many differences between ecosystems and human communities. Not everything we need to teach can be learned from ecosystems. Ecosystems do not manifest the level of human consciousness and culture that emerged with language among primates and then came to flourish in evolution with the human species.

Sustainability in the Language of Nature

By applying systems thinking to the multiple relationships interlinking the members of the earth household, we can identify core concepts that describe the patterns and processes by which nature sustains life. These concepts, the starting point for designing sustainable communities, may be called principles of ecology, principles of sustainability, principles of community, or even the basic facts of life. We need curricula that teach our children these fundamental facts of life.

These closely related concepts are different aspects of a single fundamental pattern of organization: nature sustains life by creating and nurturing communities. Among the most important of these concepts, recognized from observing hundreds of ecosystems, are "networks," "nested systems," "interdependence," "diversity," "cycles," "flows," "development," and "dynamic balance."

Networks

Because members of an ecological community derive their essential properties, and in fact their very existence, from their relationships, sustainability is not an individual property, but a property of an entire network.

At the Center for Ecoliteracy, we understand that solving problems in an enduring way requires bringing the people addressing parts of the problem together in networks of support and conversation. Our watershed restoration work, for example (see "'It Changed Everything We Thought We Could Do'" in Part III), began with one class of fourth-graders concerned about an endangered species of shrimp, but the work continues today because it evolved into a network that includes students, teachers, parents, funders, ranchers, design and construction professionals, NGOs, and government bodies. Each part of the network makes its own contribution to the project, the efforts of each are enhanced by the work of all, and the network has the resilience to keep the project alive even when individual members leave or move on.

Nested Systems

At all scales of nature, we find living systems nesting within other living systems—networks within networks. Although the same basic principles of organization operate at each scale, the different systems represent levels of differing complexity.

Students working on the Shrimp Project, for example, discovered that the shrimp inhabit pools that are part of a creek within a larger watershed. The creek flows into an estuary that is part of a national marine sanctuary, which is included in a larger bioregion. Events at one level of the system affect the sustainability of the systems embedded in the other levels.

Within social systems such as schools, the individual child's learning experiences are shaped by what happens in the classroom, which is nested within the school, which is embedded in the school district and then in the surrounding school systems, ecosystems, and political systems. At each level phenomena exhibit properties that do not exist at lower levels. Choosing strategies to affect those systems requires simultaneously addressing the multiple levels and recognizing which strategies are appropriate for different levels. For instance (see "Sustainability—A New Item on the Lunch Menu" in Part IV), the Center recognized that changing schools' food systems required moving from working with individual schools to working at the district level and then to the larger educational and economic systems in which districts are nested.

Interdependence

The sustainability of individual populations and the sustainability of the entire ecosystem are interdependent. No individual organism can exist in isolation. Animals depend on the photosynthesis of plants for their energy needs; plants depend on the carbon dioxide produced by animals and on the nitrogen fixed by bacteria at their roots. Together, plants, animals, and microorganisms regulate the entire biosphere and maintain the conditions conducive to life.

Sustainability always involves a whole community. This is the profound lesson we need to learn from nature. The exchanges of energy and resources in an ecosystem are sustained by pervasive cooperation. Life did not take over the planet by combat but by cooperation, partnership, and networking. The Center for Ecoliteracy has supported schools such as Mary E. Silveira (see

"Leadership and the Learning Community" in Part III) that recognize and celebrate interdependence.

Diversity

The role of diversity is closely connected with systems' network structures.
A diverse ecosystem will be resilient because it contains many species with
overlapping ecological functions that can partially replace one another. When
a particular species is destroyed by a severe disturbance so that a link in the
network is broken, a diverse community will be able to survive and reorgan-
ize itself because other links can at least partially fulfill the function of the destroyed species. The more complex the network's patterns of interconnections
are, the more resilient it will be.

On the other hand, in communities lacking diversity, such as monocrop
agriculture devoted to a single species of corn or wheat, a pest to which that
species is vulnerable can threaten the entire ecosystem.

In human communities ethnic and cultural diversity may play the same
role as does biodiversity in an ecosystem. Diversity means many different relationships, many different approaches to the same problem. At the Center for
Ecoliteracy, we have discovered that there is no "one-size-fits-all" sustainability
curriculum. We encourage and support multiple approaches to any issue, with
different people in different places adapting the teaching of principles of ecology to differing and changing situations.

Cycles

Matter cycles continually through the web of life. Water, the oxygen in the
air, and all the nutrients are continually recycled. Communities of organisms
have evolved over billions of years, using and recycling the same molecules
of minerals, water, and air. Mutual dependence is much more existential in
ecosystems than in social systems because the members of an ecosystem actually eat one another. Ecologists recognized this from the very beginning of ecology. They focused on feeding relations and discovered the concept of the food

chain that we still use today. But then they realized that those are not linear chains but cycles, because the bigger organisms are eaten eventually by the decomposer organisms, the insects and bacteria, and so matter cycles through an ecosystem. An ecosystem generates no waste. One species' waste becomes another species' food. As I noted in the preface, one reason for the Center's enthusiasm for school gardens is the opportunity that gardens afford for even very young children to experience nature's cycles.

The lesson for human communities is obvious. A conflict between economics and ecology arises because nature is cyclical, while industrial processes are linear. Businesses transform resources into products plus waste, and sell the products to consumers, who discard more waste after consuming the products. The ecological principle "waste equals food" means that—if an industrial system is to be sustainable—all manufactured products and materials, as well as the wastes generated in the manufacturing processes, must eventually provide nourishment for something new. In such a sustainable industrial system, the total outflow of each organization—its products *and* wastes—would be perceived and treated as resources cycling through the system.

Flows

All living systems, from organisms through ecosystems, are open systems. Solar energy, transformed into chemical energy by the photosynthesis of green plants, drives most ecological cycles, but energy itself does not cycle. As it is converted from one form of energy to another (for instance, as the chemical energy stored in petroleum is converted into mechanical energy to drive the pistons of an automobile), some of it—often much of it—inevitably flows out and is dispersed as heat. We are therefore dependent on a constant inflow of energy.

A sustainable society would use only as much energy as it could capture from the sun—by reducing its energy demands, using energy more efficiently, and capturing the flow of solar energy more effectively through solar heating, photovoltaic electricity, wind, hydropower, biomass, and other forms of energy that are renewable, efficient, and environmentally benign. Among the complex reasons that the Center for Ecoliteracy promotes farm-to-school food programs (see "Rethinking School Lunch" in Part IV) is that buying food grown close by reduces the unrenewable energy that is required to ship tons of food over thousands of miles to supply school lunches.

Development

All living systems develop, and all development invokes learning. During its development, an ecosystem passes through a series of successive stages, from a rapidly growing, changing, and expanding pioneer community to slower ecological cycles and a more stable fully exploited ecosystem. Each stage in this ecological succession represents a distinctive community in its own right.

At the species level, development and learning are manifested as the creative unfolding of life through evolution. In an ecosystem, evolution is not limited to the gradual adaptation of organisms to their environment, because the environment is itself a network of living organisms capable of adaptation and creativity.

Individuals and environment adapt to one another—they coevolve in an ongoing dance. Because development and coevolution are nonlinear, we can never fully predict or control how the processes that we start will turn out. Small changes can have profound effects. For instance, growing their own food in a school garden can open students to the delight of tasting fresh healthy food, which can create an opportunity to change school menus, which can create a systemwide market for fresh food, which can help sustain local family farms.

On the other hand, nonlinear processes can lead to unanticipated disasters, as occurred with DDT and the development of "superorganisms" resistant to antibiotics, and as some scientists fear could happen with genetic modification of organisms. A sustainable society will exercise caution about committing itself to practices with unknown outcomes. In "The Slow School" (in

Part I), Maurice Holt describes the unforeseen consequences of schools' wholesale commitment to standards-measurement techniques derived from manufacturing and industry.

Dynamic Balance

All ecological cycles act as feedback loops, so that the ecological community continually regulates and organizes itself. When one link in an ecological cycle is disturbed, the entire cycle brings the situation back into balance, and since environmental changes and disturbances happen all the time, ecological cycles continually fluctuate.

These ecological fluctuations take place between tolerance limits, so there is always the danger that the whole system will collapse when a fluctuation goes beyond those limits and the system can no longer compensate for it. The same is true of human communities. Lack of flexibility manifests itself as stress. Temporary stress is essential to life, but prolonged stress is harmful and destructive to the system. These considerations lead to the important realization that managing a social system—a company, a city, or an economy—means finding the *optimal* values for the system's variables. Trying to maximize any single variable instead of optimizing it will invariably lead to the destruction of the system as a whole.

Every living system also occasionally encounters points of instability (in human terms, points of crisis or of confusion), out of which new structures, forms, and patterns spontaneously emerge. This spontaneous emergence of order is one of life's hallmarks and is where we see that creativity is inherent in life at all levels.

One of the most valuable skills for utilizing ecological understanding is the ability to recognize when the time is right for the emergence of new forms and patterns. For example, out of frustration with the failure of piecemeal hunger intervention to have much long-term impact, "community food security" programs are emerging across the country. This movement addresses the overall systems—from energy and transportation to government commodities purchasing to the effect of media on children's food preferences—that permit communities to meet (or prevent them from meeting) their needs for nutritious, safe, acceptable food.

It is no exaggeration to say that the survival of humanity will depend on our ability in the coming decades to understand these principles of ecology and to live accordingly. Nature demonstrates that sustainable systems are possible. The best of modern science is teaching us to recognize the processes by which these systems maintain themselves. It is up to us to learn to apply these principles and to create systems of education through which coming generations can learn the principles and learn to design societies that honor and complement them.

Solving for Pattern

Wendell Berry

We are grateful to David W. Orr for introducing us to "Solving for Pattern," from Wendell Berry's The Gift of Good Land *(1982). In this essay, Berry beautifully articulates what the Center for Ecoliteracy had previously sensed, but did not have the vocabulary to describe. Within a few pages, he describes a way of agriculture—a way, really, of life—grounded in the ecological processes enumerated by Fritjof Capra in the previous essay. Nested systems, interdependence, diversity, cycles, flows, and dynamic balance are all invoked here, though not always by those names.*

CEL has especially taken two key concepts from this essay. The first is embedded in the title. The projects described in this book (STRAW, the Food Systems Project, Rethinking School Lunch, Literacy for Environmental Justice, and so on) share an assumption that long-lasting change requires looking beyond "problems" to the patterns that connect them.

Second is the insight that the criterion for the success of solutions and systems is health, particularly the health of land and the health of communities. Health, wholesome, holy, and wholeness, which are of course related etymologically, remain the surest tests of a system's sustainability.

Wendell Berry farms in Henry County, Kentucky, where his family has lived and worked the land for more than two hundred years. For many years he contributed regularly to The New Farm *magazine, where a version of this essay first appeared more than twenty years ago. He is an honored writer who excels as an essayist, as a poet, and as a novelist. He is one of America's most eloquent defenders of rural communities and small-scale family farms. As he says in the foreword to* The Gift of Good Land, *"[The small farm's] justification is not only agricultural, but is part of an ancient pattern of values, ideas, aspirations, attitudes, faiths, knowledges, and skills that propose and support the sound establishment of a people on a*

30

land. To defend the small farm is to defend a large part, and the best part, of our cultural inheritance."

OUR DILEMMA IN AGRICULTURE NOW is that the industrial methods that have so spectacularly solved some of the problems of food production have been accompanied by "side effects" so damaging as to threaten the survival of farming. Perhaps the best clue to the nature and the gravity of this dilemma is that it is not limited to agriculture. My immediate concern here is with the irony of agricultural methods that destroy, first, the health of the soil and, finally, the health of human communities. But I could just as easily be talking about sanitation systems that pollute, school systems that graduate illiterate students, medical cures that cause disease, or nuclear armaments that explode in the midst of the people they are meant to protect. This is a kind of surprise that is characteristic of our time: the cure proves incurable; security results in the evacuation of a neighborhood or a town. It is only when it is understood that our agricultural dilemma is characteristic not of our agriculture but of our time that we can begin to understand why these surprises happen and to work out standards of judgment that may prevent them.

To the problems of farming, then, as to other problems of our time, there appear to be three kinds of solutions.

There is, first, the solution that causes a ramifying set of new problems, the only limiting criterion being, apparently, that the new problems should arise beyond the purview of the expertise that produced the solution—as, in agriculture, industrial solutions to the problem of production have invariably caused problems of maintenance, conservation, economics, community health, etc., etc.

If, for example, beef cattle are fed in large feed lots, within the boundaries of the feeding operation itself a certain factory-like order and efficiency can be achieved. But even within those boundaries that mechanical order immediately produces biological disorder, for we know that health problems and dependence on drugs will be greater among cattle so confined than among cattle on pasture.

And beyond those boundaries, the problems multiply. Pen feeding of cattle in large numbers involves, first, a manure-removal problem, which becomes at some point a health problem for the animals themselves, for the local watershed, and for the adjoining ecosystems and human communities. If the manure is disposed of without returning it to the soil that produced the feed, a serious problem of soil fertility is involved. But we know too that large concentrations of animals in feed lots in one place tend to be associated with, and to promote, large cash-grain monocultures in other places. These monocultures tend to be accompanied by a whole set of specifically agricultural problems: soil erosion, soil compaction, epidemic infestations of pests, weeds, and disease. But they are also accompanied by a set of agricultural-economic problems (dependence on purchased technology; dependence on purchased fuels, fertilizers, and poisons; dependence on credit)—and by a set of community problems, beginning with depopulation and the removal of sources, services, and markets to more and more distant towns. And these are, so to speak, only the first circle of the bad effects of a bad solution. With a little care, their branchings can be traced on into nature, into the life of the cities, and into the cultural and economic life of the nation.

The second kind of solution is that which immediately worsens the problem it is intended to solve, causing a hellish symbiosis in which problem and solution reciprocally enlarge one another in a sequence that, so far as its own logic is concerned, is limitless—as when the problem of soil compaction is "solved" by a bigger tractor, which further compacts the soil, which makes a need for a still bigger tractor, and so on and on. There is an identical symbiosis between coal-fired power plants and air conditioners. It is characteristic of such solutions that no one prospers by them but the suppliers of fuel and equipment.

These two kinds of solutions are obviously bad. They always serve one good at the expense of another or of several others, and I believe that if all their effects were ever to be accounted for they would be seen to involve, too frequently, if not invariably, a net loss to nature, agriculture, and the human commonwealth.

Such solutions always involve a definition of the problems that is either false or so narrow as to be virtually false. To define an agricultural problem as if it were solely a problem of agriculture—or solely a problem of production or technology or economics—is simply to misunderstand the problem, either inadvertently or deliberately, either for profit or because of a prevalent fashion of thought. The whole problem must be solved, not just some handily identifiable and simplifiable aspect of it.

Both kinds of bad solutions leave their problems unsolved. Bigger tractors do not solve the problem of soil compaction any more than air conditioners solve the problem of air pollution. Nor does the large confinement-feeding operation solve the problem of food production; it is, rather, a way calculated to allow large-scale ambition and greed to profit from food production. The real problem of food production occurs within a complex, mutually influential relationship of soil, plants, animals, and people. A real solution to that problem will therefore be ecologically, agriculturally, and culturally healthful.

Perhaps it is not until health is set down as the aim that we come in sight of the third kind of solution: that which causes a ramifying series of solutions— as when meat animals are fed on the farm where the feed is raised, and where the feed is raised to be fed to the animals that are on the farm. Even so rudimentary a description implies a concern for pattern, for quality, which necessarily complicates the concern for production. The farmer has put plants and animals into a relationship of mutual dependence, and must perforce be concerned for balance or symmetry, a reciprocating connection in the pattern of the farm that is biological, not industrial, and that involves solutions to problems of fertility, soil husbandry, economics, sanitation—the whole complex of problems whose proper solutions add up to *health*: the health of the soil, of plants and animals, of farm and farmer, of farm family and farm community, all involved in the same interested, interlocking pattern—or pattern of patterns.

A bad solution is bad, then, because it acts destructively upon the larger patterns in which it is contained. It acts destructively upon those patterns, most likely, because it is formed in ignorance or disregard of them. A bad solution solves for a single purpose or goal, such as increased production. And it is typical of such solutions that they achieve stupendous increases in production at exorbitant biological and social costs.

A good solution is good because it is in harmony with those larger patterns—

and this harmony will, I think, be found to have the nature of analogy. A bad solution acts within the larger pattern the way a disease or addiction acts within the body. A good solution acts within the larger pattern the way a healthy organ acts within the body. But it must at once be understood that a healthy organ does not—as the mechanistic or industrial mind would like to say—"give" health to the body, is not exploited for the body's health, but is *a part* of its health. The health of organ and organism is the same, just as the health of organism and ecosystem is the same. And these structures of organ, organism, and ecosystem—as John Todd [see his book *From Eco-Cities to Living Machines—Ed.*] has so ably understood—belong to a series of analogical integrities that begins with the organelle and ends with the biosphere.

It would be next to useless, of course, to talk about the possibility of good solutions if none existed in proof and in practice. A part of our work at *The New Farm* magazine has been to locate and understand those farmers whose work is competently responsive to the requirements of health. Representative of these farmers, and among them remarkable for the thoroughness of his intelligence, is Earl F. Spencer, who has a 250-acre dairy farm near Palatine Bridge, New York.

Before 1972, Earl Spencer was following a "conventional" plan which would build his herd to 120 cows. According to this plan, he would eventually buy all the grain he fed, and he was already using as much as thirty tons per year of commercial fertilizer. But in 1972, when he had increased his herd to 70 cows, wet weather reduced his harvest by about half. The choice was clear: he had either to buy half his yearly feed supply or sell half his herd.

He chose to sell half his herd—a very unconventional choice, which in itself required a lot of independent intelligence. But character and intelligence of an even more respectable order were involved in the next step, which was to understand that the initial decision implied a profound change in the pattern of the farm and of his life and assumptions as a farmer. With his herd now reduced by half, he saw that before the sale he had been overstocked, and he had been abusing his land. On his 120 acres of tillable land, he had been growing 60 acres of corn and 60 of alfalfa. On most of his fields, he was growing corn three years in succession. The consequences of this he now saw as

* KNOWING WHAT TO DO NEXT....

symptoms, and saw that they were serious: heavy dependence on purchased supplies, deteriorating soil structure, declining quantities of organic matter, increasing erosion, yield reductions despite continued large applications of fertilizer. In addition, because of his heavy feeding of concentrates, his cows were having serious digestive and other health problems.

He began to ask fundamental questions about the nature of the creatures and the land he was dealing with, and to ask if he could not bring about some sort of balance between their needs and his own. His conclusion was that "to be in balance with nature is to be successful." His farm, he says, had been going in a "dead run"; now he would slow it to a "walk."

From his crucial decision to reduce his herd, then, several other practical measures have followed:

1. A five-year plan (extended to eight years) to phase out entirely his use of purchased fertilizers.

2. A plan, involving construction of a concrete manure pit, to increase and improve his use of manure.

3. Better husbandry of cropland, more frequent rotation, better timing.

4. The gradual reduction of grain in the feed ration and the concurrent increase of roughage—which has, to date, reduced the dependence on grain by half, from about six thousand pounds per cow to about three thousand pounds.

5. A breeding program which selects "for more efficient roughage conversion."

The most tangible results are that the costs of production have been "dramatically" reduced and that per cow [milk] production has increased by fifteen hundred to two thousand pounds. But the health of the whole farm has improved. There is a moral satisfaction in this, of which Earl Spencer is fully aware. But he is also aware that the satisfaction is not *purely* moral, for the good results are also practical and economic: "We have half the animals we had before and are feeding half as much grain to those remaining, so we now need to plant corn only two years in a row. Less corn means less plowing, less fuel for growing and harvesting, and less wear on the most expensive equipment." Veterinary bills have been reduced also. And in 1981, if the schedule holds, he will buy no commercial fertilizer at all.

From the work of Earl Spencer and other exemplary farmers, and from the understanding of destructive farming practices, it is possible to devise a set of critical standards for agriculture. I am aware that the list of standards which follows must be to some extent provisional, but am nevertheless confident that it will work to distinguish between healthy and unhealthy farms, as well as between the oversimplified minds that solve problems for some *x* such as profit or quantity of production, and those minds, sufficiently complex, that solve for health or quality or coherence of pattern. To me, the validity of these standards seems inherent in their general applicability. They will serve the making of sewer systems or households as readily as they will serve the making of farms.

A good solution accepts given limits, using so far as possible what is at hand. The farther-fetched the solution, the less it should be trusted. Granted that a farm can be too small, it is nevertheless true that enlarging scale is a deceptive solution; it solves one problem by acquiring another or several others.

A good solution accepts also the limitation of discipline. Agricultural problems should receive solutions that are agricultural, not technological or economic.

A good solution improves the balances, symmetries, or harmonies within a pattern—it is a qualitative solution—rather than entangling or complicating some part of a pattern at the expense or in neglect of the rest.

A good solution solves more than one problem, and it does not make new problems. I am talking about health as opposed to almost any cure, coherence of pattern as opposed to almost any solution produced piecemeal or in isolation. The return of organic wastes to the soil may, at first glance, appear to be a good solution *per se*. But that is not invariably or necessarily true. It is true only if the wastes are returned to the right place at the right time in the pattern of the farm, if the waste does not contain toxic materials, if the quantity is not too great, and if not too much energy or money is expended in transporting it.

A good solution will satisfy a whole range of criteria; it will be good in all respects. A farm that has found correct agricultural solutions to its problems will be fertile, productive, healthful, conservative, beautiful, pleasant to live on. This standard obviously must be qualified to the extent that the pattern of the life of a farm will be adversely affected by distortions in any of the larger patterns that contain it. It is hard, for instance, for the economy of a farm to maintain its health in a national industrial economy in which farm earnings are apt to be low and expenses high. But it is apparently true, even in such an economy, that the farmers most apt to survive are those who do not go too far out of agriculture into either industry or banking—and who, moreover, live like farmers, not like businessmen. This seems especially true for the smaller farmers.

A good solution embodies a clear distinction between biological order and mechanical order, between farming and industry. Farmers who fail to make this distinction are ideal customers of the equipment companies, but they often fail to understand that the real strength of the farm is in the soil.

Good solutions have wide margins, so that the failure of one solution does not imply the impossibility of another. Industrial agriculture tends to put its eggs into fewer and fewer baskets and to make "going for broke" its only way of going. But to grow grain should not make it impossible to pasture livestock, and to have a lot of power should not make it impossible to use only a little.

A good solution always answers the question, How much is enough? Industrial solutions have always rested on the assumption that enough is all you can get. But that destroys agriculture, as it destroys nature and culture. The good health of a farm implies the limit of a scale, because it implies a limit of attention and because such a limit is invariably implied by any pattern. You destroy a square, for example, by enlarging one angle or lengthening one side. And in any sort of work there is a point past which more quantity necessarily implies less quality. In some kinds of industrial agriculture, such as cash grain farming, it is possible (to borrow an insight from Professor Timothy Tay-lor) to think of technology as a substitute for skill. But even in such farming that possibility is illusory; the illusion can be maintained only as long as the consequences can be ignored. The illusion is much shorter lived when ani-mals are included in the farm pattern, because the husbandry of animals is so insistently a human skill. A healthy farm incorporates a pattern that a single human mind can comprehend, make, maintain, vary in response to circum-stances, and pay attention to. That this limit is obviously variable from one farmer and farm to another does not mean that it does not exist.

A good solution should be cheap, and it should not enrich one person by the distress or impoverishment of another. In agriculture, so-called "inputs" are, from a different point of view, outputs—*expenses*. In all things, I think, but especially in an agriculture, struggling to survive in an industrial econ-omy, any solution that calls for an expenditure to a manufacturer should be held in suspicion—not rejected necessarily, but *as a rule* mistrusted.

Good solutions exist only in proof and are not to be expected from ab-sentee owners or absentee experts. Problems must be solved in work and in place, with particular knowledge, fidelity, and care, by people who will suffer the consequences for their mistakes. There is no theoretical or ideal *practice*. Practical advice or direction from people who have no practice may have some value, but its value is questionable and is limited. The divisions of capital, man-agement, and labor, characteristic of an industrial system, are therefore utterly alien to the health of farming—as they probably also are to the health of man-ufacturing. The good health of a farm depends on the farmer's mind; the good health of his mind has its dependence, and its proof, in physical work. The good farmer's mind and his body—his management and his labor—work to-gether as intimately as his heart and his lungs. And the capital of a well-farmed farm by definition includes the farmer, mind and body both. Farmer and farm are one thing, an organism.

Once the farmer's mind, his body, and his farm are understood as a sin-gle organism, and once it is understood that the question of the endurance of this organism is a question about the sufficiency and integrity of a pattern, then the word "organic" can be usefully admitted into this series of standards. It is a word that I have been defining all along, although I have not used it. An organic farm, properly speaking, is not one that uses certain methods and substances and avoids others; it is a farm whose structure is formed in imitation of the structure of a natural system; it has the integrity, the independence, and the benign dependence of an organism. Sir Albert Howard [the British agriculturalist who has been called the founder of the organic farming movement—*Ed.*] said that a good farm is an analogue of the forest which "manures itself." A farm that imports too much fertility, even as feed or manure, is in this sense as inorganic as a farm that exports too much or that imports chemical fertilizer.

The introduction of the term "organic" permits me to say more plainly and usefully some things that I have said or implied earlier. In an organism, what is good for one part is good for another. What is good for the mind is good for the body; what is good for the arm is good for the heart. We know that sometimes a part may be sacrificed for the whole; a life may be saved by the amputation of an arm. But we also know that such remedies are desperate, irreversible, and destructive; it is impossible to improve the body by amputation. And such remedies do not imply a safe logic. As *tendencies* they are fatal: you cannot save your arm by the sacrifice of your life.

Perhaps most of us who know local histories of agriculture know of fields that in hard times have been sacrificed to save a farm, and we know that though such a thing is possible it is dangerous. The danger is worse when topsoil is sacrificed for the sake of a crop. And if we understand the farm as an organism, we see that it is impossible to sacrifice the health of the soil to improve the health of plants, or to sacrifice the health of plants to improve the health of animals, or to sacrifice the health of animals to improve the health of people. In a biological pattern—as in the pattern of a community—the exploitive means and motives of industrial economics are immediately destructive and ultimately suicidal.

It is in the nature of any organic pattern to be contained within a larger one. And so a good solution in one pattern preserves the integrity of the pattern that contains it. A good agricultural solution, for example, would not pollute or erode a watershed. What is good for the water is good for the ground, what is good for the ground is good for plants, what is good for plants is good for animals, what is good for animals is good for people, what is good for people is good for the air, and what is good for the air is good for the water. And vice versa.

But we must not forget that those human solutions that we may call organic are not natural. We are talking about organic *artifacts*, organic only by imitation or analogy. Our ability to make such artifacts depends on virtues that are specifically human: accurate memory, observation, insight, imagination, inventiveness, reverence, devotion, fidelity, restraint. Restraint—for us, now—above all: the ability to accept and live within limits; to resist changes that are merely novel or fashionable; to resist greed and pride; to resist the temptation to "solve" problems by ignoring them, accepting them as "trade-offs," or bequeathing them to posterity. A good solution, then, must be in harmony with good character, cultural value, and moral law.

The Power of Words

Ernest Callenbach

This essay and "Values," which follows it, are taken from Ernest Callenbach's Ecology: A Pocket Guide *(1998), a compact introduction to fundamental ecological terms, whose publication was supported by the Center for Ecoliteracy. Callenbach's 1975 novel* Ecotopia, *a portrait of a future ecologically sustainable society, became an underground classic, selling a million copies. His 1996* Bring Back the Buffalo! A Sustainable Future for America's Great Plains *applies ecotopian principles to a proposal to restore the Great Plains. "Chick" Callenbach served for thirty-six years on the staff of the University of California Press, as founder and editor of* Film Quarterly *and as editor of film books and the California Natural History Guides series. He speaks regularly around the world on environmental topics.*

A vocabulary, Callenbach says, implies a story of how the world works, and why. Words and the meanings we give them help to define "reality." (Politicians are particularly adept at this use, or misuse, of language. When the Bush administration termed its proposal for increasing logging in national forests the "Healthy Forests Initiative," it not only claimed ownership of the definition of "healthy" but implied that a vote against the initiative was a vote against healthy forests.)

Giving surprising definitions to familiar words is also a way to change or expand imagination and perspectives. For instance, when the Center for Ecoliteracy is asked for its "sustainability curriculum," the questioner usually imagines a binder containing a prescribed set of lessons. Instead, "curriculum" to CEL means the totality of a student's experiences, a mix of content and context. Organizing classes around projects rather than academic subjects is curriculum—such as in the STRAW Project described in Michael K. Stone's "'It Changed Everything We Thought We Could Do'" (in Part III). Teaming first-graders and fourth-graders as "buddies" at Mary E. Silveira School is curriculum (see "Leadership and the Learning Community" in Part III). When David W. Orr says in his foreword, "by what is included or excluded we teach the young that they are part of or apart from the natural world," he's talking about curriculum.

An overlapping term, "hidden curriculum," coined by Brian Jackson in the 1960s, points to the fact that schools transmit not just "knowledge" but also norms and values (such as respect, manners, fair play, and other traits needed to maintain a civil society). Sometimes hidden curriculum is intentional: in CEL terms, changing the context from the four walls of the classroom to include the culture and the community of the school, experiences in the garden, faculty talking to one another respectfully, or the use of a tablecloth in the dining room at The Edible Schoolyard are all hidden curriculum. Sometimes the hidden curriculum's lessons are not intentional, but reveal unspoken, and often unconscious, values: the soda machine in the hallway outside the classroom where nutrition is being taught is hidden curriculum. In his book The Nature of Design (2002), David W. Orr describes how even a campus's buildings—whether they're all right angles and squareness; how they are supplied with energy and water; how they dispose of waste; whether they demonstrate connections to their historical, cultural, and geographic settings or display any relationship to a larger set of environmental issues—become part of the school's hidden curriculum.

VOCABULARIES ARE NEVER NEUTRAL. Things that are included in a vocabulary gain a familiar reality; things that are left out are ignored or even have their existence denied. Moreover, a vocabulary implies a story of how the world works and why. Such stories always serve the interests of established institutions or classes. In science, politics, or art, a new way of talking about the world threatens to displace established ideas and the groups that espouse them, so it encounters vigorous opposition.

Today, the struggle for control of the basic terms of public discourse takes place in the media and in the work of scientists, educators, philosophers, moralists, preachers, economists, and politicians. Both leaders and ordinary citizens exposed to new ideas slowly accept or reject them. Thus our thinking continually changes to meet changing social needs—sometimes in ways that prevent crises, sometimes not.

During the past few centuries, we developed elaborate special vocabularies for higher mathematics, physics, chemistry, and biology. These provided a way of understanding the world as a set of mechanical causes and effects. Intuitively appealing, these also proved immensely useful in the deployment of industrial technology and gained wide public as well as scientific acceptance.

But in the last fifty years, something extremely strange has happened to these formerly straightforward-appearing ways of understanding and controlling the world. With the more sophisticated analysis possible through modern science, we've learned that the world is in reality more a fuzzy network of interconnected energies than a set of separate objects with neat mechanical relationships. There is no such thing as a "thing"—that is, a separate, disconnected, independent thing. Not only in biology but also in physics, the world is now described as made up of complicated overlapping and interacting patterns. The apparently solid objects and beings we see around us are in fact mostly empty space, in which systems of energetic patterns manifest themselves. There is no fixity or permanence. In mathematics, a special field now deals with chaotic phenomena. All is constant change, cycles without end, the birth and rebirth of stars, rocks, trees, humans, and microbes.

In a parallel development, during the industrial era, we also invented economics, an elaborate language deploying terms such as "profit," "marginal cost," and "market" to describe and justify the mechanisms of capitalist business. Some people think the traditional economics can also provide a reliable basis for government policies and private lives. However, something similar to the displacement of the old mechanical worldview in science is happening in economics. Economics enjoyed much prestige for the past half century, but the realization is now spreading that it deals with only a limited part of reality—things that are bought and sold. (Its vocabulary disconnects us from ecological reality; animals become "farm products" or "fur crops," mountains become "mineral resources.") Economics cannot yet conceptualize the biological world outside its abstract formulas or even deal with the complexities of how economic behavior is controlled by cultural institutions. If economics is to be useful for a sustainable future, it will have to be fundamentally overhauled, as science has been.

The ecological view of the world is the polar opposite of the narrow economic view. It recognizes that a nation's true gross national product is biological, not industrial: it is created by the blue-green bacteria that are ultimately earth's only producers. It values every aspect of the formidably complex web of life that has prevailed on earth for four billion years—and now sustains humans. Ecological thinking aims to use all the resources of science to see how life operates and how we can fit responsibly into its patterns. This profoundly different view of the world will influence both the terms we use to talk about life and how we live. Nothing will ever be the same. As the twenty-first century unfolds, we must take our guidance from new and better understandings of our glorious living world.

Values

Ernest Callenbach

The Center for Ecoliteracy's work has been grounded in values since its beginning. Speaking to a 2003 Bioneers workshop led by the Center, CEL cofounder and board member Peter Buckley said,

> At the Center for Ecoliteracy we believe that at their heart, the ecological problems we face are problems of values. We've noticed over the years that it's very hard to change the values of adults, while at the same time we've noticed that children are born with certain values intact—namely their sense of wonder and their affinity for nature. David W. Orr reminds us that the biologist E. O. Wilson calls this "biophilia." We all share that trait, but it seems particularly strong in children. It's undiminished when they're young. And one of our philosophies is that we think that, properly nurtured, biophilia can develop into ecological literacy and eventually lead toward a more sustainable society.

The central place of values is overt in "Fast-Food Values and Slow Food Values," the essay by Alice Waters that follows this one, but it permeates virtually every essay in the book. Even the commitment to education for long-term sustainability represents a choice to think beyond personal survival and to value the whole of life on earth. Our decision to focus on certain ecological principles—those by which nature sustains life—is also a values choice.

In this essay, Ernest Callenbach reminds readers that "While conflicts over environmental issues are often argued on 'practical' grounds, most environmental debates ultimately involve value conflicts." The resolution of seemingly hopeless differences can sometimes begin, he suggests, if those caught in conflict will examine and understand each other's values, perhaps discovering that they are not so far apart on fundamental matters, and then searching for common ground on which to begin working.

VALUES ARE BASIC IDEAS that guide us in how we should behave. We humans act on instinct most of the time, just like nonhuman animals. We seek food, protection, and sex without having to stop and think about these goals. If we lacked such instinctive strategies of actions, surviving would require constant rethinking and decision-making. But we are also capable, through language, of making rules about what we do and why we do it. Whether we recognize it or not, all individual humans and all human cultures possess such rules, or values. The Golden Rule, "Do unto others as you would have others do unto you," expresses the value of behaving in ways that recognize and support interdependence. In some form, it is found in all the world's religions. But values can clash with ecological reality. The idea that all other species are here solely for the good of humans, though contradicted by a wealth of scientific evidence and practical experience, is still a widespread if often unacknowledged value.

Values can conflict with each other. Take, for example, the value that an important part of being alive is to experience, understand, and enjoy nature. Honoring this value, we would preserve wilderness for our children and others in the future. But this value directly opposes a value at the root of much economic thinking that the primary goal of human beings is to maximize their individual welfare, usually monetarily—for instance, when owners cut down ancient wilderness forests to make profits from lumber.

Value conflicts occur within a person as well as between people, though we don't always want to acknowledge such conflicts. People frequently say they want both low taxes and generous government services, or both protection of natural areas and freedom to do whatever they want in them—even though they may realize deep down that they can't have both at the same time.

The environmental movement is fundamentally based not on economic or scientific arguments but on moral and aesthetic values about what is right, fitting, beautiful, or satisfying. While conflicts over environmental issues are often argued on "practical" grounds, most environmental debates ultimately involve value conflicts. Some fundamentalists believe that the end of the world will come soon, so it really doesn't matter if we humans cause terrible damage to the biosphere. People who believe that all animals have rights hold that human beings are wrong to eat other animals, to keep them in cages, or to do damaging medical experiments on them. Ecologically oriented citizens believe that we have a moral obligation to achieve sustainability, so that we do not diminish the chances of future generations to meet their needs. Some economists believe that we can trust the working of economic laws to replace used-up resources and solve pollution problems.

Such conflicting views can seem hopelessly at odds. However, there is often a possibility of mutual understanding and cooperation if we realize that although values exist inside our heads, they have consequences in the real world. We all share the consequences of value-based decisions. Religious people generally believe that their values are justified by religious texts or by the decisions of their churches, yet they can sometimes work with nonreligious people who feel that their values are justified by science—if both sides are willing to talk about the actual results of policy decisions. You often gain a new perspective on a value if you see what its concrete consequences are. Sometimes, too, when people talk respectfully together, it turns out that their values are not so far apart as they thought, or they find they can work together on behalf of one value they share although they disagree on others.

At some great turning points in history, dominant values become exhausted or problematic, and people work out new values that they hope will enable them to survive better. With the rise of capitalism, Western peoples have adopted the belief that technology can solve all of our problems and is the most important thing in life while religious and cultural matters become secondary. At the moment, many Americans are seeking ways to escape the values of expansionist industrialism (embodied in the key idea of growth) and live by new values associated with ecology (embodied in the key idea of sustainability). They don't let the earning and spending of money become their top priority. They dress simply but with flair and eat healthy foods. They focus on activities that have personal meaning to them, not just status appeal.

They are conscientious about recycling, lessening consumption, and generally reducing their impacts.

Transitions in values normally take centuries to work themselves out, through the practical experiences and rethinking of millions of people. This leisurely pace of value change may prove too slow to save us from catastrophes of desertification, deforestation, famine, and disease—brought on by global warming, ozone thinning, overpopulation, and drastic declines in primary productivity in the seas and on land. Thus it is urgent that we develop a widespread ethic of ecological responsibility.

Fast-Food Values
and Slow Food Values

Alice Waters

Alice Waters is the founder and owner of Chez Panisse restaurant in Berkeley, California. Named best restaurant in the United States by Gourmet magazine in 2001, Chez Panisse exemplifies her philosophy of serving the most delicious organic products, only when they are in season—the practice that has become known worldwide as California Cuisine. Over three decades, the restaurant has developed a network of local farmers and ranchers whose dedication to sustainable agriculture assures it a steady supply of pure and fresh ingredients. Waters is author of eight books, the most recent of which is Chez Panisse Fruit *(2002).*

The Edible Schoolyard (ESY), which Waters initiated in 1995 at Berkeley's Martin Luther King Middle School and for which the Center for Ecoliteracy was one of the initial funders, has played a central role in CEL's work with food in schools (see "Revolution Step-by-Step: On Building a Climate for Change" in Part III and "Sustainability—A New Item on the Lunch Menu" in Part IV). ESY has received international attention by demonstrating that garden experiences and cooking classes can be integrated into a whole curriculum, and that the way to convince young people to eat nutritious food is not to lecture them, but to say, "Try this and see if it doesn't taste better."

In 1996 Waters created the Chez Panisse Foundation, with a mission to transform public education and to support projects that integrate gardening, cooking, daily lunches prepared on campus with fresh ingredients, and the core academic curriculum. In 2003 the Chez Panisse Foundation and the Berkeley Unified School District, partnering with the Center for Ecoliteracy and Children's Hospital Oakland

Research Institute, entered into an agreement to design and implement a districtwide school lunch curriculum initiative.

Alice Waters is a vice president of Slow Food International, which she introduces here and which Maurice Holt invokes in the essay that follows hers. Slow Food describes its members as "eco-gastronomes," devoted to the pleasure that food brings, but also committed to maintaining respect for and a balance with nature, preserving the environment, and acting out of the conviction that their pleasure is connected with that of others, which leads them to do charity work in places where pleasure is hard to find. This essay, drawn from talks that Waters gives across the country and around the world, displays the clarity and depth of her thinking about what we can learn from food and what we can learn about ourselves from the ways we prepare, serve, and eat food.

NOT LONG AGO, I spotted a bumper sticker that said, "If you are what you eat, I'm fast, cheap, and easy." Is this really who we want to be? I don't think so, but we've been swallowed up by a fast-food culture that promotes and celebrates just those values.

The choices that each of us makes about food matter at every level. We may think that they're about our own good nutrition and our own personal pleasure, but they're really about the health of our entire society—in fact, they're about the health of human culture itself.

A cynic is supposed to be somebody who knows the price of everything and the value of nothing. By that definition, we've turned into a nation of cynics, at least as far as our food supply goes. We have values, all right, but what are they? After Eric Schlosser wrote *Fast Food Nation*, I started thinking about the ubiquity of the fast-food culture. Drive through the suburbs of any American city, and what do you see? Mile after mile of franchises. It's hard not to feel that we're the victims of a giant conspiracy. In fact, industrial farming and fast food operate hand-in-glove, very much like a vast conspiracy. Together they suppress variety, limit our choices, and manipulate our desires by hooking us on sugar and salt.

Fast-Food Values

What do our children learn from fast food? What lessons do they absorb when they eat a Happy Meal? What are the values that fast food inculcates in them? Here are some of the most important fast-food values and assumptions:

Food is cheap and abundant, and this abundance is permanent. We act as if we believe that because food is cheap and accessible to most Americans today, it will remain so without our having to change our ways of growing, selling, and preparing it. Food should be affordable and available, but the way we're going, to give just one example, California's Central Valley is going to lose its fertility within the next twenty or thirty years. Farmers know that living soil is precious and must be cared for and replenished, and that doing that isn't cheap. Fast food is cheap only because we haven't yet reckoned the real cost of farm subsidies, dependence on Middle Eastern oil, and depleted soil. We're only beginning to wake up to the health consequences of cheap food. A national diet heavy with processed foods and meat is leading to obesity and diabetes at record levels, and to a health crisis that we will still be paying for decades from now, in terms of health care costs and lost productivity.

Resources are infinite, so it's perfectly okay to waste. "There's always plenty more where that came from," our actions say. This glorification of disposability is reflected everywhere in our culture. But farmers and others who work intimately with food know that people are much more likely to think twice about whether or not they really need something if they have to dispose of it themselves.

Eating is primarily about fueling up in as little time as possible. We drive in, order, pick it up, eat it in the car, and dump what's left in the garbage can. Food is supposed to be fast and available twenty-four hours a day. And yet we all know, or should know, that anything worth doing takes time.

Meat, french fries, and sodas are actually good for us—and they should taste exactly the same everywhere. By our actions' logic, diversity is totally undesirable. But any nutritionist will say that what's really good in any diet is variety.

Where food comes from, or how fresh it is, doesn't matter. We act as if the seasons are of no particular consequence and the qualities of the places where the food is raised and where it is eaten are of no particular consequence. But the seasons connect us to nature. They punctuate the passage of time and they teach us about the impermanence of life—something that our society hasn't wanted to look at.

Advertising confers value. Better advertising means better food, says our behavior as consumers. Publicity denotes worth. Celebrity is the most virtuous quality of all. And yet we know that the ultimate sign of worth is *not needing* any advertising—something's value is self-evident, or we've discovered it by word of mouth from people we know and trust. And can we have forgotten that modesty was once a virtue?

Work is to be avoided at all costs. We treat preparation as drudgery. Besides, other people are better at it than we are. Cleaning up is drudgery, too. There are more important things to do. We have been told that work is here and pleasure is there. But in fact real pleasure comes from *doing*. Work can feed our imaginations and educate our senses. If somebody else does it all for us, we miss out on the real juice of life. Even the hard physical work we're so eager to delegate to others can change us for the better. I think it's terrible when people slave their whole lives in order to take a vacation somewhere on a cruise ship. They miss out on the pleasure that could be theirs every day if only they would pay attention to what they do and what they eat. The one thing we all have to do every day is eat, and the rituals of cooking and eating together constitute, in the words of Francine du Plessix Gray, our "primal rite of socialization, the core curriculum in the school of civilized discourse. The family meal ... is a set of protocols that curb our natural savagery and our animal greed, and cultivate a capacity for sharing and thoughtfulness" [Gray, p. 51].

These fast-food values permeate our homes, our institutions, and particularly our schools. They drive us away from the table. But they fly in the face of thousands of years of human experience growing, preparing, and eating as central expressions of life and community.

Slow Food Values

So what about *anti*-fast-food values? Is there a future for "slow food" values that make us aware of food's real costs? That tell us that real food should be available to everyone, rich and poor? That cooking and eating are not drudgery? That concentrating on a task is okay? That everything is woven together? Can we pass on to our children the magic of hospitality and generosity? Can we teach our children the values that transform our lives and the world around us? We can, but we must first change our attitudes toward food. As the growing Slow Food movement, with sixty thousand members in over one hundred countries, has demonstrated, food can teach us the things that really matter—care, beauty, concentration, discernment, sensuality, all the best that humans are capable of—but only if we take the time to think about what we're eating.

For me, life is given meaning and beauty by the daily ritual of the table—a ritual that can express tradition, character, sustainability, and diversity. These are values that I learned, almost unconsciously, at my family table as a child. But the family meal has undergone a steady devaluation from its place at the center of human life, when it was the daily enactment of shared necessity and ritualized cooperation. Today, as never before, the meals of children are likely to have been cooked by strangers, to consist of highly processed foods produced far away, and to be taken casually, greedily, in haste, and, all too often, alone.

Cultural institutions *could* honor the centrality of slow food values, but they often do the opposite. Fast-food values are pervasive and often appear where they least belong. Museums of natural history, for example, celebrate the astonishing diversity of world cultures, the beauty of human workmanship, and the wonders of nature. They even house impressive collections of artifacts relating to food: tools and depictions of hunting, foraging, agriculture, food preparation, and the hearth.

But in the museum cafeteria, crowds of people queue up in a poorly lit, depressing space as if in a diorama of contemporary life, surrounded by the unmistakable steam-table smell of precooked, portion-controlled food. In this marvelous museum, surrounded on all sides by splendid exhibits that celebrate the complexity of life and the diversity of human achievement, people appear to have stopped thinking when it comes to their very own everyday experiences. People appear to be oblivious that the cafeteria represents the antithesis of the values celebrated in the museum.

A museum cafeteria could delight the senses. It could be beautiful and could make its patrons think. It could serve delicious meals that teach where food comes from and how it is made. When diners return their trays, they could learn about composting and recycling. They could even have a little friendly human interaction, were the cafeteria designed to encourage it. The museum could inspire visitors to see the world in a different way. Instead it functions like a filling station.

Our system of public education operates in the same strange, no-context zone of hollow fast-food values. In school cafeterias, students learn how little we care about the way they nourish themselves—we've sold them to the lowest bidder. At best we serve our children government-subsidized agricultural surplus; at worst we invite fast-food restaurants to operate on school grounds. Soda machines line the hallways. Children need only compare the slickness of the nearest mall to the condition of their school and the quality of its library and its cafeteria to learn that our culture considers them more important as consumers than as students.

Still, the public school system is our last best hope for teaching real democratic values that can withstand the insidious voices of those who would have us believe that life is all about personal fulfillment and personal consumption. A slow food education is an opportunity that should be universally available. There are countless ways to weave a food program into the curriculum at every level of education. The depth and breadth of the subject—its relevance to ecology, anthropology, history, physiology, and art—assures that it could easily be integrated into the academic studies of every school, from the kindergarten to the university.

Change the food in the schools, and we can influence how children think. Change the curriculum and teach them how to garden and how to cook, and we can show that growing food and cooking and eating together give lasting richness, meaning, and beauty to our lives.

To do this will take the kind of dedication embodied by many of today's farmers. Thomas Jefferson had a vision of a nation of independent farmers. But it was Alexander Hamilton's vision of a nation of factories that prevailed. Maybe it's not too late to rethink our national purpose, after all. The ideals and the authenticity we've been craving in our lives still exist. We can still have them. They're not lost. They're right under our noses.

The Slow School:
An Idea Whose Time Has Come?

Maurice Holt

We understand from indigenous people that diversity is one of the core attributes of sustainable communities, but Maurice Holt argues here, in an essay adapted from a convocation of professional educators, that the drive toward standards-based schooling has forced education in North America and Britain into a "curriculum straitjacket." He also illuminates the systems-thinking perceptual shift from quantity to quality that Fritjof Capra describes above in "Speaking Nature's Language." It is possible, Holt says, to make both teachers and students accountable, without resort to a flawed system of quantitative measurement. He invokes the power of metaphor to create a vision for education inspired by "the quiet material pleasures of a civilized meal" as an antidote to what he calls "the hamburger model of schooling."

We are grateful to Alice Waters for introducing us to Maurice Holt and his work. His 1978 book The Common Curriculum: Its Structure and Style in the Comprehensive School *described a broad curriculum based on choice within subject groupings rather than between subjects, using a variety of learning strategies. It is credited with helping to shape an English education reform movement grounded in comprehensive schooling and whole-curriculum planning.*

Holt has served as first principal of Sheredes School in Hertfordshire, directed a master's degree program for Exeter University, and directed the American Academy, Cyprus. In 1991 he joined the graduate school at the University of Colorado at Denver as professor of curriculum theory. He has coedited the Journal of Curriculum and Supervision, *the publication of the Association for Supervision and Curriculum Development. As an emeritus professor now residing in Oxford,*

U.K., he has focused on the politics of curriculum change and on promoting the concept of slow schools.

WHEN THE YOUNG COLE PORTER left his elementary school in Indiana for a prep school on the East Coast, his mother gave his age as twelve, although he was in fact two years older. She had always encouraged his musical gifts and evidently decided that two more years at home, practicing the piano and entertaining passengers on the passing riverboats, was a better way of fostering his songwriting abilities. We should all be grateful for her foresight.

In today's school climate, Kate Porter's deception appears both unlikely and unwise. The pressure to proceed from one targeted standard to another as fast as possible, to absorb and demonstrate specified knowledge with conveyor-belt precision, is an irresistible fact of school life. Parents are encouraged to focus on achievement, not self-realization. A present-day Porter would soon be labeled a nerdy slow learner if he flunked the math test and preferred the keyboard to a baseball bat. It's curious that, in an age when the right of adults to shape their own lifestyle is taken for granted, the right of children to an education that will help them make something of themselves is more circumscribed than ever.

This curriculum straitjacket is the price exacted for believing that education is about assessed performance on specified content. The most obvious flaw in all this is that we have a category error. It's one thing to talk of standards in manufacturing crankshafts, and a very different thing to talk of standards in educating a person. Yes, Toyota has high standards of manufacture, because its machines ensure a high degree of precision. But it's quite another matter to assign a precise value to the result of an educational encounter. We're dealing with two utterly different practices, with two different kinds of problems. One is technical, the other is moral. School is a place where students develop their minds. You can't put a number on that. Indeed, in 2002 France's President Jacques Chirac made the general point: "To consider works of art and cultural goods to be ordinary merchandise is a profound mental aberration that nothing can justify." Very French, and very true. Education and attributes like creativity, resilience, motivation, enthusiasm, and compassion are cultural goods that can't be weighed or measured.

But for the standards fraternity, it's all very simple. Measure performance (numerically if possible), put schools in rank order, and set targets for improvement. Let the market loose on schools, and see who survives! This is a hard-nosed view of accountability, red in tooth and claw. Performance and compliance are the key concepts, and they've had a profound effect on the professional life of teachers. Managerial accountability means that management isn't just something that people in suits do in offices; it invades teachers' professional lives. And it turns teachers into double agents. As professionals, they want to inspire students, pursue new ideas, and shape the program to meet their interests. But as employees, they're haunted by that high-stakes test next week.

So what's the appeal of this approach? The underlying assumption here is that the system is deterministic. Set tougher targets and the scores will go up. Ah, if only it were that simple! If it were, the standards movement would have done its job years ago. The fact is that when you're faced with complex practical problems, rich in uncertainties, the direct, commonsense route rarely works. As economist and management guru W. Edwards Deming points out, common sense tells us that the earth is flat. The counterintuitive approach, like the slow school, calls for more imagination, more thought and discussion, but it may be the one that works in the end.

Consider the case of the Canadian Pacific Railroad and the Rogers Pass. As the builders headed westward, they encountered the challenge of the Selkirk Mountains. There was no obvious pass—no way of avoiding an expensive detour. Major A. B. Rogers took up the challenge with an open mind, examined the results of earlier attempts, and found the pass, not by going west—but by veering off to the southeast! Not the intuitive solution. He's sending us a message.

Management writers James Collins and Jerry Porras, in their book *Built to Last* (1997), concluded that approaching problems the indirect way also works in business. Hewlett-Packard became more profitable than Texas Instruments by concentrating on electronics rather than profits—on process rather than outcomes. The man who built Boeing into a hugely successful company, Bill Allen, did it because he and his engineers were obsessed by aeronautics. This led them to a major challenge and a huge gamble—designing and building the 747 jumbo jet. If the accountants had been in charge, it would never have happened.

An Alternative Metaphor

The metaphor of standards is extremely potent, very seductive, but it's educational poison. We need to find another. Like Major Rogers, I shall take a non-intuitive route, by looking at the world of food. Eating is about nourishing the body, and education is about nourishing the mind. And that's how I came to realize that there are striking similarities between standards-based schools and hamburger restaurants. Both offer standardized fare; what's on offer is not a great source of nourishment, and both the school and the burger bar work best with compliant staffs that don't challenge the system. In a McDonald's, it's best to leave your brains at the door. In a standards-based school, you can forget about curriculum development—what matters is test enforcement. The burger restaurant is designed to maximize profit; the standards-led school is programmed to maximize test scores. One produces fast food; the other might be labeled a "fast school."

Back in 1986, a McDonald's franchise opened in Rome, and journalist Carlo Petrini walked past with some friends. He made a joke that turned into a movement: "There's fast food, so why not slow food?" Now there's an international Slow Food Congress, a Slow Food university, and Slow Food convivia (local grassroots offices) all over North America. In Italy, there are sixty slow cities pursuing "slow politics," by calming traffic, keeping out big supermarkets, and persuading restaurants to use organic ingredients.

Even better, the slow food movement has ideals. Its literature declares that it is, "above all, a movement for cultural dignity," it is "a battle against a way of life based solely on speed and convenience," and it seeks to save "the cultural inheritance of humanity." These three aims have a lot in common with education, where respect for our cultural inheritance is linked with long-term implications. Slow food also emphasizes community, as do good schools.

The slow food movement is important because it sprang from civil society and not from a committee room full of businessmen and politicians. It's a genuine grassroots construction, an expression of a public good, and it has a definite philosophical position—that life is about more than a yogurt and half-a-dozen cell-phone calls for lunch. It draws upon tradition and character, and it honors complexity—how you combine and cook familiar ingredients enhances the pleasure of eating. And slow food is also about moral choices—we need time to reflect upon what Carlo Petrini called "quiet material pleasure."

In essence, "slow" has become a metaphor for a particular approach to practical problems. Hence the idea of a "slow school," which doesn't mean reading in slow motion for slow learners. The slow school attends to philosophy, to tradition, to community, to moral choices. Students have time not just to memorize, but also to understand.

In a slow school, you have some theory about what you want to do, but it is embodied in practice and itself animates practice. The fast school is very different—it's like fast food, where theory is kept separate from practice. Hamburger theory is simple—put fried beef in a bun and it will taste good. The practice is a defined set of procedures, and where the beef comes from is no concern of the consumer's. The fast school's theory is also simple theory: education is about assessed performance on specified content. Nobody knows where the theory came from—there's no research that supports this view of education, and a lot to suggest that it isn't education.

In fact, the crucial aspects of the slow school—a philosophical approach, a respect for complexity and community, and making moral choices—are prominent in the work of the curriculum theorist Joseph Schwab. Schwab argues, in his 1969 speech "The Practical: A Language for Curriculum," that the field of curriculum suffers from a surplus of theories about practice, when what is needed is theory embodied within practice. Developing a rich curriculum that actually works calls for deliberation—finding the real problem, reviewing relevant facts, considering alternative solutions. The school renews itself; change is not some abstraction, it's right in there as part of the deliberative process.

This is where the metaphor of the slow school has its real strength. It's a big tent, with lots of room for a great variety of approaches. And just as slow food is tied to a broad social concept—the quiet material pleasures of a civilized meal, of conversation that transcends class or creed—so the slow school is tied to broad social acceptance, through a curriculum that aims to offer all students the same chance.

There is no canonical slow school: they can all be different, as their communities are different. But one or two aspects are likely to be in evidence. First, the school must be contextualized—it must understand its community, socially and politically, and work with it. Second, it needs to look critically at coverage—less is definitely more. Much can be achieved by linking kindred subjects, integrating the learning around common themes. The three sciences—physics, chemistry, and biology—can be unified by using a theme such as "patterns," cutting down on overlap and clutter. Putting English, history, and geography together in a five-year humanities program, grades 7 to 11, makes a great deal of sense. It can be a powerhouse for promoting cultural breadth and respect for others. Similar amalgamations are possible in the creative arts and in the performing arts—areas that get seriously neglected when the dogma of standards moves in. The key point is to ensure that the theme gives adequate scope, under its umbrella, for the specialist teachers who make up the team. Without specialist input, you lose intellectual rigor.

Accountability and the Slow School

Fundamentally, accountability means giving an account, explaining what one has done. There's nothing punitive about this—it's about finding out what's happened. In education, it means teachers describing and explaining to parents a program of activities and their children's responses to them; it's justified by professional teacher status, employment by a responsible authority, and the ethos of the school. It's based on informal monitoring, not tests. The intention is to achieve understanding, not compliance. This is the concept of professional accountability.

The bad news is that the standards movement has replaced this with managerial accountability, but here's the good news. The slow school lends itself to a different, and vastly better, form of accountability that builds on the professional model. As in slow food, you construct a climate within a community such that different ideas about a professional activity can be devised, incorporated in practice, and used to create "quiet, material pleasure." The participants implicitly render an account to each other as the activity unfolds, and the explicit result is not only a satisfying meal or lesson—it's the discovery of a form of life with lots of possibilities. Fast food is about a recipe; slow food is about a story. The standards-led school is about a quickie menu of content and procedures; the slow school is a narrative, a deliberative practice that drives narrative accountability.

With narrative accountability, teachers impart their ideas to parents, who respond with their own views. Each respects the other's perspective. Parents and other stakeholders are inside the tent and part of the action. How can slow-school students express, in a way that can be adjudicated, the benefits the school has brought them? It's a pity that the idea of graduation from American public schools is being displaced by qualification based on high-stakes tests. Graduation is a much better concept, and it can be based on personal demonstrations. A panel of stakeholders judges a student's presentation, drawing as necessary on outside opinion. No enlightened school district could dismiss such arrangements out of hand.

Should the slow school be a small school? It's safe to say that for a slow school to flourish, the climate will be more secure in a school of three hundred than in a school of three thousand. A school of eight hundred or so would be my personal limit. The record for small schools is good, but they need to be big enough to sustain a staff that covers the main specialties.

At the heart of the educational enterprise lies the school curriculum. In broad terms, there are two ways of thinking about the curriculum, and there will always be some tension between them. On the one hand, the school can be seen from the outside, as an institution created by society for its benefit. The emphasis is on acquiring knowledge: the skills, dispositions, and competences as defined by external agencies. The curriculum is fixed and procedural, and we judge its success by asking: Have the students absorbed the required content? When people talk about "delivering the curriculum," it's this that they have in mind: a systematic model of curriculum, with the focus on product. This is standards-based education—the hamburger model of schooling.

On the other hand, we can choose to look at the school from the inside, and focus on the practice of curriculum—on the engagement between teacher and learner in a given context and the issues it generates. Curriculum is then not a matter of applying predetermined answers, but of solving these interactive problems so as to benefit all students, using the method of deliberation. The focus is on process, on students influencing their own learning. This is a deliberative model of curriculum, and we judge its success by asking: How do our students see themselves? Can they make moral judgments? Have they made something of themselves? The metaphor of the slow school is an attempt to animate this model of liberal education.

There is no reason why the phrase "slow school" should not acquire the cachet associated with "slow food." In many aspects of life, doing things slowly is associated with profound pleasure. Fast sunbathing is not regarded as particularly enjoyable. If we want to understand a striking baseball catch, we replay it in slow motion. Why try to absorb the treasures of Florence in a brief guided tour, if you can spend a month appreciating them for yourself? If we want our children to apprehend the variety of human experience and learn how they can contribute to it, we must give them—and their teachers—the opportunity to do so. Let the slow times roll!

Part II

Tradition/Place

Indian Pedagogy:
A Look at Traditional California
Indian Teaching Techniques

Malcolm Margolin

Malcolm Margolin embodies commitment to the preservation of tradition from a place-based perspective. He is owner and publisher of Heyday Books, which he founded in 1974 to publish books on California history, literature, travel, and Native American life. Heyday has remained a vital independent press, one of the most important publishers of works on Native American topics and one of those most respected by native peoples. He is also founder, publisher, and coeditor of News from Native California, *a quarterly magazine devoted to the history and culture of California Indians, and cofounder of* Bay Nature, *a quarterly that focuses on the natural history of the San Francisco Bay Area. He cofounded the Native California Network, a foundation that raises money for traditional California Indian culture, and founded and chairs the Clapperstick Institute, a nonprofit organization devoted to deepening the public's understanding of California's cultural and natural heritage.*

His 1978 book The Ohlone Way *established him as a sensitive and observant reporter on Native American life. His other books include* The Earth Manual: How to Work on Wild Land without Taming It *(1975; revised 1985),* The Way We Lived: California Indian Reminiscences, Stories, and Songs *(1981; revised and expanded 1993), and* The East Bay Out: A Personal Guide to the East Bay Regional Parks *(1974).*

Margolin wears his erudition lightly and takes in the world the same way that he writes here, with patience, humility, and attention to the small details that together make big pictures. The big picture in this essay includes the profound distinction be-

tween teaching and learning, which he says is a basic element of California Indian pedagogy. He quotes an Indian saying, "When you teach someone something, you've robbed the person of the experience of learning it. You need to be cautious before you take that experience away from someone else." The Center for Ecoliteracy, working primarily outside of native cultures, has been guided by a similar belief; for instance, former CEL curriculum coordinator Juan Carlos Collins cites educational researcher Edgar Dale, who makes the point (from a Western statistics-oriented perspective) that people remember only 10 percent of what they have read, 20 percent of what they have discussed, and 90 percent of what they have experienced (Dale).

In this essay, Margolin describes a way of teaching that couldn't be farther from the prevalent mode in most Western schools, which follow what Brazilian educator and philosopher Paolo Freire has called the "banking model": "The teacher issues communiqués and makes deposits which the students patiently receive, memorize, and repeat" (Freire, p. 72). His findings illustrate Fritjof Capra's point in "Speaking Nature's Language" (Part I) that the new approach to education based on the theory of living systems shares much with ancient practice; educators can learn a lot by attending to the ways of cultures that have sustained themselves for thousands of years.

TO THOSE WHO DON'T KNOW MUCH about Indian cultures, the phrase "Indian pedagogy" might seem like a stretch. Granted, native cultures in California did not have what a modern resident would recognize as a formal educational system—designated teachers with specialized training, a defined curriculum, places and times set aside for instruction, clear standards for attainment, and so on. If we could have wandered into an Indian village a couple of hundred years ago, we might very well have concluded (as did other early visitors) that native children learned simply by following their parents and other relatives around from one chore to the next, accumulating knowledge by absorption, imitation, and, at best, casual ad hoc instruction. Seeing no schools, courthouses, churches, or farms, we, like other early observers, might have concluded that these "simple" hunting-and-gathering cultures had little in the way of educational, governmental, religious, agricultural, or economic practice or philosophy, and what little they did have was "underdeveloped" and "primitive." In other words, they weren't like us.

It would be impossible in this brief essay to tackle all these ethnocentric assumptions—the arrogant belief, so deeply embedded in Western culture, that we occupy the pinnacle of human achievement and that others are to be ranked according to how close they come to us. Recent generations of anthropologists and other scholars have steadily underscored the fact that so-called primitive people led lives of considerable complexity that included highly evolved, sophisticated, self-aware systems of governance, religion, and landscape manipulation, as well as of education, even if these systems are not easily recognizable through the prism of modern Western culture.

Education, in short, was not something that incidentally and passively happened to native children as they grew up. In fact the perceived need to properly educate children was striking, and considerable effort and skill were expended on it. Native California cultures had no writing; with no way to record knowledge—whether geographic, technical, artistic, social, or religious—transmitting and securing that knowledge deeply and accurately in the minds of a younger generation was of great concern. These cultures passed on knowledge with care, with strategy, with a self-conscious and articulated sense of educational theory. It is no exaggeration to say there was indeed a native pedagogy.

Being neither Indian nor an educator, I don't claim the authority or the background to explore this subject in the depth it deserves. I am, however, able to draw on thirty years of research, writing, and publishing about California Indian communities. Here are a few observations that may be of value to educators (including parents) now. At the least, an open-minded consideration of these traditional techniques and the assumptions underlying them may prove thought-provoking and may point to places where our own methods and educational system are overly narrow or even dangerously ineffective.

Repairing Feathers

In 1987 I cofounded a magazine devoted to California Indian culture, *News from Native California*, with two friends: Vera Mae Fredrickson, an anthropologist living in Berkeley, and David Peri, a Coast Miwok Indian who taught at Sonoma State University. In our first issue we ran an article by Harry Roberts, who had long been associated with the San Francisco Zen Center.

Although non-Indian himself, Harry had grown up near the mouth of the Klamath River and had lived closely with the Yurok. Robert Spott of the village of Requa, a man Harry referred to as "Uncle," was a well-known Yurok political and cultural leader. One morning, Harry recalled, he was watching Uncle repair the feathers on the long headdress wands used for a healing ceremony called the Brush Dance. Uncle was working hard, meticulously smoothing old feathers and regluing new feathers in places where young Harry could scarcely discern any damage. Why all the finickiness, Harry asked. The damage was hardly visible in the daylight, and the Brush Dance would be held at night; no one, neither dancers nor audience, would ever notice all of Uncle's demanding, scrupulous work. For a long time Uncle Spott avoided answering the question. Instead he asked that young Harry work on the answer himself, while he gave Harry only occasional prods, hints, and stories. Only after Harry had been forced to think hard about his question did Spott discuss it at all, and even then not so much directly as by telling a story that would lead to understanding.

I remember my coeditor David Peri remarking at the time that this was an excellent example of how the older generation conveyed important information. Robert Spott could have answered the question easily and directly, David observed, but he hadn't. By refusing to answer the question and refusing even to have much to do with Harry until Harry was on the way to figuring it out himself, Robert first put pressure on the youngster so that he'd know that what he had asked was important. Then he let him work on it, and when young Harry seemed closer to figuring it out Robert told a story that made it all come clear. Did I understand what was going on, David asked. Did I understand the difference between teaching and learning? In fact, David noted, there was a saying: When you teach someone something, you've robbed the person of the experience of learning it. You need to be cautious before you take that experience away from someone else.

This distinction between teaching and learning forms a basic element of what I am calling traditional California Indian pedagogy.

Initiation

Among the most powerful memories of an older generation of Indians was that of their initiation. Among many tribes a girl at her first menstruation would be sequestered, sometimes in a specially built shelter away from the family dwelling. Here she would eat special foods, perform certain rituals, and act in prescribed ways. Elders observed her closely, monitoring her gestures and her motions—there was only one approved way, for example, of scratching herself if her skin itched—and questioning her about her thoughts, even her dreams. Older women—her grandmother, her aunt, sometimes her mother, and others—would also lecture her, revealing secret knowledge that was kept from younger girls. After a period of time the initiate would be brought out in a public dance and celebration, transformed from a girl into a woman.

Boys often had a similarly dramatic and defined coming of age. In southern California boys reaching puberty would often be removed from their families and put under the care of spiritual leaders who would reveal secrets and transmit esoteric knowledge, often with the aid of powerful hallucinogens. Sometimes the initiate, in an altered state of consciousness, would be brought to a specially made sand painting, the patterns of which provided an explanation of how the powers of the world are aligned—nothing less than the blueprint of the universe. In northern California a young man might be invited to join the men's society of the roundhouse. He might in fact spend an entire winter in a subterranean roundhouse where he would learn songs, sacred dances, rituals, and other arcane (as well as practical) knowledge before emerging in the spring as an adult.

Today we like to think that we live in a society marked by open access to knowledge, but even in this age of the World Wide Web, this is hardly the case. All kinds of information—nuclear secrets, military secrets, commercial secrets, private medical records, and so on—are kept out of reach of the uninitiated, often at considerable effort and expense. It is not unusual to visit a public archive to view someone's papers and discover that the papers are under seal until fifty years after the person's death, because they contain "sensitive material." And we all know that once we discover that something is secret we are all the more eager to learn about it. Traditional societies used this universal human trait—our eagerness to reach out for withheld knowledge—in a very successful pedagogical practice.

Children learn differently from adults, the Indians felt, and therefore learning had to be paced. If exposed to adult knowledge while too young, people would misunderstand and devalue it. Children learn in a particular way, it was said, and you needed to respect that way. Once they reached the threshold of adulthood and were judged ready for the complex knowledge one needed to be a fully functioning adult, the knowledge was carefully prepared and presented to them: not thrown at them, nor left around for them to pick at, but handed to them in a highly ritualized setting that made the recipients feel that what they were being given was long sought, highly valued, and would consequently be cherished, remembered, and likewise passed on.

Paradoxically, making certain kinds of knowledge scarce helped ensure that it would be conveyed carefully from one generation to the next in a manner that reinforced its importance. For example, the creation myth is arguably the most important piece of knowledge in any culture, and transmitting it with total accuracy, with even the smallest details intact, is of major concern, especially for cultures that depend entirely on the spoken word and human memory. One would imagine that the best way of doing this would be to make sure that the creation story was told as often and in as many circumstances as possible, but this was not the case. Many tribes severely restricted the time and manner of telling. In some areas of California, for example, the creation story could be told only during the winter months, only at night, only in a sanctified space, only by a particularly trained and authorized person who had to fast for so many days, who had to sit in a particular posture, and so forth. Because the telling of the creation story was rare and difficult, its importance was emphasized, its recitation made keener and the audience's listening more intense.

What a Song Means

In southern California a few people still sing what are called "bird songs," linked verses that used to be sung for four nights straight during the winter.

They recount the wanderings of divinities over the world in the earliest moments of creation. My friend Ernest Siva, a Serrano and Cahuilla Indian from Banning, is one such singer. Once after he had sung an especially lovely verse, I summoned up the courage to ask him what it meant. After some thought, he responded something like this: If I was asking what the words meant, he'd be glad to translate them for me. But that's not really what the song meant, at least to him. What gave the song its meaning was not just the words but who had taught it to him, when it could be sung, who could sing it, all the other times it had been sung, to whom he had or would be teaching it. When it was sung at a funeral, for example, that circumstance added to the memory and thus the meaning of the song.

Traditional societies personally transmit and personally use knowledge. It doesn't exist in books that can be shelved; songs are not recorded on CDs that can be played at will. Knowledge exists only because one person gave it to another, and it is kept alive only by repeated use and personal transmission. How one learns something and uses that knowledge is important in traditional societies, more than in ours. We seem to feel that whatever is to be learned exists independently from the way it is transmitted. If, for example, one person learns one thing from a parent, another from a teacher, a third from a computer, we like to assume that they all know the same thing. You simply know as a fact that the earth revolves around the sun, whether you absorbed that fact in early childhood, learned it in adulthood, figured it out on your own, had to reject religious belief to get there, or learned it in English or in some other language. No matter how you learned it, it's a fact, and in our culture facts are seen as solid little building blocks, unchanged by how they are acquired or used.

In traditional cultures that does not seem to be the case. Knowledge, transmitted orally from generation to generation, comes with much more history, more personal interaction, more flavor if you will, and perhaps is felt with greater depth and emotional complexity. I remember that in my grammar school a teacher I had a crush on would read us books such as *Heidi*. I still think of the Swiss Alps with a great yearning and great love that I can't help but think would not be there had I picked the book up from the local library and read it myself. Native pedagogy concerns itself not just with what is taught but with who teaches it and under what circumstances. Teaching is not, in other words, just a means of conveying knowledge and information; it is an integral part of that knowledge and information as well.

The Center of the World

Jaime de Angulo, a linguist and collector of folklore, was once working in the high, lonely country between Redding and Alturas in northeastern California, interviewing elders who still spoke the Achumawe and Atsugewi languages. When one old man began telling him the story of how Silver Fox created the world, Jaime interrupted. What do you mean Silver Fox created the world? I just heard from your neighbors that it was Coyote who created the world. The old man didn't pause. Well, he shrugged, over there they say it was Coyote, here we say it was Silver Fox, and he went on with the story.

I've witnessed the same thing many times. In northwestern California, for example, the Hupa have their world-renewal rituals at a place they consider the center of the world—the spot from which humans first emerged—Takimildin. A neighboring tribe, the Yurok, likewise have a center-of-the-world place, Kenek. And not far from them are the Karuk, with Katamin as their center of the world. And it is not unusual these days for a member of one tribe to visit another's rituals and even dance at their world center.

In Western cultures this level of tolerance would be almost inconceivable. Were this Europe, we would likely have witnessed centuries of religious warfare, with lands laid waste and countless "heretics" massacred, until the location of the "real" center of the world was resolved. Western culture seems to crave certainty; we demand it from our religious beliefs and from our educational system alike. We seem to feel that questions have answers and that these answers are exclusive—answering "yes" precludes answering "no." Things are true or they are false. Although we pay lip service to mystery, we construct educational systems around the assumption that things are knowable, and students are rewarded for knowing, for having the correct answer. If we don't know something, it's because we're ignorant, rather than because some things—often the most important things—are simply not knowable.

Built into California Indians' traditional teaching methods, and indeed their overall philosophy, is, I feel, a marvelous acknowledgment that much in the world around us is fundamentally mysterious and cannot be known with certainty. In fact, an important aspect of Indian pedagogy is something that I find heartbreakingly beautiful—a sense of humility: a sense that the world is far bigger, more complex, and more mysterious than the human mind can ever encompass, and that to be a full human being you need to learn to live with ambiguity and a tolerance for the unknown. The alternative is to live with brittle delusions of certainty.

Building a Roundhouse

Throughout much of north central California—from Mendocino and Sonoma Counties east to the Sierra foothills—the roundhouse was (and in places still is) a major cultural and architectural attainment. In traditional times, this large communal building was mostly underground and served variously as a place of worship, a community center, and a university.

A few years ago I was at Chaw'se State Park, where the Sierra Mewuk community erected an especially graceful roundhouse in about 1970, then rebuilt it in the early 1990s. It is well used, especially at an annual September event called Big Time, when people come from all over California to celebrate the fall harvest, using the roundhouse for dancing, singing, praying, and otherwise honoring their culture. Here, especially at dawn when dancers enter the roundhouse to greet the rising sun, one can feel the mystery, beauty, ongoing vitality, and truthfulness of California's oldest cultures.

One day I was talking with my friend Dwight Dutschke, whose family had taken part in the original construction and who himself has been actively engaged in the annual Big Time. Our conversation turned to how the roundhouse had been constructed, and I was questioning him about certain details: how the entranceway had been oriented, how the posts had been put in, how the rafters had been secured, and so on. Finally he said, "I know what you are

getting at. You're getting at the fact that we could have constructed it better."
"No, no," I protested, "that's not at all what I was getting at." "Well," he went
on, "we could indeed have constructed it better. A lot of the people who
worked on it were into construction, and we know how to build. We could
have put creosote on the posts when they went into the ground. There's nothing in the old laws that says you can't do that. There's nothing in the old laws
that says you have to tie the rafters with grape vine; we could have used wire
and nails. We could have built it so that it would last a hundred years. But we
didn't. We didn't because there was another law we had to follow. When you
build a roundhouse you construct it so that it falls apart every twenty years.
That way every generation has the chance to rebuild it. Every generation has
to learn the songs, the ceremonies, the techniques. If you want to make a building last you do it one way. But if you want to make the knowledge last, you
do it another way."

Sometimes at these annual Big Times a group such as the Pomo dancers
from Elem Colony near Clear Lake will perform a Big Head dance. The Big
Head is a mysterious figure, at least to me. Associated with a divinity called
Kuksu, in some places it is whistled out of the forest where it dwells, entering the roundhouse with a grand halo of a feathered headdress, pounding the
floor with bare feet in a rhythmic and repetitious dance, while the fire from
the middle of the roundhouse casts great shadows on the ceiling. Powerful
and awe-inspiring, both the dance and the regalia associated with it are protected by ritual, rules, and cultural proscriptions. I once asked one of the Big
Head dancers to explain it to me. His response was, "I'm not sure what it means;
all I know is that when I do the dance, it puts my head in the big way."

Both these phenomena—building the roundhouse and the Big Head
dance—point to yet another aspect of traditional pedagogy, a need not just to
"know" but to experience. Knowledge is not just something to be stored and
talked about; it's something to be lived. It's got to be "cooked into you," as they
say. It's not enough to have a lot of information, to have the "right" ideas, to
be able to answer the question correctly. Knowledge apart from experience cannot be trusted and won't last, certainly not in a culture without writing. A
Western theologian might very well research and assemble facts about what

the Big Head dance means; the dancer, however, knows something more important and lasting: that it puts his head in the "big way."

Mourning Dove

Walk almost anywhere in the forested lands of northwestern California and you will hear the plaintive call of the mourning dove. On at least four separate occasions, when I was with Indian friends, this call triggered the telling of the story of Mourning Dove, *o'row'e* in the Yurok language. It is perhaps the most popular and widely told of the old-time stories.

Like other such mythic tales, the story of *o'row'e* takes place in the distant past, shortly after the creation, when all the animals of the world were a kind of divine people (*woge* in Yurok). They seem to have lived and even looked much like people, and long ago their deeds established the world as we know it today.

In that old world, *o'row'e* was a gambler. Once he was deeply involved in a gambling game with others. He was on a great winning streak, piling up around himself great stores of Indian treasure: white deerskins, huge obsidian blades, red woodpecker scalps, long dentalia shells, in short all the wealth and beauty of the Indian world. He was interrupted by a messenger who had come to fetch him, to tell him that his grandfather was dying and that he needed to come immediately to the deathbed. Just a few more hands, just a few more hands, said *o'row'e*, and I'll be right there. He continued to play, continued to win, and his grandfather died. When the time of metamorphosis occurred, when the *woge* of old took on the animal forms by which we now know them, *o'row'e* was transformed into the mourning dove. To this day you can see glistening around his neck the treasures he had won in that gambling game. And you can hear the call he will make through eternity as he mourns forever the grandfather he once ignored.

Even today, every time someone hears *o'row'e* cry, it calls to mind that ancient story and with it a constant reminder that one cannot let material gain get in the way of more essential human obligations. If you do, you will pay eternally for the lapse: just listen to *o'row'e*.

Stories like this were embedded everywhere in traditional culture: animals, plants, mountains, stars, even big rocks, had a past, and wherever you went the sight of an animal, the call of a bird, the presence of a rock reminded you of an instructional story. You could not go anywhere without being informed, educated, lectured to by the world around you. This was not a soulless world that worked on principles of evolutionary biology, chemistry, and physics. It was a world alive with strands of consciousness. It had history, and it was profoundly moral.

We might, I suppose, view this simply as a pedagogical strategy. In cultures without writing, instruction can best be preserved by packaging it as a story and then attaching the story like a billboard to an animal, plant, or place so that people will constantly be reminded of it. That's valid, but I think there is something more: a sense that animals, plants, and everything else we see have something to teach us, that the important lessons in life are not just held by people but are part of the larger world. The world contains things that we need to know that are too important to be left solely to human beings, and these essential lessons are embedded in the animals, plants, mountains, and rivers around us. Learning, in short, does not just take place only in deliberate teaching situations between people. The entire world is a teacher.

Knowledge Comes to You

I'm not entirely certain, but I think I heard the following story a long time ago from a Hupa friend, Jack Norton. Jack told of a man, depressed and miserable, who sat by a creek. He had been sitting by the creek a long time when he was surprised to hear that the creek was singing him a song. He had never heard the song before, but when he went back home and sang it for an elder, the elder recognized it as a song that once belonged to someone who had died decades before. "How did the creek get the song?" asked the man. "I don't know," answered the elder, "but sometimes songs are like that. If they don't have anyone to sing them, they'll give themselves over to a creek for safekeeping."

I don't want to make too much of this—it's subtle, perhaps fragile, and I'm not sure how well I understand it—but many things, such as songs, dances, stories, and prayers, that our culture sees as strictly human fabrication seem to be viewed by some traditional cultures as entities that exist on their own. The song in the preceding story had a life outside the human race; if humans were to disappear, the song would still exist in the stream. To some degree, much of what people need to know is seen as residing in the world around them, with a mind and spirit of its own; in certain situations such knowledge gives itself over to people.

This is, I think, qualitatively and significantly different from the way we view knowledge—as something we acquire and we own. In our society, where commodity and marketplace are the dominant metaphors, we see knowledge as something to be grabbed, possessed, controlled. This sense of going after knowledge wasn't foreign to Indian pedagogy. When, for example, a woman training to be a shaman wanted a certain power, she often went out to try to capture it. But perhaps more typically, the shaman-in-training would put herself out in the world, perhaps fasting or undergoing other deprivation, and the power might take pity on her, see that she was a good person, and voluntarily come to her. The world was alive, and the knowledge and teachings you needed were not necessarily yours because you wanted them or even worked directly for them. Knowledge often came as a gift, and the goal of Indian pedagogy was to teach people the respect and alertness necessary so that they could recognize, receive, and in the end use the gifts that the world had given them.

On the subject of gifts, let me conclude by gratefully acknowledging that my thirty-year involvement with the California Indian community has been an extraordinary gift. I hope these thoughts on traditional California Indian pedagogy are helpful to others. They certainly worked for generation after generation in traditional cultures, where they kept alive not only cultural information, technical know-how, artistic skills, and religious belief, but also an understanding of how to be a full human being in the natural world. Perhaps within this traditional pedagogy are hints as to how we too might devise a system of education that doesn't just produce people who can take tests, but who have a chance of becoming "real persons."

Okanagan Education
for Sustainable Living:
As Natural as Learning to Walk or Talk

Jeannette C. Armstrong

One of the key ecological principles guiding the Center for Ecoliteracy is nested systems, reflecting the insight that each living system forms a whole itself, while at the same time it is part of a series of larger systems. In her essay "En'owkin" (Part I), Jeannette Armstrong, an Okanagan Indian born on the Penticton Indian Reserve in British Columbia, describes how, in Okanagan culture, each individual is always understood as a single facet of a family. Family systems, in turn, are understood to be the foundation of a network called the community, which uses its collective knowledge to secure the well-being of all its members. The community exists within the "vast and ancient body of intricately connected patterns, operating in perfect unison," called the land.

In this essay, Armstrong describes how these nested systems interacted in the process of education in the Okanagan ancestral system and how she and others within her community are working to preserve that system's traditions in the face of pressures to assimilate that have been forced on their community since colonization, as its young people have often been sent away to nonnative schools.

Since 1985, Armstrong has served as a faculty member, director of programs, and executive director of the En'owkin Centre in Penticton. En'owkin Centre is an indigenous cultural, educational, ecological, and creative arts post-secondary institution that practices and implements indigenous knowledge and systems. Its offerings include an indigenous fine arts program, an indigenous political development and leadership certificate program, and an Okanagan adult language program. The Centre hosts regional, national, and international indigenous conferences and forums, and houses Theytus Books, the first publisher in Canada under aboriginal ownership and control. For more information about Jeannette Armstrong, see the introduction to "En'owkin."

IN MY OKANAGAN ANCESTRAL SYSTEM, education occurred as a natural part of family and community in everyday living. Unlike today, education was not segregated into institutions of schooling separate from the family. Different families had different specialized skills and knowledge, which they transmitted from generation to generation with great pride, while embedding values necessary to sustain the community. Imparting skills and knowledge necessary for living well was as important then as it is today; the difference may be in how families presented sustainability principles in terms of communal behavior necessary to maintain healthy resources and food systems. As with most peoples who have developed highly sophisticated systems of sustainable land use, Okanagan family systems, operating within village communities, placed a high value on collaboration and sharing among village members.

Sharing resources and labor for security and sustenance was an esteemed responsibility modeled most stringently by the Chief family, or *qalth*, who spoke for the community and maintained peace. "Sharing" means something quite different in the Okanagan language from what it means in English. It constitutes "a manifestation or demonstration of how-to-be" rather than "possessions being divided among others." The clear imperative that individuals within the community must cooperate willingly to demonstrate sustainability values ensures the survival and well-being of the whole. Community exists to be shared with, rather than to be competed against.

In our language, we think of "community" as a living organism. The whole earth needs to be healthy for families to be healthy and for individuals to thrive. We recognize family systems, or *qalth*, as different parts of a body with different functions, just as the hands, the heart, and the head have different but necessary functions. One *qalth* might be skilled in craft, another *qalth* might be skilled in herbal knowledge, another might study land and food systems, and so on.

Having identity as part of a *qalth* offered deep assurance and a sense of belonging to individuals. *Qalth* systems alleviated social pressure on individuals and established cohort systems supportive of learning the special skills necessary to the whole. All older members shared responsibility for transferring
the *qalth*'s skills to its young. Mothers, fathers, older siblings, and cousins,
aunts, uncles, and grandparents were all seen as teachers, modeling good practice. The eldest were the most treasured teachers because, as they became physically frail, they were more available for advice and guidance. Therefore, they
enjoyed the constant attentions of younger people.

Survival knowledge and skills were acquired through real-world learning, modeling how the whole community must carry out work and sustenance
with future needs in mind, no matter how difficult the conditions. The belief
system, which celebrates life, places high value on careful taking of the land's
resources. It demonstrates how "sharing with community" extends to "our
relatives on the land." We think of the plants, fish, birds, and animals as "relatives," who share their lives with each other and with us. Every day, elder
qalth members show how these "relatives" share their gifts with us and therefore require our respect, love, and protection.

Learning useful skills and information, from that perspective, was as natural as learning to walk or talk. Children couldn't help but learn. They were
guided into enjoyment of their family's work of gathering berries and roots,
fishing, hunting, or making clothing and tools. Particular skills acquired by
different family members were sources of pride and enjoyment to be lovingly
handed down to the young as marks of identity.

The benefits consequently shared by the community included security and
support for those who might be disadvantaged by age, physical limitation, or
circumstance, since whole family systems compensated and produced all that
was required by the community. Higher value was placed on how well individuals learned to share and their willingness to collaborate rather than on the
mastery of everyday skills.

Settlement in the Okanagan occurred during my grandmother's early adult
years. The transition to ranching and farming occurred during our parents'
early adult years, and the introduction of "schooling" occurred during my older

siblings' youth. Harvesting from the land as hunters, gatherers, and as farmers remains very much a central practice of traditional families of the Okanagan. I have been fortunate in having experienced all that which my ancestors
learned, shared, and practiced. It is easy for me to see where the gaps are in our
present social system. Living in a village community that has retained some
of the practices and principles required for living sustainably makes my work
easier. But the practice of "schooling" has meant the loss of a good way of life
that was embedded in good community and land-based values.

Forced assimilation into the colonizing culture of schooling has taken its
toll on many of our communities, but the remnants of our family and community values can be relied upon to reconstruct good practice, which reinforces our tried and tested traditional system.

Our ecoliteracy program at the En'owkin Centre attempts to reconstruct
a way that shows how family, community, and land must interact in celebration and appreciation of the gift of life. At En'owkin, ecoliteracy means that
we must find ways to integrate academic and practical skills into a curriculum,
demonstrating principles of collaboration, sharing, and sustainable land use.
It means that we must strive to permeate all learning with opportunities for
family and community to create lasting systems. It means programs that continuously give place for ritual and recognition of the individual within family and community. It means a curriculum consciously focused on experiencing happiness through meaningful service and on collaboration as the highest
pleasures. It means that elders, parents, and community members are continually engaged in all aspects of programs and projects to ensure the full participation of all.

To meet these challenges, En'owkin Centre has had to evolve in a way
that is organic, while expressing a clear educational intent. We have the advantage of having good family and community culture to guide our work in
developing curricula that serve our goals. "Schooling" and "academics" are
connected directly to achieve healthy family, community, and land. Because
our programs and projects are ecoliteracy-based, they must demonstrate real-
world outcomes. We work on community-relevant projects that engage children, parents, and elders in the restoration of land, culture, and celebration.

For instance, EcoAction, one of our projects, restores a black cottonwood riparian ecosystem that is home to many endangered species. We bring children from various schools together with adult volunteers from our community and from environmental and civil organizations. The volunteers teach and share work and resources on restoration and stewardship. We organize work and outings to learn from our elders, who are our knowledge keepers. They teach us how to collect indigenous seeds at the right places and times of the season. Together, young people and old people propagate, care for, and transplant the seedlings. They learn and celebrate the work together.

While our resources are small, the Centre has drawn the surrounding community in, as a part of our practice of connecting land and people. The gatherings and celebrations are becoming traditions eagerly attended by huge numbers of new friends finding joy and peace in being. Our work is a fervent prayer for peace and sustenance of family, community, and land.

Place and Pedagogy

David W. Orr

"Place and Pedagogy" and "Recollection," the essay that follows, offer two perspectives on one experience. "Place and Pedagogy" was written while David W. Orr was in the midst of living and working at the Meadowcreek Project in Fox, Arkansas, which he had helped found in 1979. The intensely personal "Recollection" looks back at the Meadowcreek experience from the vantage point of 2004. These two approaches to the same general theme, place-based education, show us Orr's unwillingness to reach a conclusion about a subject, declare the problem solved, and be done with it. They also show his ability to come at the same issue from many directions.

Kenny Ausubel once said, when introducing David Orr to a Bioneers audience, that he "is simply the most important innovator in environmental education in the country and quite probably the world, and one of the great visionary educators of this time."

Orr has served on the Center for Ecoliteracy board since CEL's founding. His 1992 book Ecological Literacy *(from which the first essay is taken) and the ideas expressed in it are the source of the Center's name and the inspiration for many of its core practices, especially the centrality of education grounded in place.*

Orr has been instrumental in putting the concept of environmental literacy on the map and in inspiring a reexamination of the university and other educational institutions in addressing our civilization's environmental crisis. His books, Earth in Mind *(1994),* The Nature of Design *(2002), and* The Last Refuge: Patriotism, Politics, and the Environment in the Age of Terror *(2004), as well as* Ecological Literacy, *are seminal texts that will continue to have impact for generations.*

He is now a professor and chair of the Environmental Studies Program at Ober-

lin College. He has published over 120 articles in scientific and professional jour-
nals and serves as a contributing editor to the journal Conservation Biology.

Orr is perhaps known best in recent years for leading the effort to design and
build a $7.2 million environmentally intelligent Environmental Studies Center at
Oberlin, a building described by the New York Times *as "the most remarkable" of*
a new generation of college buildings. The building, which was conceived and designed
through a unique collaboration of students, staff members, and some of the most in-
novative designers and architects in the world, was selected as one of the thirty "mile-
stone buildings in the twentieth century" by the U.S. Department of Energy.

In Orr's work, as these essays show, there is no disconnection between theory
and practice. His writing is eco-design in action, and his practice is embodied theory.
Neither is there division within his work among functionality, ethics, ecology, aes-
thetics, and nourishment of the human spirit. Speaking about building design and
construction at a Bioneers workshop, he remarked, "You begin to think about the aes-
thetics starting all the way out at the wells, the mines, the manufacturing establish-
ments, by asking who's downwind and who's downstream. And if [the artifact] causes
ugliness there, you can't say that this artifact is beautiful. If it causes ugliness at some
later place, and some later time, you cannot say that the artifact itself is beautiful."
Orr's writing, as these essays and this book's foreword show, is beautiful, and hon-
est, and full of heart, and wise.

(Footnotes that were part of the original essay have been converted to in-text
citations, with a reference list at the end of the piece.)

THOREAU WENT TO LIVE by an ordinary pool on the outskirts of
an unremarkable New England village, "to drive life into a corner, and reduce
it to its lowest terms." Thoreau did not "research" Walden Pond, rather, he
went to live, as he put it, "deliberately." Nor did he seek the far-off and the ex-
otic, but the ordinary, "the essential facts of life." He produced no particularly
usable data, but he did live his subject carefully, observing Walden, its environs, and himself. In the process he revealed something of the potential lying
untapped in the commonplace, in our own places, in ourselves, and the rela-
tion between all three.

In contemporary jargon, Thoreau's excursion was "interdisciplinary."

Walden is a mosaic of philosophy, natural history, geology, folklore, archeology, economics, politics, education, and more. He did not restrict himself to any academic pigeonhole. His "discipline" was as broad as his imagination and as specific as the $28.12 he spent for his house. Thoreau lived his subject. *Walden* is more than a diary of what he thought; it is a record of what he did and what he experienced. If, as Whitehead put it, "The learned world . . . is tame because it has never been scared by the facts," one finds little that is tame in *Walden*. For Thoreau, the facts, including both Walden Pond and himself, goaded, tempered, and scared his intellect. Nor is this the timid objective observer whose personhood and intellect remain strangers to each other. For Thoreau, philosophy was important enough "to live accordingly to its dictates . . . to solve some of the problems of life, not only theoretically, but practically." Ultimately, Thoreau's subject matter was Thoreau: his goal, wholeness; his tool, Walden Pond; and his methodology, simplification.

Aside from its merits as literature or philosophy, *Walden* is an antidote to the idea that education is a passive, indoor activity occurring between the ages of six and twenty-one. In contrast to the tendencies to segregate disciplines, and to segregate intellect from its surroundings, *Walden* is a model of the possible unity between personhood, pedagogy, and place. For Thoreau, Walden was more than his location. It was a laboratory for observation and experimentation; a library of data about geology, history, flora, and fauna; a source of inspiration and renewal; and a testing ground for the man. *Walden* is no monologue, it is a dialogue between a man and a place. In a sense, *Walden* wrote Thoreau. His genius, I think, was to allow himself to be shaped by his place, to allow it to speak with his voice.

Other than as a collection of buildings where learning is supposed to occur, place has no particular standing in contemporary education. The typical college or university is organized around bodies of knowledge coalesced into disciplines. Sorting through a college catalogue, you are not likely to find courses dealing with the ecology, hydrology, geology, history, economics, politics, energy use, food policy, waste disposal, and architecture of the campus or its community. Nor are you likely to find many courses offering enlightenment to modern scholars in the art of living well in a place. The typical curriculum is reminiscent of Kierkegaard's comment after reading the vast, weighty corpus of Hegel's philosophy, that Hegel had "taken care of everything, except perhaps for the question of how one was to live one's life." Similarly, a great deal of what passes for knowledge is little more than abstraction piled on top of abstraction, disconnected from tangible experience, real problems, and the places where we live and work. In this sense it is utopian, which literally means "nowhere."

The importance of place in education has been overlooked for a variety of reasons. One is the ease with which we miss the immediate and the mundane. Those things nearest at hand are often the most difficult to see. Second, for purists, place itself is a nebulous concept. Yet Thoreau understandably spent little time trying to define the precise boundaries of his place, nor was it necessary to do so. *Walden* is a study of an area small enough to be easily walked over in a day and still observed carefully. Place is defined by its human scale: a household, neighborhood, community, forty acres, one thousand acres.

Place is nebulous to educators because to a great extent we are a deplaced people for whom our immediate places are no longer sources of food, water, livelihood, energy, materials, friends, recreation, or sacred inspiration. We are, as Raymond Dasmann once noted, "biosphere people," supplied with all these and more from places around the world that are largely unknown to us, as are those to which we consign our toxic and radioactive wastes, garbage, sewage, and industrial trash. We consume a great deal of time and energy going somewhere else. The average American moves ten times in a lifetime and spends countless hours at airports and on highways going to places that look a great deal like those left behind. Our lives are lived amidst the architectural expressions of deplacement: the shopping mall, apartment, neon strip, freeway, glass office tower, and homogenized development—none of which encourage much sense of rootedness, responsibility, and belonging.

Third, place by definition is specific, yet our mode of thought is increasingly abstract. The danger of abstraction lies partly in what Whitehead described as the "fallacy of misplaced concreteness": the confusion of our symbols with reality. The results are comparable, as someone put it, to eating the menu instead of the meal. Words and theories take on a life of their own, independent of the reality they purport to mirror, often with tragic results. At its worst, as Lewis Mumford describes it:

> The abstract intelligence, operating with its own conceptual apparatus, in its own self-restricted field is actually a coercive instrument: an arrogant fragment of the full human personality, determined to make the world over in its own oversimplified terms, willfully rejecting interests and values incompatible with its own assumptions, and thereby depriving itself of any of the cooperative and generative functions of life—feeling, emotion, playfulness, exuberance, free fantasy—in short, the liberating sources of unpredictable and uncontrollable creativity. (Mumford, "Utopia, the City, and the Machine," p. 10)

By capturing only a fragment of reality, unrelieved abstraction inevitably distorts perception. By denying genuine emotion, it distorts and diminishes human potentials. For the fully abstracted mind, all places become "real estate" or mere natural resources, their larger economic, ecological, social, political, and spiritual possibilities lost to the purely and narrowly utilitarian.

The idea that place could be a significant educational tool was proposed by John Dewey in an 1897 essay. Dewey proposed that we "make each of our schools an embryonic community . . . with types of occupations that reflect the life of the larger society." He intended to broaden the focus of education, which he regarded as too "highly specialized, one-sided, and narrow." The school, its relations with the larger community, and all of its internal functions, Dewey proposed to remake into curriculum.

The regional survey, which reflected a broader conception of the role of place in education, was developed by Lewis Mumford in the 1940s. In Mumford's words, the regional survey was

> not something to be added to an already crowded curriculum. It is rather (potentially) the backbone of a drastically revised method of study, in which every aspect of the sciences and the arts is ecologically related from the bottom up, in which they connect directly and

constantly in the student's experience of his region and his community. Regional survey must begin with the infant's first exploration
of his dooryard and his neighborhood; it must continue to expand
and deepen, at every successive stage of growth until the student is
capable of seeing and experiencing above all, of relating and integrating and directing the separate parts of his environment, hitherto
unnoticed or dispersed. (Mumford, *Values for Survival*, pp. 151–52)

The regional survey (Mumford cites *Walden* as a classic example) involved
the intensive study of the local environment by specialists and every member
of the community, including schoolchildren. As the focal point for education,
the regional survey was intended to create habits of thinking across disciplines,
promote cooperation, and dissolve distinctions between facts and values, the
past and the future, and nature and human society. Beyond education, Mumford regarded the regional survey as the basis for rational coordination and planning and as a vehicle for widespread public participation.

The integration of place into education is important for four reasons. First,
it requires the combination of intellect with experience. The typical classroom
is an arena for lecture and discussion, both of which are important to intellectual growth. The study of place involves complementary discussions of intellect: direct observation, investigation, experimentation, and skill in the application of knowledge. The latter is regarded merely as "vocational education."
But for Mumford and Dewey, practical and manual skills were an essential aspect of experience, good thinking, and the development of the whole person.
Both regarded the acquisition of manual skills as vitally important in sharp-
ening the intellect. Dewey again:

We cannot overlook the importance for educational purposes of the
close and intimate acquaintance got with nature at first hand, with real
things and materials, with the actual processes of their manipulations,
and the knowledge of their special necessities and uses. In all this there
[is] continual training of observation, of ingenuity, constructive imagination, of logical thought, and of the sense of reality acquired through

firsthand contact with actualities. The educative forces of the domestic spinning and weaving, of the sawmill, the gristmill, the cooper ship, and the blacksmith forge were continually operative. (Dewey, p. 457)

Similarly, Whitehead states that:

There is a coordination of senses and thought, and also a reciprocal influence between brain activity and material creative activity. In this reaction, the hands are peculiarly important. It is a moot point whether the human hand created the human brain, or the brain created the hand. Certainly, the connection is intimate and reciprocal. (Whitehead, p. 50)

In the reciprocity between thinking and doing, knowledge loses much of its abstractness, becoming in the application to specific places and problems tangible and direct.

Second, the study of place is relevant to the problems of overspecialization, which has been called a terminal disease of contemporary civilization. It is surely debilitating to the individual intellect. Mumford's remedy for the narrow, underdimensioned mind is the requirement to balance analysis with synthesis. This cannot be accomplished by adding courses to an already overextended curriculum or by fine-tuning a system designed to produce specialists. It can be done only by reconceptualizing the purposes of education in order to promote diversity of thought and a wider understanding of interrelatedness. Places are laboratories of diversity and complexity, mixing social functions and natural processes. A place has a human history and a geologic past; it is part of an ecosystem with a variety of microsystems, it is a landscape with a particular flora and fauna. Its inhabitants are part of a social, economic, and political order: they import or export energy materials, water, and wastes, they are linked by innumerable bonds to other places. A place cannot be understood from the vantage point of a single discipline or specialization. It can be understood only on its terms as a complex mosaic of phenomena and problems. The classroom and indoor laboratory are ideal environments in which to narrow reality in order to focus on bits and pieces. The study of place, by contrast, enables us to widen the focus to examine the interrelationships between disciplines and to lengthen our perception of time.

It is important not to stop learning at the point of mere intellectual comprehension. Students should be encouraged to act on the basis of information from the survey to identify a series of projects to promote greater self-reliance, interdisciplinary learning, and physical competence, such as policies for food, energy, architecture, and waste. These provide opportunities for intellectual and experiential learning involving many different disciplines working on tangible problems. If the place also includes natural areas, forests, streams, and agricultural lands, the opportunities for environmental learning multiply accordingly.

Finally, for Mumford and Dewey, much of the pathology of contemporary civilization was related to the disintegration of the small community. Dewey wrote in 1927: "The invasion and partial destruction of the life of the [local community] by outside uncontrolled agencies is the immediate source of the instability, disintegration, and restlessness which characterize the present epoch." The study of place, then, has a third significance in reeducating people in the art of living well where they are. The distinction between inhabiting and residing is important here. A resident is a temporary occupant, putting down few roots and investing little, knowing little, and perhaps caring little for the immediate locale beyond its ability to gratify. As both a cause and effect of displacement, the resident lives in an indoor world of office building, shopping mall, automobile, apartment, and suburban house, and watches television an average of four hours each day. The inhabitant, in contrast, "dwells," as [Ivan] Illich puts it, in an intimate, organic, and mutually nourishing relationship with a place (Illich). Good inhabitance is an art requiring detailed knowledge of a place, the capacity for observation, and a sense of care and rootedness. Residence requires cash and a map. A resident can reside almost anywhere that provides an income. Inhabitants bear the marks of their places, whether rural or urban, in patterns of speech, through dress and behavior. Uprooted, they get homesick. Historically, inhabitants are less likely to vandalize theirs or others' places. They also tend to make good neighbors and honest citizens. They are, in short, the bedrock of the stable community and neighborhood that Mumford, Dewey, and Jefferson regarded as the essential ingredient of democracy.

Paul Shepard explains the stability of inhabitants as a consequence of the interplay between the psyche and a particular landform. "Terrain structure," he argues, "is the model for the patterns of cognition" (Shepard, pp. 22–32). The physical and biological patterns of a place are imprinted on the mind so the "cognition, personality, creativity, and maturity—all are in some way tied to particular gestalts of space." Accordingly, the child must have an opportunity to "soak in a place, and the adolescent and adult must be able to return to that place to ponder the visible substrate of his own personality." Hence, knowledge of a place—where you are and where you come from—is intertwined with knowledge of who you are. Landscape, in other words, shapes mindscape. Since it diminishes the potential for maturation and inhabitance, the ravagement of places is psychologically ravaging as well. If Shepard is right, and I believe that he is, we are paying a high price for the massive rearrangement of the North American landscape of the past fifty years.

For deplaced people, education in the arts of inhabitation is partly remedial learning: the unlearning of old habits of waste and dependency. It requires, first, the ability to perceive and utilize the potentials of a place. One of the major accomplishments of the past several decades has been the rediscovery of how much ordinary people can do for themselves in small places. The significance of this fact coincides with the growing recognition of the ecological, political, and economic costs, and the vulnerability of the large-scale centralized systems, whether publicly or privately controlled. Smaller-scale technologies are often cheaper and more resilient, and they do not undermine democratic institutions by requiring the centralization of capital, expertise, and political authority. Taken together, they vastly expand the potential of ecologically designed, intensively developed places to meet human needs on a sustained basis.

Education for reinhabitation must also instill an applied ethical sense toward habitat. Again Leopold's standard—"A thing is right when it tends to preserve the integrity, stability, and beauty of the biotic community. It is wrong when it tends otherwise"—is on balance a clear standard for most de-

cisions about the use we make of our places. From the standpoint of education, the stumbling block to development of an ethic of place is not the complexity of the subject; it is the fact, as Leopold put it, "that our educational system is headed away from . . . an intense consciousness of land" (Leopold, pp.
224, 225).

Critics might argue that the study of place would be inherently parochial
and narrowing. If place were the entire focus of education, it certainly could
be. But the study of place would be only a part of a larger curriculum which
would include the study of relationships between places as well. For Mumford, place was simply the most immediate of a series of layers leading to the
entire region as a system of small places. But parochialism is not the result of
what is studied as much as how it is studied. Lewis Thomas, after all, was able
to observe the planet in the workings of a single cell (Thomas).

At issue is our relationship to our own places. What is the proper balance between mobility and rootedness? Indeed, are rootedness and immobil-
ity synonymous? How long does it take for one to learn enough about a place
to become an inhabitant and not merely a resident? However one chooses to
answer these questions, the lack of a sense of place, our "cult of homelessness,"
is endemic, and its price is the destruction of the small community and the resulting social and ecological degeneracy (Brownell). We are not the first foot-
loose wanderers of our species. Our nomadism, however, is on a larger and
more destructive scale.

We cannot solve such deep problems quickly, but we can begin learning
how to reinhabit our places, as Wendell Berry says, "lovingly, knowingly, skill-
fully, reverently" (Berry, p. 281), restoring context to our lives in the process.
For a world growing short of many things, the next sensible frontiers to explore are those of the places where we live and work.

References

Berry, Wendell. *The Gift of Good Land*. San Francisco: North Point Press, 1981.
Brownell, Baker. *The Human Community*. New York: Harper Brothers, 1950.
Dewey, John. "The School and Social Progress." In J. McDermott, ed., *The Philosophy of John Dewey*.
    Chicago: University of Chicago Press, 1981.
Illich, Ivan. "Dwelling." *CoEvolution Quarterly* 41 (Spring 1984).

Leopold, Aldo. *A Sand County Almanac*. New York: Oxford University Press, 1987; orig. pub. 1949.

Mumford, Lewis. "Utopia, the City, and the Machine." In Frank Manuel, ed., *Utopias and Utopian Thought*. Boston: Beacon Press, 1966.

Mumford, Lewis. *Values for Survival*. New York: Harcourt, Brace and Co., 1946.

Shepard, Paul. "Place in American Culture." *North American Review* (Fall 1977): 22–32.

Thomas, Lewis. *The Lives of a Cell*. New York: Viking Press, 1974.

Whitehead, Alfred North. *The Aims of Education*. New York: Free Press, 1967; orig. pub. 1929.

Recollection

David W. Orr

> Once in his life a man . . . ought to give himself up to a particular landscape
> in his experience, to look at it from as many angles as he can, to wonder
> about it, to dwell upon it. He ought to imagine that he touches it with his
> hands at every season and listen to the sounds that are made upon it. He
> ought to imagine the creatures there and all the faintest motions of the wind.
> He ought to recollect the glare of noon and all the colors of the dawn and
> dusk. —N. Scott Momaday, *The Way to Rainy Mountain*, p. 83

WE CAME AS INTERLOPERS to a place to which we had neither
attachments nor roots. What we had were ideas, energy, a bit of cash, and a
belief that we might do great and good things. We found this place quite by
serendipity, and it was a good choice for reasons that we could not have known
in advance and a poor choice for obvious reasons we did not see. Of course,
we became the first students and the place itself became both our tutor and the
curriculum.

Our intent was to create an environmental educational center without
disciplinary blinders, shortsightedness, and the bureaucracy of conventional
educational institutions. The idea behind the Meadowcreek experiment was
that we would draw a line around the 1,500 acres we'd bought in the Arkansas
Ozarks and make everything that happened inside that line curriculum: how
we farmed the 250 acres of bottom land, how we built, how we managed
the 1,200 acres of forest, the applied ecology necessary to manage the place,
how we supplied ourselves with energy. Rather like Henry Thoreau going to
Walden in order to drive some of the problems of living into a corner where
they might be more easily studied, we intended this three-mile-long valley to
be a laboratory in which to study some of the problems of living and liveli-

hood on a finite planet. Our curriculum coalesced around sustainable agriculture, forestry, applied ecology, rural economic development, and renewable energy technology, delivered through internships with college graduates, January terms, conferences, seminars, and scholar-in-residence programs. Broadly, if it had to do with the subject of sustainability, it was fair game for us. Over a decade the number of conference guests, students, and visitors rose to several thousand per year, and the list of attendees, visiting faculty, and conference participants included a roster of most of the prominent thinkers and activists in the field.

But the place itself became an agent in the curriculum in ways we did not always anticipate. The land, as Thoreau noted, had its own expectations and priorities lurking below all of our confident talk about education and our efforts to render place into pedagogy. Land has a mind of its own to which we are not privy. The curriculum of that place came to include particular happenings that we did not anticipate (such as a five-hundred-year flood, the hottest and driest summer ever, and the coldest winter on record), along with the mysterious processes that we pigeonhole with academic words like ecology, forestry, botany, soil science, and animal behavior.

We'd come from one of the centers of wealth and power in American society, Chapel Hill, North Carolina. By every measure Fox, Arkansas, is at the periphery. The world of power, wealth, and influence looks very different from the outside looking in. I'd arrived full of self-assurance, thinking myself well educated, knowledgeable, and armed with a compelling point of view. Eleven years later I knew how phony that assurance can be. We set out to create an educational experiment, influenced by places like Black Mountain College, Deep Springs College, and a few others at the periphery of American education and imagination. I thought my education and background would be adequate to the challenge. From the age of five onward I had been in or around higher education as the son of a college president, a student, and a faculty member. I soon discovered much of that experience to be irrelevant. In all of my time as a student or teacher I recall few serious conversations about the purposes and nature of education and none at all about the adequacy of formal education relative to our role as members in the community of life. It was assumed that mastery of a subject matter was sufficient in order to teach others, and that those very subjects are properly conceived and important.

In that void I had grown disillusioned by the rigid separation of disciplines in the academy and its indifference to big questions about the human future. I was disillusioned, too, about what I perceived to be the separation of head, hands, and heart in the learned world. Education, it was assumed, began at the neck and worked up, but dealt with only half of that. Study of the other half, that part of mind where feeling, humor, poetry, and integration originate, was considered lacking in rigor by people who were often, I thought, unable to distinguish between rigor and rigor mortis. The resulting wars between head, hands, and heart, and between the worlds of theory and of practical experience, were fought, but without much awareness, in every classroom, school, and college in the land, and in the minds and lives of every student. Problems we often diagnose as ones of bad behavior and low motivation among those to be educated or those doing the educating more likely reflect the miscalibration between schooling and something deep inside trying to break free. On the political science faculty at the University of North Carolina I found only two colleagues, out of thirty-six, sympathetic to such woolly ideas, one who worked as a poet in his spare time and the other a man who'd spent his academic life thinking about connections and systems. It was not considered appropriately rigorous to discuss the directions or adequacy of knowledge and research and certainly not as these applied to, or perhaps even contributed to, problems of human tenure on earth.

Confronted by the mysteries of a place in the Ozarks that I did not know, and slightly bookish by nature, I also read avidly all of those writers on education that I had avoided in my earlier years as a college teacher, including John Dewey, Albert Schweitzer, Maria Montessori, J. Glenn Gray, and Alfred North Whitehead, and others like Gregory Cajete, Thomas Merton, Parker Palmer, and Chet Bowers. There is, I discovered, a profound criticism of the foundations of contemporary education in their writings that emphasizes the importance of place, individual creativity, our implicatedness in the world, reverence, and the stultifying effects of "second-hand learning," as Whitehead once put it. From a variety of sources, we know that the things most deeply embedded in us are formed by the combination of experience and doing with the practice of reflection and articulation. And we know, too, that what Rachel Carson called "the sense of wonder" requires childhood experience in nature and constant practice as well as early validation by adults. The cultivation of the sense of wonder, however, takes us to the edge of mystery where language loses its power to describe and where analysis, the taking apart of things, is impotent before the wholeness of Creation, where the only appropriate response is a prayerful silence.

In the late fall of 1983 we moved into a passive solar house that we built on the site of what had once been a steam-powered sawmill. Little of the mill remained but the rock pad where the boiler and steam engine once sat, along with rusted pipes, wrenches, axe heads, and bolts, all overgrown with greenbrier, cedar, and sweet gum. The place had become so overgrown that it was an eyesore to the few who traveled the dirt road that ran along the east edge of the site at the foot of a steep hill. The house was nestled in the arm of a steep hill to the east and a low boulder-strewn wooded hill to the north. Looking to the west through a patch of second-growth trees, across what local people called the "sand field," past Meadowcreek, the west ridge rose six hundred feet to rock bluffs and chimney rocks at the top. To the south the house looked down the three miles of the Meadowcreek Valley to the gorge of the Middle Fork of the Little Red River and the bluffs beyond. At night the only visible evidence of human occupation was a light at a Methodist church camp seven miles distant.

I began to clear the site in spare time in the late fall, mostly because it offended my idea of what an edge ought to look like. Farm boundaries, fencerows, and the edge of fields, I'd learned, should be neat and manicured. Descartes would have liked it that way. This was a conviction for which I was prepared to shed blood. Those familiar with greenbrier may know about how much blood can be shed in the clearing of roughly an acre of land overrun with it. As the brush, vines, briers, and small trees gave way, traces of the old sawmill became apparent. The owners of the mill had dug out a basin, now overgrown, that collected water from a natural seep at the back of the site. This water was used to cool the boiler which sat on a rock pad about fifteen feet long by five feet wide, now anchored at one end by a giant sycamore tree. Heat had made the upper layers of rock brittle so that they could be broken apart by hand. Still, most of the rock was useful for building retaining walls around the house.

Remnants of rusty hand-forged tools and metalware lay all about: head blocks from the sawmill, battered buggy-wheel rims, pipes, and things I could not identify. My collection, carefully cleaned and painted with Rustoleum, was eventually nailed up to the side of my woodshed. The collection testified to human ingenuity and perseverance in the face of necessity. Some nameless person, for example, had taken two pieces of strap metal, hot-welded them together, and beveled one edge to make a workable chisel. We discovered dozens of wrenches, perhaps made by the same person, with similar homespun resourcefulness. I showed one piece of rusty pipe split at the seams to an itinerant philosopher with a keen sense of place and a compassionate heart. He uttered a low sigh and said he hoped that whatever child had forgotten to drain the boiler some frosty night long past was not rebuked too harshly. So did I.

While I was clearing the site, the place was working on me in its own fashion. Often I would stop work to gaze down the valley or look up at the bluffs to the west. I wondered who had owned the mill. What were they like? What kind of life did they have in this place? Why did they leave? Several hundred yards to the south at the end of the sand field, where Meadowcreek had once run diagonally across the valley floor, was the site of an ancient Osage Indian village recently excavated by local archeologists. What were their lives like here? Were they, in some sense, still here? The place, I tell you, had voices.

It also had sounds. Across the sand field, Meadowcreek, on its way to the Gulf of Mexico via the Middle Fork, White River, and Mississippi, tumbles over and around boulders the size of cars. The first heavy rains in the late fall raise the water level and the sound of rushing water would again fill the valley. In the late evening owls in the woods across the field would begin their nightly conversations. Occasionally I'd join in until they discovered that I had nothing sensible to say, at which point they would descend into a sullen silence so as not to encourage me further. In the spring and early summer the chuck-will's widows and tree frogs would hold their evening serenades. Once a month or so a pack of coyotes would interrupt their raids on the local chicken houses to hold a symposium in the valley. Unlike owls, who converse patiently throughout the night, coyotes handle their business quickly, seldom taking longer than thirty minutes, and then it's back to work. The wind blows hot straight up the valley from the south all summer long The winter wind comes cold down the valley out of the Bear Pen. Pieces of ancient seabed raised to bluff height would sometimes be heard breaking loose and crashing to the forest floor below. Except for an occasional pick-up truck, however, few human-made sounds intruded on the symphony of wind and rushing water. And although humans in the past century had taken a terrible toll on the valley, the wounds were healing. One could imagine this as a wilderness in the re-making.

I do not recall when the thought of building a house in this place first came to Elaine or me. Once we had made our decision, however, the logic of the location became clear. The site was sheltered from the north wind yet open to the summer sun and summer winds to the south. It was shaded from the summer sun by woods on the west. It was located in the valley, where summer heat was tempered by cooler air descending in the night, yet it was high enough to be out of the flood plain. And the view down Meadowcreek Valley framed by high ridges on either side was an endless and ever-changing delight. But logic was just a rationalization for holding a deeper conversation with a particular place and its nameless guardian spirits. We *had* to build there.

Once I invited a cosmopolitan woman writer of note from San Francisco to give a talk to our students and staff on the theme of the importance of place. Her talk was sophisticated, smart, and full of allusions to great writers and big ideas. But she was honest enough to admit that she had no sense of place, only words and thoughts about it. By her own admission, place was an abstraction. In the back of the room, listening intently, were several Ozark women whose daily life was lived to the rhythms and demands of place. They lived the reality, privations, and joys that the other woman for the most part could only talk about. They could, however, no more intellectualize about place and its importance than they could repeal the law of gravity. Afterward, I asked several of them what they thought about the talk, to which they responded that they did not understand a word of it. "One who knows does not say and one who says does not know"—Lao Tzu.

Attachment to place grows by a stealth by which mere words and thoughts give way to something deeper. In time the boundary of the person and the place can become almost indistinguishable. There are people who die quickly when uprooted from their ancestral homes. I have come to believe that driving people from the places in which they are rooted is about the most cruel punishment that one human can inflict on another. But I do not believe that one can plan to become attached or centered in a place. It takes time, patience, perhaps poverty, but most certainly a great deal of necessity. And like combining hydrogen and oxygen to make water, it takes some nameless emergent third thing by which novelty comes about. It cannot happen during a vacation, although a kind of infatuation with a place can occur in that length of time. It will not likely happen without something akin perhaps to a marriage vow, a commitment to a particular location for better or for worse. Can it happen in a city? Not likely, at least not likely in the cities that we've built. My urban friends will protest that they too have a sense of place. By my reckoning, however, what they have is a sense of habitat shaped by familiarity for human-made places. The sense of place is the affinity for what nature, not humankind, has done in a particular location, and the skill to live accordingly.

One moonlit night I decided to walk south down the valley toward the Middle Fork, about an hour-long walk. On my return through the tree breaks, the moon rising above the eastern ridge, I was aware of being followed. Heart racing, I quickened my pace through a tree break dividing one field from another, went another twenty paces or so, and then turned around. Close behind was a lone coyote perhaps crossed with a bit of red wolf, the largest I'd ever seen. I had no weapon and wasn't nearly fast enough to outrun him. But when I stopped, he stopped and then did not budge. We were eye to eye in the awkward wordless boundary between species. His intentions were unknown to me, and, I suppose, mine were to him. Trying to calm myself and not knowing what else to do, I spoke a few words, assuming language to be an advantage of sorts. The coyote cocked his head to one side, ears perked up. He would occasionally look away and then look back with what I interpreted

hopefully as a quizzical but slightly interested look on his face. I was encouraged and greatly relieved. After a few minutes of monologue and perked ears,
I decided to sit down; he reciprocated. I took this as a good sign and continued to talk softly, even tried to sing a bit, and from time our eyes would meet
and I heard him make something like a low yip, yip sound that sounded
friendly enough. By now the moon was nearly overhead and we were fully
visible to each other. After what may have been five or ten minutes, I stood
up and he stood as well. I took one slow step forward, he responded by splay-
ing out his feet ready to bolt. With my next step he bounded off toward the
woods, paused to look back and then disappeared into the night. I stood and
watched him fade into the trees along the creek and then walked home, blessed
in some way that I could not describe.

I had ventured into the coyote's world of night foraging and mating, and
I think he was simply curious about this lone, misplaced human. I had no
weapon and no machine, which made me more approachable. Perhaps it is van-
ity, but I think we did communicate in a fashion. Extending a bit further, he
was both curious and courteous. And those who profess not to believe that
animals think have never ventured alone and vulnerable into a conversation
with one on its terms and in its native habitat. Being vulnerable requires a degree of agility and openness that is alien to the enclosed curriculum of the academy where the matters of greatest consequence have to do with grade-point
averages, tenure, and *US News and World Report*'s annual ranking of colleges.

I doubt that we can ever come to love the planet as some claim to do, but
I know that we can learn to love particular places. I believe that the evolution
of a humane, just, and durable civilization will require a great deal of love and
competence and restraint that love requires for particular places. I believe that,
far from being a quaint relic of a bygone age, the love of place and the acceptance of the discipline of place will prove to be essential to a decent future.

After eleven years at the periphery, wrestling with busted fences, recalcitrant
cows, and the relationship between place and pedagogy on the back forty, I returned to the academy to teach in the Environmental Studies Program at Oberlin College. In the transition I discovered how much the previous eleven years

had changed my own views of the process and substance of education. I had a Ph.D. but had not been educated to think about education, the Latin root for which means to draw forth. But who is qualified and by what standards to mid-wife the birth of personhood in another or spark another's mind into the state of awareness or to properly appraise the results? What does it mean to be edu-cated and by what standard is that mysterious process to be judged? In some cir-cles, great stock is placed on mastery of routine knowledge, what Brazilian ed-ucator Paulo Freire described as the banking model of education. Others, deemed more progressive, emphasize the process of learning, which mostly means the cultivation of a kind of disciplined curiosity. Both, however, conceive education as a form of "anthropolatry," in the philosopher Mary Midgley's word, the worship of human accomplishments, history, and mastery of nature (see "Sus-tainability and Moral Pluralism," in Midgley). As anthropolatry, the study of nature is mostly intended to fathom how the world works so as to permit a more complete human mastery and a finer level of manipulation extending down into genes and atoms and outward into the far reaches of space.

My experience in the Ozarks opened the door to the different possibility that education ought, somehow, to be more of a dialogue requiring the capac-ity to listen to wind, water, animals, sky, nighttime sounds, and what a native American once described as earthsong . . . the very sorts of things dismissed by Midgley's anthropolators as romantic nonsense.

Had I been asked during my initial interview for the position at Oberlin to summarize my views of education based on my eleven-year sojourn in the Ozarks, my answer would have been something like this:

I believe that humankind, a precocious upstart ape, has a long way to go and a short time to get there, as country philosopher Jerry Reed once put it. We are rather like the passengers hearing the pilot over the intercom say that the flight is running ahead of schedule, but is lost.

I believe that as a species we are promising in many ways—as we assume in moments of self-congratulation—but no one can say for certain exactly what that promise might be. Opinions tend to divide between those who think us like some kind of cosmic dandelion destined to send our seed out to fill every nook and cranny of the universe and those who would prefer a more modest

and spiritually deeper evolutionary course. I believe these to be mutually exclusive paths. But celebration of humankind, Midgley's "anthropolatry," is
deeply, perhaps fatally, embedded in both.

I believe that the world is one and indivisible and that every attempt to
reduce it to its components, however useful in the short term, distorts reality and misleads us into thinking ourselves to be smarter than we are in fact.
Discovering "the pattern that connects," or systems thinking, is hard for us,
particularly when it includes nonquantitative elements of values, time, and
rights. Beyond reductionism, other modes of knowing characteristic of other
cultures and other times have little or no standing within the prevailing view
of what constitutes rigorous thinking. Across its various departments and programs the academy is a methodological monoculture.

I believe that our serious problems are first and foremost problems of
heart and empathy, and only secondarily problems of intellect. In other words,
mere smartness is much overrated and is not, as is widely believed, entirely
synonymous with intelligence. But good-heartedness is a kind of long-term
intelligence.

I believe education properly conceived can help each of us overcome the
centripetal tug of greed, illusion, and ill will, but that is a lifelong process that
only begins with formal schooling.

I believe that that part of education initiated in classrooms ought to equip
us, as J. Glenn Gray once said, to understand our implicatedness in life—that
no person can be an island or should want to be.

I believe that the idea that the truth sets us free is just a slogan. Truth, I
suspect, is furtive, seldom showing itself in air-conditioned rooms, as someone once put it. When it shows itself, it is likely to be daunting, confusing,
conflicting, ironic, perhaps even terrifying, but not necessarily liberating as
we understand that word. It is more likely to be hard, demanding, and elusive.
The path of least resistance is to seek smaller truths and live comfortably in
denial of larger ones. The proper role of education is to jar us out of that som-
nambulant state and prepare the learner to be worthy for the encounter with
truth if and when so graced.

I believe that what is advertised as the "explosion of knowledge" is largely fraudulent. What has exploded, as Jacques Barzun noted in *The American University*, is mostly "(1) repetition in swollen fragments of what was known more compactly and elegantly before; (2) repetition, conscious or not, of new knowledge found by others; (3) repetition of oneself in diverse forms; and (4) original worthlessness" (Barzun, p. 222). Certainly our technological prowess, hence our capacity to muck around in lots of things and lots of ways, has exploded, but that should not be confused with knowledge, a more complicated thing.

I believe that the best thing we can do for students is to help open them to the world of ideas, the "Great Conversation." The worst thing we can do is to make them technicians of one sort or another in preparation for successful careers. I've always thought that Thomas Merton was on to something when he advised students, in *Love and Living*, to "Be anything you like, be madmen, drunks, and bastards of every shape and form, but at all costs avoid one thing: success" (Merton, p. 11). We've had enough success and it's just about ruined us.

I believe that the world is rich in possibilities. I do not think that we are fated to poison ourselves or to destroy the earth. I believe that we can rise above division, hardheartedness, greed, illusion, and ill will. And I believe that we are capable of becoming citizens in the larger community of life and that doing so would ennoble humankind.

And I believe that once in a lifetime we ought to give ourselves up to a particular landscape, to dwell on it, wonder about it, imagine it, touch it, listen to it, and recollect.

On Watershed Education

Robert Hass

In 1997, the year he completed his term as poet laureate of the United States, Robert Hass described the position: "The job of poet laureate doesn't have much definition. The position was created by Franklin Roosevelt and Archibald MacLeish over drinks sometime in 1938 or '39. . . . You're given a small stipend and a beautiful office; you're expected to set up a literary series for the community of Washington, D.C.; the rest is pretty much a blank slate. You are not expected to write a lot of poetry—no odes on nuclear submarines are required."

Using this blank slate, Hass combined two of his passions: children's education and the celebration of wild places. He invited poets, scientists, novelists, essayists ("as many of the writers in the country who write about 'place' as I could gather") to come to Washington, read their work, and discuss the American tradition of environmental writing. And, with Pamela Michael, he founded River of Words (see Michael's essay "Helping Children Fall in Love with the Earth," which follows).

It was Hass's genius to focus the River of Words program on watersheds, rather than skip from year to year among different environmental topics. In the present essay, which appears in slightly different form as the introduction to River of Words, *a collection of art and poems by participants in the program, edited by Pamela Michael, he expands on his insight that "water is everywhere, and everywhere is local." Watersheds are also, in terms of the principles of ecology, a prime example of nested systems: pool ecosystems exist within stream ecosystems, which frequently flow into creeks and rivers, all within watersheds. Watersheds constitute nature's boundaries, and ultimately feed into the planet's great bodies of water.*

Robert Hass is a two-time winner of the National Book Critics Circle Award and recipient of a MacArthur fellowship. He has published numerous books of poetry and essays, including Praise *(1979),* Human Wishes *(1989),* Sun Under Wood *(1996), and* Twentieth Century Pleasures *(1984). Currently professor of English at the University of California, he serves on the board of the International Rivers Network and cofounded the national environmental education project. His awards include the Yale Younger Poets Award, the William Carlos Williams Award, an Award of Merit from the American Academy of Arts and Letters, and a Guggenheim Fellowship. In 1997 the North American Association for Environmental Education named him Educator of the Year.*

IF YOU PUT THE EARTH'S WATER—so I've read—into a gallon jug, just over a tablespoonful would be available for human use. Ninety-seven percent of the planet's water is in the ocean, and two percent is locked in ice-caps and glaciers. A good deal of what's left lies in aquifers, often at inaccessible depths. But at any given moment in the earth's great hydrological cycle, about ninety thousand cubic kilometers of fresh water flow through rivers and lakes. It is this water, renewable but also contaminable and unpredictable and unevenly distributed, on which all earthly life depends. And it is this water we need to know how to preserve and share, if we are going to protect the quality of life on earth. That's why you're holding this book in your hands; our children, with their quick minds and sensuous aliveness, need to be educated to this task, and encouraging them to make art and poetry out of their experience of their own watersheds is one way to do this.

Water is everywhere, and everywhere it is local. In Yokohama Bay it is local to Yokohama, and in San Francisco Bay it is local to San Francisco. The survival of many Pacific life forms depends upon the behavior of people who live beside those bays. The Mississippi River is local when it flows through Minneapolis and local when it flows past St. Louis and local when it widens to a delta at New Orleans. Water is local in an Ecuadorian lake in the Andes where a flock of Baird's sandpipers, not yet an endangered species, is wintering; and it is local in the pond where they summer in northern Vermont, where local dairy farmers are in conversation with environmentalists about the once-clear water now burdened with algal blooms caused by the feces of the dairy cattle who produce the milk that produces the sharp cheddar cheese that someone in a café in New York is nibbling just now with a glass of wine made from grapes full of water that fell, locally, on a field in Bordeaux on a warm gray day five years ago.

The history of this country is so much a history of the culture of rivers. It doesn't matter whether children are urban or suburban or live in the country, their relationship to water is fundamental. The first posters put out by River of Words said, "What is your ecological address?" so that they could get into the habit of locating themselves and the place they live by understanding how water flowed through, how it was used, what other life forms were supported and were there because of the waters that flowed through the places they lived.

Rivers are a deep and sentimental part of American lore. On the one hand, there is this almost religious and eschatological dimension to the idea of a river in American culture; and on the other hand there are the actual rivers—canalized, abused, polluted, much used and much denied. There's that joke, "Denial is a river in Egypt." Well, denial is every river in America. We don't like to look at how we've treated them and what it says about our relationship to the land. In a way, a river is a kind of symbol of the repressed ecological problems in American society.

Water is local and global and complicated because different distributions of water and weather in different geographies have made for different animal and plant species, and human beings symbolize themselves through the plants and animals they live among—in one landscape raven is trickster, in another coyote; people are tough as oak in European forests, tough as ironwood on African savannas. "Races of birds, subspecies of trees, and types of hats or raingear," as Gary Snyder has remarked, "often go by watershed" (Snyder, p. 229): it is old knowledge that we make and are made by the places where we live.

And it is a new imperative—born of the many pressures on the planet and its biological life—that our children understand this. It is not something that the world we have created will necessarily teach them. The media that dominate our public life are always selling something: the news shows need to sell the news to deliver the audiences to the sellers of goods and services, and the other programs do the same, all at more or less the same feverish pitch. It's not exactly a public culture we intended, but it's the one that has come about. We have so far an only semi-articulated convention that we would not let this culture, which deluges our children in their daily lives, selling them mostly toys and sweetened foods, penetrate too deeply into our schools.

Meanwhile, many, many teachers are trying to figure out how to educate a new generation to the world they are going to inherit and how to do it in more useful and imaginative ways than most of us experienced. This is a movement that comes from the bottom up, from the life of a nation, its concerns and its ideals. Most of it is going on outside our schools of education and their certification programs, outside the public debate, such as it is, about the quality of our schools. Some of it is happening in the education programs of parks, in museums of social and natural history, in alliances between departments of natural resources and local activists, and educators. Most of it is the work of dedicated and imaginative classroom teachers and of the environmentally concerned folk who work in local and national nonprofits. They have students in Pacific Northwest schools dancing the life cycles of salmon and classrooms in Florida mapping the flow pattern of the Everglades. The poems and works of art collected by River of Words come from classrooms all over the world, and they are part of the record of this upwelling.

If you think about the world's water supply, about access to clean water as a human right, about the enormous pressures of population growth and economic development, about the growing gap between rich and poor, about skeins of migrating birds flying toward their memory of feeding and nesting grounds, about the schools of fish in the bays where we load and unload our oil, about the difficulty of making even small changes in human behavior, and, thinking about these things, seeing as children see and understanding the concerns that have moved their teachers, you will feel the force of what these teachers are doing.

Helping Children
Fall in Love with the Earth:
Environmental Education and the Arts

Pamela Michael

Understanding the world systemically, a major premise of ecological literacy, entails a shift in emphasis from contents to patterns. "Whether we talk about literature and poetry, the visual arts, music, or the performing arts," says Fritjof Capra, "there's hardly anything more effective than art for developing and refining a child's ability to recognize and express patterns" ("Speaking Nature's Language," in Part I).

CEL is a longtime major supporter of River of Words (ROW), recognizing its ability to integrate the arts and sciences. ROW practices place-based learning by inviting children to use the arts to explore and express their understanding of and connection to their home places. In doing so, as ROW's cofounder and executive director Pamela Michael explains here, ROW also enables children to engage the natural world with their whole selves—conscious and unconscious, emotional and cognitive.

Before she cofounded River of Words with then U.S. Poet Laureate Robert Hass, Pamela Michael's career spanned, among other areas, writing, teaching, curriculum development, radio journalism, and advocacy for the arts and environmental education. She did curriculum development for the Discovery Channel, directed the United Nations—sponsored International Task Force on Media and Education, and developed rural educational programs in Upper Egypt. Wild Writing Women: Stories of World Travel, which she edited, won the National Association of Travel Journalists Award for Best Travel Book of 2002. Most recently she served as editor for River of Words: Images and Poetry in Praise of Water, *which won the*

2004 Skipping Stones Award for Best Book on Nature or Ecology. Her other books include The Gift of Rivers *(2000), coedited with Robert Hass, and* A Woman's Passion for Travel *(1999) and* A Mother's World: Journeys of the Heart *(1998), both coedited with Marybeth Bond.*

Michael teaches writing workshops on both nonfiction and poetry, and leads teacher training workshops all over the world, instructing classroom teachers, park naturalists, and other youth leaders in ways to incorporate nature exploration and the arts in their work. She brings to everything she touches an indefatigable enthusiasm and open heart. When CEL and ROW shared contiguous offices, we felt her excitement as she lovingly celebrated each newly arrived entry of art or poetry for ROW's annual environmental art and poetry contest.

CHILDREN ARE EXPERTS at creating visions of places they've seen only in their imaginations—places made real by the act of creation. What happens when you invite them to "imagine" real places, to find the poetry in water and earth and stone—not just to explore the beauty of a place, but to feel their connection to it?

You get children finding their places in the natural world, children who know that water doesn't just come from a tap, who can name the plants and animals around them, understand the challenges of living sustainably on the earth, and gain the tools and imagination to address those challenges. You get children who know their "ecological addresses" as well as the names of their streets or towns. You get hope.

A desire to nurture that hope gave birth a decade ago to River of Words (ROW), an international K–12 program, whose supporters have included the Center for Ecoliteracy, that invites students to explore their own watersheds, discover those watersheds' importance in their lives, and express through poetry and art what they've observed, felt, and learned.

Words and Watersheds

In 1995, poet and scholar Robert Hass and I began meeting weekly to discuss ways to leverage Hass's new position as U.S. poet laureate to advance environmental literacy. We invited an unconventional mix of artists, business people, teachers, writers, and a feisty bunch of dam fighters from International Rivers Network (IRN) to join us.

The Academy of American Poets had announced that they were declaring April as an annual National Poetry Month. Looking for a way to engage people's attention in the months before the following April, we decided to create a national (later to become international) environmental poetry and art contest. I imagined a different theme each year, beginning with rivers, hoping that IRN would agree to sponsor the contest. Instead, suggested Robert Hass, "Let's make the theme 'watersheds,' and keep it watersheds. Learning about our own watersheds gets to the essence of how we have to understand our home grounds, which is critical if we're ever to have a hope of managing them effectively. Let's get kids' imaginations working from that perspective right from the start." We named our organization River of Words; Hass brought in the Library of Congress Center for the Book as a sponsor, giving us important validation. Having a contest on the theme of watersheds required that we give teachers background on watersheds, why they're important and how students might explore them. With the help of poets, scientists, educators, artists, and conservationists, we developed a "Watershed Explorer" educator's guide, which we distributed free to teachers across the country, with sections on teaching about watersheds, bioregions, poetry, and art.

Our strategy was to create rich sensory experiences for students, encouraging them to explore their communities and imaginations—weaving in natural and cultural history—and to synthesize what they had learned and observed into line and verse. We sought to help children to become keen observers of their own "place in space," as Gary Snyder calls it, in the hope that they would develop a sense of belonging to a particular place.

We chose an exploration model, based on children's experiencing nature firsthand, for its ability to capture the imagination and for its focus on observation, which enables children to seek consciously for information that will extend their ideas. [For examples of Watershed Explorer activities, see "The Loupe's Secret" in Part IV and the essay that follows this one, "Finding Your Own Bioregion."—*Ed.*] We tried to add elements of wonder, discovery, interpretation, dexterity, and surprise to learning, and to promote our belief that while not everyone can be an artist, everyone can be artistic.

Our idea was to connect schools with as many facets of the community as possible in exploring and learning about their places. Who lived here long ago? How did they feed themselves? Where does our water come from? Where does our garbage go? What stories, songs, poems, tall tales, and art has this place inspired? We provided every state arts council in the country with ROW materials, encouraging them to do outreach to the schools in their regions. We offered bookstore owners ideas for in-store displays of local poetry and natural history, afternoon children's poetry readings, sidewalk art events, and the like.

Five months later, thousands of entries began to pour into our office, from a wide cross-section of America's youth representing nearly every state—from public, private, and parochial schools and home-schooling families; from after-school programs, 4-H clubs, Girl Scouts, nature centers, youth clubs, and libraries. We posted our favorite poems and paintings in the mailroom, alongside the usual office clutter of announcements, flyers, reminders, and jokes. Staff meetings at International Rivers Network, which provided us office space, often began with reading a newly arrived poem or two.

Poems like this one confirmed our belief in children's ability to use art to connect with place in striking and beautiful ways:

The Art of Creeks

When the sun sets,
the creek turns
shiny yellow,
which I paint.

When the moon
is in the sky,
the creek is shiny white,
which I paint.

Slithering water
keeps going,
keeps going.
While under
the water,
the shiny gold rocks
live.
The water is their blanket.

The creek of coldness
shakes your hand
as it turns
blue.
Quickly I pull out
with cold
ripples
where I was.

The winter chills
the quiet creek.
That blizzard
rushed away
the noise.
I need the
Spring
to come.

—LYLE LODER FRIEDMAN, AGE 8
    Wyndmoor, Pennsylvania
    Teacher: Jane McVeigh Schultz
    1996 River of Words Grand Prize winner

Response to the contest convinced us that that we had discovered an un-
met need. Our curriculum helped children experience the world with curiosity

and wonder, enhancing their sensitivity to nature as well as their expressiveness in responding to the environment. It was welcomed by teachers, especially those attempting to introduce ecological principles to their students. "Finally, someone put some art, some heart, into environmental education!" one exclaimed.

Combining science and the arts, as we do in our educator's guide, makes pedagogical sense. Both disciplines rely on observation, pattern recognition, problem solving, experimentation, and thinking by analogy. Both artists and scientists observe, record, imagine, and create. At first we thought we'd come up with a novel pairing. Further research showed that, in fact, nineteenth- and early twentieth-century natural history texts were brimming with art, poetry, songs, and even splashes of spirituality. We found a respect and love for nature and beauty in these earlier lessons that seemed worth emulating, especially in a world often lacking in these qualities.

Because environmental education, like much education, often fails to acknowledge the crucial role of emotions in the learning process, activities that both inform the mind and engage the heart proved to be a powerful and effective combination. We soon began defining our mission as "helping children fall in love with the earth." Because people protect what they love, this is a powerful prescription for stewardship, and ultimately, we hope, kinship.

This poem from 1999 radiates understanding, respect, and affection for the natural world:

Reflections

Sometimes,
when the mountains
reflect on rivers,
you can find out things
you never knew before.
There are flowers up there,
rocks like clouds,
a little snow becomes a creek and grows into a river.

—LINDSAY RYDER, age 11
   Bend, Oregon
   Teachers: Vicki Ball and Ashley Kaneda
   1999 River of Words Finalist

At a time when most children (in the United States, at any rate) can identify more than a thousand corporate logos but cannot name the plants or trees
or birds in their own neighborhoods, or say who lived in their towns a hundred years ago, or describe where their drinking water comes from, finding
ways to make the world a vibrant and interesting—and a meaningful—place
for kids is critical.

Nature is specific: living things inhabit or visit certain ecosystems and
not others. And so language must be specific, too, as the best poetry is; this
ROW poem from 2000 illustrates the richness of experience, observation,
and expression that comes with knowing the things' names.

Rockefeller Wildlife Preserve: Mid-August

The air is moist
The water bittersweet
A southern Gulf breeze sighs
Laughing gulls call
And cicadas click their
Luminous song
I smell the death scent
Of beached gars
And see the dreamy haze
Of oil on water
Nearby an alligator stares
With tabby eyes
A great heron startles
From its marsh bed
Standing on the rip-rap,

I peer at the water
And slowly hoist
The turkey neck on string
A blue-point crab
Grips the bait
I slyly dip the net
A good two feet away
And scoop up the crustacean
Without warning
And drop it into a bucket
To meet many friends.
Gifts of the Mississippi,
The day has reached its climax
Animals sleep through the heat,
Hiding in the wax myrtles
A snowy egret,
White plumage glistening,
Glides into the Roseau cane.

—KEVIN MAHER, age 12
Lafayette, Louisiana
Teacher: Charles Mire
2000 River of Words Grand Prize

The River of Words contest has become the largest such competition in the world, drawing entries from more than a dozen countries. From the beginning, however, we viewed the contest as just the "hook," the inducement for getting the attention of (overworked) teachers and (mightily distracted) students. We knew that we could achieve our goal of connecting kids to their watersheds and their imaginations only if we could find a way into the tightly scheduled and protected classroom environment, and into the annual routine of schoolchildren around the world.

Aware of the evidence that cooperation rather than competition is a hallmark of sustainable natural and human communities, we were ambivalent about inserting the element of competition into the classroom and the creative process (where, of course, it already existed to some degree). In the early years, before River of Words had proved itself to be wholeheartedly respectful of our young participants and their work as well as an excellent tool for getting students (particularly underachieving students) excited about learning, we often had to defend our strategy.

Over ten years, my defensiveness has shifted to a strong endorsement of the model of limited competition. For one thing, because our educator's guide was introduced to support a *contest*, we serendipitously did an end run around the very formidable curriculum gatekeepers in state after state. Moreover, the contest format exposes young people to standards of excellence and opportunities for recognition. This is especially important in the United States, where instructional practices of recent decades, originally intended to encourage children and build their self-esteem, have wrought the unintended consequence of convincing quite a few children that anything that comes out of their mouths or pens is praiseworthy, if not perfect. For many students this obviates the need to revise, to strive for improvement, or to labor to find just the right word or image.

Any doubts I may have had about the effects of the contest on kids vanished after hearing story after story from teachers and parents: the "slow" learner who blossomed once he started writing poetry, the shy child whose artwork gained her respect and a circle of friends, the immigrant child who was able to share with his new classmates the rural culture he had left behind. The father of one of our finalists told us, still amazed, "I've never seen Adam work for four hours straight on anything before."

The fact that so many of our winners and finalists have been students with enormous challenges, not the kids who usually win the prizes, is another benefit of adding the arts to environmental education. Our winners have included quite a few autistic, Down's syndrome, blind, deaf, and developmentally disabled children. Because kids have many different styles of learning, as Howard Gardner and others have described (see Gardner's *Frames of Mind: The Theory of Multiple Intelligences*), a truly multidisciplinary curriculum like

River of Words maximizes the chance for students with varying learning styles and abilities to succeed.

River of Words has been particularly effective in reaching urban youth, young people whose connections to the natural world are often tenuous and fragmented. In honor of our affiliation with the Library of Congress we award the "Anacostia Watershed Prize" to a Washington, D.C., student each year. (The Anacostia is the District of Columbia's *other* river, a poor, polluted step-sister to the Potomac.)

Thirst
Thirst, how I thirst to be loved.
To be held
To be full like a river after the snow melts.
Or a puddle after the rain.
Thirst.
My grandmother says blessed are those who thirst
after righteousness for they will be filled.
Oh how I want to be full
Thirst.

—CLARENCE ADAMS, age 17
    Washington, D.C.
    Teacher: Margot DeFerranti
    2004 Anacostia Watershed Prize

Wonder, Not Catastrophe

In recent years, environmental education has too often focused on environmental problems and crises such as pollution and species extinction. For example, in *Beyond Ecophobia: Reclaiming the Heart in Nature Education*, David Sobel argues that emphasizing environmental problems with children, especially young ones, can leave them feeling disempowered and hopeless about the state of the world and their ability to affect it. ROW's approach allows children to immerse themselves in nature and asks them to observe carefully, creating an opening for emergence of the joy and wonder that the natural world can evoke. We believe that children who come to understand and to love their home places will grow into engaged, effective citizens committed to preserving those places. As Fyodor Dostoevsky said, "Beauty will save the world." (This is not to say that the poetry and art submitted by children, especially from places such as Pakistan and Afghanistan, does not ever reflect the harsh realities of the environments in which they live.)

ROW's emphasizing direct, investigative experience and expression rather than taking sides on contentious issues has proved to be important for political as well as cognitive/emotional reasons. Beginning in the 1990s, environmental education became a battleground in some places, particularly those already torn by fights over resource use.

In Arizona, for instance, the state-mandated environmental education program was dismantled and its funding turned over to a rancher-dominated "Wise Use" group. Resource industry—sponsored books like Michael Serena and Susan Shaw's *Facts Not Fear* (Regnery Publishing, 1999) took advantage of the negative and issue-driven nature of much of the early environmental education curricula. (This book, in a much-publicized and later discredited anecdote, described a child returning home from school in tears, sobbing "Mommy, they cut down trees to make my bed!") River of Words, which eschews "politically correct" interpretations, has helped some teachers overcome objections raised by administrators who feared parent or community backlash to environmental education programs.

Because ROW's curriculum is not issue-oriented and because the arts in general honor individual experience, children are able to communicate about ideas, lifestyles, and events that might find little authentication in more traditional environmental education approaches. River of Words receives numerous poems and paintings each year that depict the branding of calves, hunting, fishing, raising chickens, and other activities that reflect the real lives of the poems' creators and their families, lives that are often misunderstood, if not demonized, by some environmental educators.

This poem about hunting geese exhibits a keen sense of place and family and a sweet affection for both. (It should be noted that hunters, particularly duck hunters, are some of the most active and effective conservationists in the United States.)

Us Men

waterproofed to the waist,
see a vision, that to us
only comes once a year.
We are grumbling, stalking
out to the shed, to the purr
of engines warming.
Our breath spirits the chilled wind.
All day, work.
For the first time I am a part of it,
deserving of the reward that will come.
We sink back into cold metal bunkers
dug along gumbo levees
the color of potter's clay.
Dried stalks & weeds sway as cover.
In the distance, floodwater
rises against the sunburst ray
of a dying day. I hear the geese faintly
honk & gaggle above me. I see silhouettes
dot the horizon. There are splashes
of touch & go, wings flapping.
Yes, I do hope they like it here.
My father reaches for his boy,
                    and I give in.

—ERIC WIESMANN, age 15
   Vicksburg, Mississippi
   Teacher: Greg Sellers
   2000 River of Words Finalist

Weaving Networks

ROW has always worked by building partnerships, beginning with our initial association with International Rivers Network. At that time—and regrettably even today—most environmental advocacy organizations paid education and youth programs little more than lip service. A few crossword puzzles in the "Kid's Corner" section of their website or an anthropomorphized furry cartoon character exhorting kids to recycle often constituted the extent of their attempts to educate the next generation of earth stewards.

Fortunately, Owen Lammers, IRN's executive director when we launched ROW, recognized in River of Words a chance to create a program for IRN that educated and inspired. He gave us a meeting place, telephones, and a copy machine, and set about raising funds for us. We are proud that our ultimate success in getting into classrooms—reaching young people, as well as parents and, ultimately, policymakers—has spurred other advocacy groups to commit resources and energy to education programs. The attitude that only the campaigners do the "real" work is slowly changing in favor of recognizing education's role in shaping values and behavior that promote sustainable living.

We have worked hard to promote collaborations within schools and between schools and their communities, encouraging teachers to partner with other teachers—a science teacher and an English teacher, say—as well as with other resources in their community: bird watchers, writers, park rangers, water department employees, photographers, farmers, and so on.

We have been heartened by the innovative ways local communities have implemented River of Words. One small town in New Mexico celebrated with a River of Words parade down Main Street, which was festooned with streetlight banners made from children's artwork. Every shop in town that day had a little basket next to the cash register where you could take a poem or leave a poem. The community also sponsored a riverbank clean-up and poetry reading, which has become an annual event.

An elementary school class in California added a multigenerational aspect by visiting a senior citizens' home that stood alongside a creek. The students conducted oral history interviews of the elders, many of whom were lifelong residents of the area. They explored the creek together, and the kids returned to their classrooms to write poems and paint about their experiences. When the seniors received copies of the children's work, they were so inspired that they invited the class to return with their families the following month. The seniors threw a wonderful party for them and read poems they had written in response to the children's work. Many were about the creek, and quite a few included childhood memories of the place.

In 2001 River of Words spun off from IRN and became an independent nonprofit. Our contest now accepts entries in Spanish, English, and American Sign Language (submitted on videotape). We honor eight national winners and an international grand prizewinner at an awards ceremony at the Library of Congress, and publish an annual book of the contest's winning entries and a 270-page *River of Words Watershed Explorer™ Curriculum Educator's Guide* (see www.riverofwords.org). In 2003 we opened Young at Art, one of the country's first art galleries devoted to children's work. The gallery and our website sell reproductions of our huge collection of children's watershed art, which is almost continually on display at some museum, library, or other public space. Several teachers' colleges have adopted River of Words as a model for interdisciplinary cooperation.

Each year we train hundreds of classroom teachers and informal educators across the country in arts-oriented place-based education. Typically, we will be invited to give a workshop by a sponsoring agency such as a water district, which may in turn invite a grassroots group, Friends of This River or That Creek, perhaps a library or park district, Fish and Wildlife personnel, arts council representatives or local museum staff members, and, of course, schools, school districts, principals, and teachers. Often, these folks have never worked together on a project before; many times the relationships endure and spark other collaborations. Individuals, institutions, and agencies develop friendships, vocabularies, trust, and working relationships—partnerships that can prove crucial when the community has to address watershed management or other civic issues. Cooperating on a noncontroversial arts and education project gives people tools and experience they can apply to more contentious issues later on.

River of Words participants have given us a unique and encompassing perspective on our world, as seen through the eyes of its children. They have expressed their concerns, dreams, wishes, and fears in words and pictures that astound and delight. We offer their thoughtful and heartfelt creations as a sign of hope for the future.

Return

Bring me home by moonlit path
Where pale moon stains the ochre earth.
Tell me where to go.
Away from the place where the yellow lanterns glow
Where the insects gather for heat
in the lonely night.
Surround me with trees
where stubborn houses refuse
To stand
Where the rain breaks delicately
against green leaves
Take me to the place
where the stars do not hide timidly
ashamed of their beauty
Where the smells that rise from the earth
guide me
Guide me home to the forest
Where I can find myself again
hidden in the leaves

—CELIA LA LUZ, age 15
    San Francisco, California
    Teachers: Tim Lamarre and Susan Terence
    2003 River of Words Grand Prize

Finding Your Own Bioregion

Peter Berg

"Finding Your Own Bioregion" is taken from Peter Berg's Discovering Your Life-
Place: A First Bioregional Workbook. *This chapter also appears as one of the
lessons in* River of Words Watershed Explorer™ Curriculum Educator's
Guide, *a compilation of the materials that River of Words (see previous essay) has
found especially useful for helping students identify and deeply experience their home
places. Berg writes in the Workbook version of "Finding Your Own Bioregion":*

> The concept of a bioregion is uniquely useful for putting ourselves back into
> nature instead of on top of it. A bioregion is a way to describe the natural
> geography where one lives. It also identifies a locale for carrying out activ-
> ities that are appropriate for maintaining those natural characteristics.
> Bioregions have distinct features such as climate, soils, landforms, water-
> sheds, and native plants and animals. They have also been sites for adap-
> tive long-term inhabitation by native peoples in the past, and they can be
> reinhabited by their present occupants. (p. 5)

When launching the Center for Ecoliteracy, rather than identify its geographic
territory by political boundaries, CEL's founders defined its geographical scope as
the Shasta Bioregion, roughly the area bounded by the Pacific Ocean on the west, the
Sierra Nevada on the east, the Klamath-Siskiyou mountains of southern Oregon
and northern California on the north, and the Tehachapi mountains on the south.

Peter Berg is founder and director of the Planet Drum Foundation, which is
devoted to grassroots ecological work emphasizing sustainability, community self-de-
termination, and regional self-reliance. He is often credited with originating the concept of bioregions. Planet Drum helps start new bioregional groups and offers projects,

publications, speakers, and workshops to organizations seeking ways to live sustain-
ably within the natural confines of bioregions. Along with Discovering Your Life-
Place *(1995), his books include* Reinhabiting a Separate Country: A Bioregional
Anthology of Northern California *(1978) and* A Green City Program for the
San Francisco Bay Area and Beyond *(1991), all published by Planet Drum Books.*

At his request, Berg's dedication in Discovering Your Life-Place *is included
here: "Dedicated to Carl O. Sauer, whose introductory overview* Man in Nature
*[Turtle Island Foundation, 1975] served to enhance his numerous contributions to
the study of geography and inspired this effort."*

AN EFFECTIVE WAY TO BEGIN acquiring a sense of your own
bioregion is by making a simple map that shows some of the basic natural
characteristics where you live. The map-making process will be an absorbing
exploration, but it is also personally empowering because it describes an immediate area for practicing reinhabitation and becoming native to your life-
place. Since this map is your own personal view, it shows a territory that has
never been drawn with these particular features before.

All you need is a fairly large piece of blank paper and several pens or pen-
cils that can produce at least six colors. Put an X in the middle of your paper.
This represents the actual dwelling place where you live. Depending on the
scale that you choose for this map, it can be as large as a city or as small as your
house or apartment building.

In the upper right-hand corner of the paper, write the letter "N" to represent the north direction. If you don't know which direction is north, try to
remember where the sun rises (east) and then visualize what lies 90 degrees
or a quarter turn of your head to the left from there. You can also find north
by remembering where the sun sets (west) and shifting your mental picture
90 degrees to the right of that direction.

Knowing compass points is important for determining major characteristics of the place where you live. For example, you'll want to know which
direction gets the most sunlight and is therefore warmer because plants and
animals respond to this phenomenon in many different ways. The warmest
direction is also essential information for positioning a new house so that it

can absorb the most heat during short winter days when the arc of the sun can become extremely low on the horizon depending on how far you are from the equator.

Compass points are also necessary for building up a dependable store of information about your life-place. Using the letter "N" to orient you, draw a few arrows on the side of the paper that matches the direction from which wind and rain usually come. This may actually be a different place depending on the time of the year, or there may be several places at any season. Hint: If you haven't thought about this before and don't know this direction, try to remember which doorstep gets wettest in a storm, which window sill inside the house gets damp, or which windows rattle when the wind blows.

Next draw in the body of water that is nearest to the X that marks the spot where you live. It may be a creek, river, lake, pond, or even a marsh or swamp. In some cases it could be the shore of an ocean. This is the time when the scale of your map will become evident. If you are fairly familiar with a large area around the place you marked X, you may want to show a very large body of water such as a major river, a very large lake, or an ocean bay. If you aren't comfortable with a scale as big as that, start with a creek or pond that you know is nearby. If you can, show how it connects to a river or marsh. Most of the land in cities has been covered over with streets or buildings, so if you are a city dweller, show the nearest river, or a lake or creek in a nearby park. Clue: The direction that rain runs in the street gutters may point to a body of water. Use a particular color such as blue for this so that the water system stands out clearly, and other colors for each of the parts of the map that follow.

The water body you drew is surrounded by high ground that causes rain or spring water to flow into it by the force of gravity. This elevated land might be hills if the scale of your map is small or a mountain range if the scale is very large. High ground sheds water, so the term "watershed" is used to describe all of the land that surrounds a particular body of water.

Draw in the hills or mountains that create the watershed where you live. Clue: Watersheds can be huge, such as that for the Mississippi River with the Rockies on one side and the Appalachian/Allegheny Mountains on the

other, or as small as the rise of ground that separates two creeks and the low hills around a pond in a park. Use a different color than the previous one showing water.

The next element to include in this map is soil. Use your memory of visits to different parts of the bioregion to draw in different types of soil such as sand, clay, or black topsoil. Usually the highest ground is rockier than lower places because the lighter soil blows or washes away. If you remember seeing exposed rocks on hilltops, draw them in. The light soil that blew or washed away settles in valleys or other low places that are usually near bodies of water. Think of where this type of soil probably lies and draw it in. Clue: Farmers prefer nutrient-rich topsoil, so it can probably be found wherever you've seen fields and farmhouses. Is there also sandy soil where you live? How about hard red clay? Use a new color (or colors) to draw these in. Add any other geological characteristics such as lava beds, granite cliffs, coral rock, caves, or salt beds that are unique to your bioregion.

Next draw in some examples of plants and animals that are native to the place where you live. "Native" means that these are wild animals rather than domestic ones like dogs and cats or horses and cows. It also means plants that are indigenous rather than most of the ones that are grown for food or were brought from other places for some other reasons. For example, oak trees are native to North American bioregions but apple trees aren't. Hint: Types of animals range from insects to fish and from birds to mammals. Plants include grasses, herbs, and shrubs as well as trees.

So far there haven't been any signs of human beings in this map. There are usually so many of them in all of the places where people live that most of them wouldn't fit. In order to focus your map on the present situation, draw in just two aspects of the human relationship to whatever other features you've drawn. The first one is a visual representation of the worst things people are doing. Hint: It could be a source of wastes that threatens to pollute all of the water. It could also be bad farming practices that are eroding soil, mining that is creating hazardous dumps, or dams that block the passage of fish in a river.

Now show the best things people are doing to try to harmonize with the natural elements in the map. Hint: These may be organic produce or permaculture farms that maintain good soil, or recycling projects that reduce wastes. Some other beneficial activities could be renewable energy projects, efforts to restore forests or rivers, and other attempts to improve the balance between human needs and those of natural systems. Of course, this will be a matter of your personal opinion at this particular time, but that's an important aspect of knowing how you perceive the place where you live.

The map you've made is a view of your bioregion. It is also a kind of a flag for the place. It shows your home base in terms of some of the natural elements that ultimately support life there. These elements need to be restored where they have been damaged and preserved where they are still intact. Some of them should be seen as appropriate sources for supplying basic human needs of food, water, energy, and materials as long as this can be done in ways that are sustainable for both people and other life.

A bioregional sense of place can become the basis for your view of the community. It's easy to see that many community issues would benefit from this. They include land use and development decisions, water supplies and sewage treatment, education and health, and even staging local celebrations to recognize unique natural events such as the seasonal flowering or fruiting of native plants and appearances of wildlife. Local problems ranging from unemployment and poverty to transportation and utilities also have a bioregional aspect. They can be partially solved by projects to convert buildings and vehicles to use renewable sources of energy, create some self-reliant food production, recycle materials and water, or restore damaged ecosystems.

You will have a much fuller ecological picture of the place where you live because of a bioregional perspective, but it can also help lead to worthwhile jobs and a future profession. Rural and suburban places can all use some degree of ecological restoration whether through reforestation, reestablishing wildlife populations, rebuilding soil, mending damaged watercourses, or other small- and large-scale projects. City environments are not ecologically sustainable at the present time and will require vast amounts of work to become so. There are many opportunities to do this through reconstruction of buildings, development of alternatives to private automobile transportation, com-

munity gardening, urban wild habitat restoration, recycling, neighborhood re-
vitalization, and social programs such as youth employment in various aspects
of sustainability.

Someone who practices living-in-place possesses a personal quality that
can't be achieved otherwise. Becoming a reinhabitant will make you an au-
thentic member of your life community.

Your map shows a territory that needs support and defense. You may eventually want to join together with other people who live in the bioregion to find
out more about it and explore ways to live there that will be appropriate for
maintaining a unique part of the earth.

Part III

Relationship

Revolution Step-by-Step:
On Building a Climate for Change

*An Interview with Neil Smith, Former Principal of Martin
Luther King Middle School, Berkeley, California*

Leslie Comnes

*One reason that changing institutions can take as long as it does is the necessity of
building relationships, though that time is often not accounted for or may be regarded
as wheel-spinning by those who are eager to see fast results.*

*The Center for Ecoliteracy is committed to relationship building, but even it can
sometimes slide over the relationship-building phase when telling abbreviated stories
about its work. In the short version of The Edible Schoolyard (ESY) story (see "Sustainability: A New Item on the Lunch Menu" in Part IV), Alice Waters meets
Neil Smith, the principal at Martin Luther King Middle School. She has a brilliant
vision for integrating classrooms, gardens, kitchens, and cafeterias. He is moved by
the vision. The Edible Schoolyard comes to life; the faculty integrates garden and
cooking classes with classroom teaching and changes the class schedule to accommo-
date the new curriculum. ESY becomes famous and helps spark a movement for curricular reform across the whole district and around the world, and everyone lives
happily and eats fresh, nutritious food for ever after.*

*That story is essentially true, but it's hardly complete. This interview fills in some
important gaps. When Neil Smith came to Martin Luther King in 1989, five years
before his meeting with Alice Waters, he arrived at a run-down, demoralized school
that had run through a series of principals. Discipline was a major problem. The faculty's recent experiences had left it wary of any new principal's ideas. During Smith's*

first October, the Loma Prieta earthquake rendered the cafeteria unusable. The ground on which The Edible Schoolyard's garden was eventually built was an ugly asphalt lot.

In this interview, Smith describes how he gained the faculty's trust and helped to nurture the kinds of relationships and on-campus community that are prerequisites to systemic reform. He talks about needing to take time when people aren't ready, about conceiving of projects in terms people can understand and believe are possible, about the one-step-at-a-time process that he and the faculty went through for two years before agreeing to restructure the class schedule.

After thirteen years as principal at King, Smith became director of curriculum, instruction, and staff development for the Berkeley Unified School District. Before his work at King, he had taught at middle schools and high schools and served as principal of Cathedral Intermediate School in San Francisco and assistant principal at San Ramon Valley High School. He was named San Francisco Private School Educator of the Year by the California Schoolmasters in 1984 and Educator of the Year in 2000 by the Berkeley Public Education Foundation.

Leslie Comnes, a freelance writer and editor based in Portland, Oregon, who specializes in education and science issues, conducted this interview with Neil Smith in 1998.

LESLIE COMNES: *I understand that you started here at King as principal in 1989, having been in administration for ten years before that. What were some of the challenges you faced coming into the school?*

NEIL SMITH: When I arrived at King, the school had been through a number of principals in a short period of time. Teachers did not feel supported at the school and felt that their voices didn't matter in the operation of the school. Student discipline was poor, and the buildings and grounds were in terrible shape.

I tried to help teachers see that we could do something about all of this. If we worked together and set goals as to what's important to us, and had agreements about that, we could change the school. But we couldn't change it overnight. Each year we could add something new to our list, but to think that in one year, or even two years, everything was going to be wonderful would be very foolish.

As a way to help teachers feel supported, one of my first goals was to get student discipline in hand. At that time, the school was a two-year school, and I expected that the eighth graders who had already been there a year would resist the new limits I set. I expected that they would never give in, but neither would I, and we would battle the whole year. I also expected that by the end of the year we could make a major impact in that area. And we did. But it was a yearlong battle and was a very tough year for me.

What else did you do to help teachers feel as though their voices were heard?

At the first staff development day we had in the fall, I divided the staff into four groups to look at the problems that the school was experiencing, such as academic failure and behavior. I asked each group of about ten teachers to examine the problem and to come up with some plans for looking at that issue. When they came back, one of the groups reported that our school needed a revolution. So, a group began to work on the revolution, and we set up the Revolutionary Committee. The committee was designed to be a fluid group of the faculty so anyone could come. It met after school and chose and defined the problems that it would address. At the beginning, there were about a dozen people who came. After some initial venting, the Revolutionary Committee began to focus on solutions. The committee would research and seek solutions that it would then bring back to the whole staff.

When a staff becomes as large as the staff at King [fifty teachers], to try to hammer things out at a faculty meeting is a laborious process, and it frustrates people. The Revolutionary Committee puts in the time and the effort to work a problem through and then runs it by the staff to be critiqued. By the time the committee presents an idea to the staff, they've spent a lot of time working on the issue and getting a lot of input, a lot of shaping from the staff.

How does the Revolutionary Committee help shape the school?

The first year the committee got some things going for the next year, and teachers really felt a part of the process. They didn't feel that anybody had forced the ideas on them, and they felt responsible for the programs that we were implementing. Anything that was put into place that impacted the school as a whole was approved by the faculty as a whole.

With the Revolutionary Committee in place, people saw that things were beginning to work that first year. The committee became a part of the fiber of the school, although some years its spark is greater than others. It seems that when the staff perceives more problems, more people attend the Revolutionary Committee, and when things are going well, fewer people come. However, this can slow down the reform effort, for dissatisfaction with the status quo often spurs people to move more quickly into reform.

We looked at our block schedule a number of years ago through the Revolutionary Committee. In forty-five minutes, say, you feel like you are racing in and racing out. When you have a ninety-five-minute period you can actually have time to do things with your class. I think the block schedule is what makes our garden and our kitchen work so well. Even walking to the garden can take fifteen minutes, with organizing your class, focusing them on task, and letting them know what you are going to do.

So in the midst of all this change at the school, you read Alice Waters's interview in the paper where she commented on the physical deterioration at King. You called her up and invited her to talk with you. Was it at that meeting when the idea for The Edible Schoolyard came about?

When I met with Alice, she already had a vision of a school garden and of integrating the garden into the school lunch program, with students using the fresh produce to make lunches. I saw her idea as one that would empower kids, one that could positively impact the school climate and the school curriculum. It seemed to make a lot of sense to me. It wasn't something I had considered before, but I thought that it really could enhance what we had going already and could make King a better school for the kids who come here.

The idea excited me, but it was also overwhelming. I didn't think I could create this project and run a school at the same time. I knew I needed someone to make this project happen—ideally a parent in the PTA who would work with Alice. I put the idea out at the PTA meeting but there was no response. I tried again the following fall, and Beebo Turman, a parent, became excited about it.

Next I talked to the faculty about it, to see if there were teachers interested as well. It definitely sparked the interest of two of our science teachers— Phoebe Tanner and Beth Sonnenberg. But Alice's vision was so far-reaching and so "out there" compared to where we were. She was talking about students serving other students lunches that they had grown in the garden, and we were looking at an asphalt urban lot that looked so bleak. People told me it was really far-out—I had to agree. I even told Alice that she was jumping to step ten before we had even gotten to step one! We needed to start with the garden before we could talk about the cafeteria and redoing the lunch program. Well, pretty soon there was a garden and then a kitchen. And now we are talking about a dining commons that's being planned!

How have you helped people see the vision to get to where The Edible Schoolyard is now?

As school people, we know that there are a lot of big ideas that come along. I think that someone has to break the ideas down into steps that most people can at least envision. To put out to everybody the idea of students serving lunch to one another was a bit far-out even for most of our faculty, and I think for most parents, but to put out the idea of a garden—they could envision that. Now when I discuss the idea of kids serving lunch to each other, it's not so far-out anymore. Now they see that they've come this far.

So you build on your successes. But there has to be some measurable, noticeable success that people can stand on before they go to the next step. Then people can say, "Okay, now this is what we see. And yes, there is this overarching vision of where we are going."

So, initially, most people saw it as "We're getting a garden"?

Yes, people could buy into the garden. Talking about building on success, a couple of years earlier, we had transformed another area of the playground—an equally horrific urban lot—into a baseball field. By using outside resources such as the North Oakland Little League and the Berkeley-Albany Softball League, along with the PTA, the school had dug up the old asphalt and put in grass and a baseball diamond.

So when we put out the idea of having a garden, people could imagine that. People looked at the baseball field, and there wasn't a feeling of hopelessness about the garden. They had seen one patch of land transformed; maybe this other patch of land would be transformed, too.

Although people would buy into the garden, they would often say, "Come on, you're going to grow produce? Kids are going to cook it? Give me a break." I'd just say, "Let's talk about that after we get the garden."

In the beginning, then, you had a few people who were excited and motivated about the garden. How did you move from that to buy-in from the rest of the staff?

A key to the buy-in has been not forcing people to do something they don't want to do. People have said to me, "You're the principal, can't you just make the teachers do this?" Well, no, you can't. And not only that, you don't want to. Because when people are forced to do something, they don't do it well. In order for something like this to be successful, the teacher has to want to do it. If the teacher wants to do it, it's going to catch on with the kids.

When a decision involves everyone schoolwide, we take a faculty vote. I look for such a sizable majority that those in the minority feel like, "The tide is moving against me. I've got to turn and go with the tide." On crucial issues, such as the double-period block schedule or implementing an organizational binder, you need buy-in from everybody and it has to be at least 80 percent if you are going to make it work. I look for 80 percent in those votes. We use a secret ballot, and I always let people know the exact vote. With other issues that are really just preference issues—like whether an assembly happens second period or fourth—then we go with a strict majority: 50 percent plus one. An example of getting buy-in would be what happened with the double-period schedule. In the first year, the science department agreed to try double periods for a year. We needed another department to go with them, so we could put those two classes back-to-back on the schedule. History agreed to try it for a semester, with the understanding that they would vote at the end of that time; if they voted to go back to traditional, we would. At the end of the semester, the history department voted 50-50 to stick with it. I told them that since science wanted to stay with it, and they were just 50-50, we would stay with it through the year and then decide what to do the next year. They were okay with that.

After that the English and math departments came to me and said they wanted double periods the next year. We had a faculty meeting to talk about what we were going to do: We could have two departments out of six on the block schedule, but we couldn't have three or four departments without the others.

At the meeting I threw it open for their ideas. The science department said they would never go back to forty-five minutes again. The history department agreed! I was so surprised, but by now they had more than half of the department who really liked it. English and math had already said they wanted to go with it. PE said they didn't want it but they wouldn't block it. That left the electives department. Two electives teachers objected, and one of them said it was probably not the best thing for a foreign language. I would agree, but you have to look at the school as a whole. The level of French and Spanish we are teaching is so elementary that three days a week would suffice. So we took the vote, and the staff voted overwhelmingly for it.

We were nervous about it. We spent time at our staff retreat in August planning how everybody would teach for ninety-five minutes. It took a while to adjust, but there was buy-in, and now there is no thought of our schedule running any other way.

Did you have a faculty vote like that for The Edible Schoolyard project?

With The Edible Schoolyard, it was slightly different. It didn't require buy-in from everybody because it didn't involve everybody. So the question for the staff as a whole was, "Here's a project that is going to go on. What do you think?"

When we make staff decisions, we sometimes use a method with eight levels of voting. This gives people a way to express their concerns, their reservations, and even their negativity toward an idea without blocking it. A person can say, "All right I'll go along with this idea. I don't like it, but I don't want to stop anybody else; and so, all right, you have my grudging 'yes.'"

The Edible Schoolyard really only impacted those teachers who were taking their kids out to the garden, primarily sixth-grade science teachers. Those teachers really wanted it, and I think among the rest of the staff there were varying views: "Nice idea, but I don't want to be involved"; "We don't want to stop you, enjoy it"; or "At some point I might like to be involved." I also think there was probably some skepticism as to what would happen. I don't think that anyone realized how it would run, how big it would become, or how successful it would be.

With the staff willing to try the project, how did things begin to get rolling?

In about March of 1995, we had a charrette and invited different people to come to the school—landscape architects, teachers, restaurateurs, food growers, and others. We asked them how to make the project happen. Out of that meeting, we selected our site from three possibilities. Through some connections we got someone to take the asphalt out. It's a toxic substance so it has to be properly removed.

However, even though we got rid of the asphalt, the soil was not good. So, in December of 1995, we had a planting. We invited people connected with the project to come to throw the first seeds. We made it ceremonial, with an Aztec dance group. They were drumming while we got lines of people to walk along and toss seeds as they went. The seeds were primarily fava beans, to put nitrogen back into the soil and to cleanse the soil.

A lot has happened with The Edible Schoolyard since you planted those first seeds in 1995. At first, just a few teachers took their kids out to the garden. As the gar-

den grew you added Edible Schoolyard staff. Then the kitchen came along in 1997, which has brought in other classes and other teachers to the project. And now you are in the midst of planning a school dining commons and garden kitchen that will make the project even more a center of the school. Are there teachers who are thinking, "Whoa, what happened?"

Yes, there probably are. But they also can see that the program is so successful and that it is obviously having such a good effect on the kids. The garden teachers who went out initially worked through a lot of the bugs, so that the second wave of teachers using the garden benefited from the initial teachers' experiences. These first teachers have been very good about sharing their experiences and about doing staff development. For example, they put together a panel of different teachers—including seasoned veterans—who have had good experiences in the garden. When someone who has taught at King for more than twenty years sits up on the panel and talks about how it has worked for her and how successful it has been with her kids, her experience speaks to the whole faculty.

The support that you have given teachers for this project is impressive, like making sure that there is staff to manage the garden. In other schools, teachers try to run the school garden in addition to their classroom duties, and that can get frustrating.

You have to compare the garden to every other good resource you have at your school, like the computer lab, for example. The computer lab becomes more successful and better used when there is a computer technician and instructor already in the lab. With this support, teachers have someone to help them to plan the lesson, to set things up in advance, to troubleshoot, and to make sure things are kept up. The same is true with the library. You can have this wonderful resource, but without a librarian, it just won't be used as well. The same is true with the garden. Just having the resource there is not enough. Having the personnel is critical to making the thing work.

With the garden, if you have to go out ahead of time to plan it, well, then you don't go. And if the garden is not just yours, but you are sharing it with other teachers, it changes even more. For it to work effectively you need that garden coordinator whose job is to facilitate the success of the garden program.

One thing that has stuck with me is the tremendous amount of communication among teachers and support staff that seems to be involved in making this project work.

Yes, the teachers and staff initially involved have spent a tremendous amount of time talking things through and getting things to work. The Center for Eco-literacy really recognizes the need to do that. They've given us a grant to allow teachers to develop curriculum, and to create the position of mentor teachers. Those mentor teachers help to shepherd their colleagues through the process. That's important, too.

How does The Edible Schoolyard fit into your notion of school reform?

For a project like The Edible Schoolyard to happen, there has to be a climate at the school where the ideas of reform are viewed positively. And reform doesn't have to start off in a big way. Sometimes when people talk about reform, it frightens people. But you have to build on small successes. You can look at something that's manageable, that's doable, and that's attractive to a lot of people; when you are successful with that, then you move to another step, and then another. When you build on other successes, people's visions begin to expand. They begin to say, "We *can* do this."

I think if ten years ago I had come to King and said, "We're going to build a school that has a garden in the back, that has a baseball field over here, we'll have a double-period schedule," you know, I wouldn't have lasted a year! Everyone would have thought that I was some crackpot coming in. And, what's more, I know that my vision would not have specifically included all those things.

My vision was definitely a reformist vision, but it was broad enough that it could encompass a lot of ways to get to the end. The end has always been clear to me: that every kid is buying into his or her education, is excited about learning, is treated well at school, and feels safe at school; and that every teacher

is empowered to help design and create this learning community. But I am open
to getting there through lots of different paths. I don't say, "This is the way
we have to go." I assume that lots of people bring lots of ideas and that the collective group is smarter than anybody in the group. By putting ideas through
the group, we hone them, make them workable for everybody, and get buy-
in from everybody, too.

*From what you are saying, reform is happening at different layers at King. You are
talking about the school being a place where kids feel safe and engaged, and it also
seems important for the teachers to feel safe to express their ideas.*

Oh, yes. That's what the Revolutionary Committee is for. People bring forth
some pretty wild ideas, and no matter how far-out an idea seems, it gets considered. Alice's idea initially seemed pretty far-out, frankly, given an urban
school. Kids serving each other lunch, growing their own carrots—that was
pretty wild. But a lot of things we have at King would have seemed wild to
people there ten years ago. Teach kids for ninety-five minutes? We used to think
they couldn't sit that long. And now, we don't even talk about it. It's part of
the culture of the school.

What are some other ways, would you say, that the culture of the school has changed?

The culture has changed drastically, which has been responsible for other things
changing as well. The culture of the school is now one where there is a lot going on for kids—a lot of learning—and it's going on in exciting ways. There
is also a feeling among the staff as a whole that we are all responsible for the
kids as a whole. I don't think there is anyone now who would just look at their
room, at just their own students, or at their own curriculum. Everyone has an
understanding of the big picture and feels some responsibility for it.

*The Center for Ecoliteracy talks about this shift from the parts to the whole, which
seems to be a critical element in reform.*

That's a big shift. It's also part of middle school reform in particular. Middle school reform is about moving away from that high school model, where I as teacher am responsible for presenting my subject to my students. It makes middle school more like elementary school, where you continue to nurture students—not pamper them as babies, but nurture them as learners—and help them in the growing process. We have a staff of teachers that is really committed to this particular age level. They really want to be at middle school.

How has The Edible Schoolyard helped in building community?

King feels more like a community than it did a few years ago, due to a number of projects, the garden being one of them. It brings people in who may not be interested in tutoring, or reading, or coaching, but who are interested in getting involved. I think the neighbors and the community really like The Edible Schoolyard. Rather than seeing a desolate landscape, they now see a beautiful garden. It has enhanced the image of the school in the neighborhood.

The sense of community goes beyond the school only because it happens within the school. Among the staff there is a real sense of community. Teachers feel respected by one another even if their opinions differ. They feel that their ideas will at least be considered, if not accepted. Among staff there is a real caring about one another and a sense that we are all working together for a big common purpose.

What advice would you give to someone embarking on a project such as The Edible Schoolyard?

First of all, you need to understand that it's not going to happen in a year, that it's a long-term project. Second, you don't have to have buy-in from the whole staff initially to get started, but you do have to have a few committed people. Third, it's good to look for support both inside and outside the school, at least initially, to make it work. You need district support. Our superintendent, Jack McLaughlin, was very supportive, and this is especially important if you are going to be using part of the land at the school. Finally, there has to be support for the teachers who participate, support in various ways like time to meet or a person who is out there guiding them.

How have parents responded to The Edible Schoolyard?

There was a worry initially that some parents might say, "You are taking away from 'real curriculum' so that my child can spend time in the garden." It was a fear that hasn't really materialized. It has come up with the occasional parent, but it has been rare. On the other hand, we've had many parents say, "My child's favorite thing about the school is the garden." Parents, of course, are pleased when their kids are happy about something at school, especially sixth-, seventh-, and eighth-graders, who are rarely happy about anything. So that has been satisfying to hear.

Have you heard from the students directly about what they think of the project?

Every year we have to survey our students as part of the Berkeley Schools Excellence Project. This spring we got close to six hundred responses. Students complete a two-sided survey, and on the backside they have to list the top six things they think should be priorities for funding at the school. They have thirty-five possible choices. At our school, the most votes went to PE/sports, the second most was for field trips, and third was for the garden— out of thirty-five possibilities! That was quite a testament from the kids' point of view—that the garden is something that they value.

Have you noticed any difference in things like test scores or other academic assessments?

Can you prove that it's making a difference? I don't know that you can. What The Edible Schoolyard has done is helped change the culture of the school. It grabs kids' interest in school by giving them a hands-on experience with their peers and their teachers. It pulls kids into the school, into learning. And it makes kids realize that learning isn't just books, but that life is about learning.

One of the tasks of middle school is to excite kids about learning, and The Edible Schoolyard is successful there. If at the end of a child's eighth-grade experience, the child has certain facts down, how long will those facts be remembered? But if the child is excited about a particular subject, he or she is going to become a real student and go on learning about it. That's really what you want to do—in middle school in particular—isn't it?

Ecological Literacy: Learning in Context

Photographs by James Tyler

A revolution in education is under way and it is starting in the most unlikely places. The revolutionaries are not professional educators from famous universities; rather, they are elementary school students, a growing number of intrepid teachers, and a handful of facilitators from widely diverse backgrounds. The goal of the revolution is the reconnection of young people with their own habitats and communities. The classroom is the ecology of the surrounding community, not the confining four walls of the traditional school. The pedagogy of the revolution is simply a process of organized engagement with living systems and the lives of people who live by the grace of those systems. . . . We need a transformed curriculum and schools as the start of a larger process of change that might eventually transform our communities and the culture beyond. If this occurs, and I believe that it will, it will begin with small everyday things: freshwater shrimp, the trees along the banks of streams, the lives of ordinary people, the stories we tell, and the excitement of children.—David W. Orr, from "A Sense of Wonder"

The following photographs illustrate the educational revolution that is occurring in many of the schools and projects described in this book. Inspired by David Orr's vision, the Center for Ecoliteracy has helped creative educators identify teaching contexts as close as a playground, a garden, or a nearby creek where children can wade into nature, develop emotional and aesthetic attachments to the natural world, and acquire and practice ecological literacy. (All quotations are from the essays published in this book.)

Learning in the School Garden

Students are supposedly addicted to fast food, but vegetables like broccoli and chard are big hits when grown, harvested, and cooked by Edible Schoolyard students.

"When . . . children grow or prepare the foods they eat, the food almost always becomes more attractive. . . . The lifelong nutrition habits that children acquire from school food programs don't end with eating better food. A food systems curriculum promotes understanding about where food comes from and the natural cycles that produce it."—Marilyn Briggs, "Rethinking School Lunch"

Learning in Watersheds

Students doing creek restoration work on ranches in Sonoma and Marin Counties learn about the interaction of species in an ecosystem while helping to preserve endangered California freshwater shrimp.

"Students can see results [from planting willows]. In four months, the sprigs they plant will have branches three to four feet long. In two years, they'll look like little trees. They stabilize the soil. They provide shade to cool the water and reduce evaporation. Birds nest in them and bring in seeds of other trees like alders and oaks."—Laurette Rogers, quoted in Michael K. Stone, "'It Changed Everything We Thought We Could Do'"

Learning in the Kitchen Classroom

In the kitchen classroom at The Edible Schoolyard in Berkeley, sharing meals around a table they have set with colorful tablecloths and vases of flowers reminds children of the role of food in enriching human community.

"Can we pass on to our children the magic of hospitality and generosity? Can we teach our children the values that transform our lives and the world around us? . . . Food can teach us the things that really matter—care, beauty, concentration, discernment, sensuality, all the best that humans are capable of— but only if we take the time to think about what we're eating."—Alice Waters, "Fast-Food Values and Slow Food Values"

Learning from the Campus Landscape

Building a straw-bale toolshed for a new school garden requires the co-operative efforts of the whole school community at Martin Luther King Middle School in Berkeley.

"[The landscape of the campus] is part of the community and it's a part of the curriculum in which children learn about the world, starting from where they are. . . . Children, staff members, and parents transform areas of the school grounds into educational resources or outdoor classrooms."—Jeanne Casella, "Leadership and the Learning Community"

Learning on the Playground

A child gets up close with life found on the playground at an urban elementary school in San Francisco.

"Close observation—mixed with wonder—is essential for the development of artist, scientist, writer, as well as mathematician, humorist, inventor, and more."—Kerry Ruef, "The Loupe's Secret"

Learning through Art in Nature

Students make art out of their engagement with tools and materials in the garden of a Berkeley middle school.

"Combining science and the arts . . . makes pedagogical sense. Both disciplines rely on observation, pattern recognition, problem solving, experimentation, and thinking by analogy."—Pamela Michael, "Helping Children Fall in Love with the Earth"

Learning on Regional Sustainable Farms

Many children have never experienced food that doesn't come from a box or can. Visits to regional farms let them experience the origins of food and put a face on the people who grow what the students eat.

"Most of our society . . . no longer knows what it's like to pull a carrot from the ground, or eat the heart out of a watermelon still warm from the sun, or munch on beans that are so fresh that they explode in your mouth." —Michael Ableman, "Raising Whole Children Is Like Raising Good Food"

Leadership and the
Learning Community

An Interview with Jeanne Casella,
Principal of Mary E. Silveira School, San Rafael, California

Zenobia Barlow, Sara Marcellino, and Michael K. Stone

A walk through the campus at Mary E. Silveira School, a multiracial school of about four hundred students in suburban San Rafael, California, gives hints as to why the Center for Ecoliteracy chose this as one of its exemplary elementary schools (and why it was named a California Distinguished School). "What am I?" asks a sign posted next to a white oak tree in the center of the campus—that week's "mystery species of the week." At one edge of the campus is a bean-shaped pond, some 6 or 8 feet by 30 feet, designed and built with the help of students, teachers, and parents. The pond, home to turtles, fish, and compatible plants, is a place of peacefulness and beauty, as well as a classroom and laboratory. A playing-field-sized garden adorns another side of the campus. In a small "Five Senses Garden," kindergarten teacher Lara Franklin has planted lemon verbena, scented geranium, sage, and mint for smell; soft lamb's ear for touch; nemesia and tulips for sight; and a variety of herbs and nasturtium for taste. Behind the cafeteria, bins of worms eat their way through table scraps and produce soil for the gardens.

About half of Silveira's students apply for jobs on one of twenty-two teams that help care for the campus and the school community. A pond team watches over the pond. Junior master gardeners assist in the garden. The energy team conducts energy audits and writes notes to teachers, providing gentle reminders to turn off the lights when a class goes to the cafeteria. On a table in the hallway lies a two-sided sign

149

crafted in the handwriting of a young student from the team that works on conflict resolution; one side reads "Talk" and the other side "Listen." Other students serve as school historians, curators, stage managers, waste managers, and in more than a dozen other roles.

The curriculum isn't as immediately visible, but the garden, pond, tanks where steelhead eggs hatch in the spring, student jobs, and community service are all part of an integrated curriculum that can focus from year to year on different ecological themes, such as "cycles."

Such schools are usually reflections of flexible, creative leaders who can fulfill their responsibilities while encouraging others to share leadership. Jeanne Casella, Silveira's principal, is one of those leaders. The Center first connected with her when she was the elementary and middle school principal in rural Laytonville, California, one of CEL's first grantees. She has taught at every grade level from preschool through eighth grade and holds teaching certificates in both regular and special education. She has served as a student teacher supervisor for Dominican University and worked with twelve school districts as development specialist for the Mendocino County Office of Education.

This interview combines talks with Jeanne both by the book's editors and by Sara Marcellino, a Center for Ecoliteracy writer, who also gathered the acccompanying quotes from teachers, students, and parents.

CENTER FOR ECOLITERACY: Fritjof Capra has observed that "Integrating the curriculum through ecologically oriented projects is possible only if the school becomes a true learning community. In such a learning community, teachers, students, administrators, and parents are all interlinked in a network of relationships as they work together to facilitate learning." Mary E. Silveira looks like that kind of learning community. How have you accomplished this?

JEANNE CASELLA: Everyone feels recognized. I make it a point to greet everyone by name. Seeing that people know the names of people in the community—and know that other people know their name—is one way to build community. I want the children to know the names of at least the teachers, instructional assistants, and custodians. We do activities to support this. For instance, at our weekly assembly a panel of blindfolded children from different classes will ask yes-or-no questions to try to figure out the identity of a "Secret Staff Person." It's a fun way to introduce staff members to the children.

We have a "buddy system" linking students, say a first-grader with a fourth-grader. The younger students feel like they have an older sibling at the school. The older students take pride in caring for their "little buddy." I'll be walking with a child, who'll say, "Oh, my buddy's in the library," or "My buddy's down in the garden." They get to know each other at a different level, by working on a book project or interview, or planting seeds in the garden together. In another way that we link across grade levels, each teacher meets for various activities a half-dozen times during the year with a group of twenty kindergarten-through-fifth-grade students.

How do you reinforce the feeling of everyone being connected to the whole community?

Some schools hold an assembly once a month, but we have one every week. It's not long, about forty-five minutes, but everyone is invited, including parents and community members. We talk about current happenings and recognize people's achievements. I'm going to try using the assembly for whole-school problem solving. If I pose a question (for instance, "Should we add two more large fish to the pond?") on Monday, and classes discuss it and report at the assembly, that might be better than just having a select few in the student council work on it. Each classroom also has a job or task that contributes to the school community, such as maintaining the pond, running a schoolwide mail system, or managing the lost-and-found.

We make sure to recognize people who contribute to the community. Because our school's logo is the star, we award "Star Cards" to encourage students to take pride in their school, care for each other, and develop positive feelings about themselves. Star Cards are given to students who do something over and above our expected behavior and academic standards, and can be turned in for special treats such as an ice cream sundae with the principal or extra recess time. During the year, every student has an opportunity to be the Star of the Week and be honored in the classroom and at assemblies, wear a special badge, and be featured in our office scrapbook.

We've been impressed by your school jobs for students. How did they come about?

Teachers at a project-based learning conference I attended talked about creating jobs in their classroom, such as the classroom historian, who captured the history of the class for the year. I thought, "Could we do that on a whole-school level?" We started with five or six jobs, and it snowballed. We now have thirty-two different jobs, "employing" about half our students. Students submit applications, just like in real-life jobs, explaining why they want the job and why they would be good at it. They even have to give references and sign a contract agreeing to fulfill the job's responsibilities.

The kids in the program feel empowered. They acquire a variety of skills. The correspondence secretaries work at my desk on Wednesday afternoons and learn how to write a friendly letter. They have to work cooperatively with three or four other students to figure out how to divide up the tasks. They learn people skills. The waste managers learn about vermicomposting and recycling, and are trained by Conservation Corps members to conduct waste audits for the school.

The Campus

Is the landscape of the campus itself part of your community?

It's part of the community, and it's part of the curriculum in which children learn about the world, starting from where they are. Children are usually given too few opportunities to observe and interact with wildlife. We want to help children build a strong environmental ethic, so that they grow up to be adults who respect and care for the earth.

Through our EcoStar program, children, staff members, and parents transform areas of the school grounds into educational resources or outdoor classrooms. What better way for students to study the life cycles and adaptations of organisms than to watch monarch butterflies emerging on milkweed plants that they have planted? What better way to learn measurement than to map the garden area on the school grounds? What better place for reading, journal writing, or sketching than a natural area that they helped to create?

> When you're inside and you're learning about plants you say, "Oh, this is this kind of plant." But if you're outside and you can feel it, see it, and observe it, you understand more. When I'm outside I can see all the beautiful scenes, and when you turn those scenes to education, that actually works for me. You use your senses to detect and feel life.
> —KAITLYN ST. JAMES, Silveira fifth-grader

Our goals include instilling a sense of place and of ownership, pride, and responsibility in students; teaching and practicing the principles of ecology; heightening children's environmental awareness and promoting earth stewardship; and integrating subject matter such as science, math, and social studies. First-graders help grow and harvest food in our garden. Second-graders participate in the STRAW program [see the next essay—*Ed.*], doing salmon habitat preservation on a creek near the school. Third-graders manage the worm bin compost boxes where we recycle fruit and vegetable waste from the cafeteria to create soil for the garden. Fourth-graders plant annual native wildflowers and maintain the school's native perennial garden. Fifth-graders are responsible for maintenance and water-quality testing in our school pond. Each classroom contributes to the garden by pulling weeds, propagating plantings from cuttings and seed, or assisting with the community plots such as the pumpkin patch.

Teachers

How do you help teachers feel that they're part of a learning community?

I use a shared leadership model. I ask for teachers' advice, and I listen to their opinions. Like the students—like everyone—teachers need to feel valued, rec-

ognized, respected, and appreciated. They need compliments, a note left in their
mailbox or on their desk, a luncheon hosted by parents, or a handmade gift
from a child. I let our parent community know how hard our teachers work,
how successful they are, and how they serve as the heartbeat of our school. I
pay tribute to teachers when I write up their formal evaluations; I want them
to know their strengths and to figure out ways for them to share their talents
with the rest of the community. Teachers also need to feel that as a school we
respect differences and value diversity. I encourage them to bring their own
ways of being into their teaching lives.

Teachers are on the same bell schedule as the children they teach. They
have to go to the bathroom at a certain time and eat at a certain time. They often
feel isolated, and don't have time during their workday to consult with one
another, as other professionals do.

What can you do to lessen this isolation?

We spend time getting to know one another. We get together at one another's
houses. We "check in" or share both school-related and personal information
at the beginning of each staff meeting. We talk about the good things that are
happening, and we make goals for ourselves.

I encourage teachers to attend conferences, to collaborate, or just to visit
each other's classrooms. I'll teach their classes, so that they can do that. When
I'm giving tours to campus visitors, I'm always proud of what I see in the classrooms. It's a really wonderful feeling, and I tell teachers that they should have
that feeling, too. One of my two principal's meetings each month is used for
grade-level collaboration. We share new materials or ideas from conferences,
workshops, or meetings.

One of the most important innovations, thanks to a grant from the Center for Ecoliteracy, was a program of roving substitute teachers who covered
classes for two hours, twice a month, to free up the teachers from each grade
to work together. It's key that this planning time came within their school days.
Unlike middle school and high school teachers, elementary school teachers

don't have preparation periods built into their daily schedules. They're often asked to do things after school, on their own time, when they're tired.

Were these planning blocks the times when the teachers integrated campus projects, in-class activities, and the curriculum?

Teachers can feel overwhelmed with curriculum requirements and feel that outdoor learning projects are an additional burden or "add-on." It is necessary to outline how a project will help meet the learning standards and curriculum requirements. The Center for Ecoliteracy grant allowed us to start the year with a planning retreat. Prior to the retreat, we sent two teachers to a training on the "Understanding by Design" process, which they then taught to the whole staff over the year. We began by asking what we wanted students to learn and experience and how we would assess that, and worked backwards from there to identifying the essential questions for each study unit. At that retreat we devised the two-hour planning blocks and agreed to take time at monthly staff meetings so that grade levels could hear what other grade levels were doing. We encouraged grade-level teams to share student work, and we left this work out in the staff room for others to see.

> Our curriculum is much more integrated now, down to applying math skills with the temperature readings [in salmon tanks]. This work is something these kids will remember when they talk about second grade. Not the geometry they are learning or the social studies report they wrote. This is what they're going to remember. That's what makes it so worthwhile.
> —LYNN COLOMBO, Silveira second-grade teacher

We chose "cycles" as an ecological concept around which to integrate curriculum for the year. I used several resources to introduce the concept. Then teachers examined the curriculum and decided how to weave the study of cycles into it. For instance, while working in the garden, first-graders studied the life cycles of beneficial garden insects such as the ladybug and the praying mantis. Students working on compost studied nature's recycling processes. Because we have used a project-based model for several years, it wasn't difficult for teachers to integrate the cycles theme into new project ideas or take something like the second-grade salmon unit and have the kids redesign it with more focus on cycles. We talked schoolwide about cycles at our assemblies, with reports from each classroom about, for example, cycles they had noticed in the garden or pond.

How can a principal help to inspire teachers with new ideas?

Change is always difficult, but if you create an atmosphere where it's safe for people to experiment and take risks, they are more willing to try new things. The principal can give teachers resources and help them look at a variety of options. But the principal doesn't have to come up with all the ideas, and it's better if they don't. Particularly when you first come to a school, you just have to listen—especially to people who have lived in that space longer than you have. Sometimes all you have to do is let teachers know that they'll be supported.

When I arrived, we had a little garden in the courtyard, and everybody kept talking about wanting something bigger and wouldn't it be nice if we could have vegetables as opposed to only flowers. Finally I just said, "Go ahead." That's all they needed to start figuring out what to do. Several of us wrote grants, and our parent community helped with donations of time, equipment, and materials.

The next year we had to add portable classrooms, and the dirt area around the portables was a muddy mess in the rainy season. I asked both the teachers and the kids, "What would you like?" We made a list and got permission to talk to the school architect. The kids said, "We don't want the portables just plunked down. We want some order, and we want some sidewalks and grassy hills, and we want a pond . . . "

That was pretty unheard of—young students telling an architect what they wanted—but it's important to invite them to become active participants in their own education and to have a say about the place they spend a good part of their day. Students surveyed possible sites for the garden. A fifth-grade classroom was in charge of the design and worked with community "experts" and the other classrooms to make sure everyone's needs were met. Fourth-graders built a shed for the tools, first- and fourth-grade buddy classes built compost bins, and everyone decorated mini-benches for the area.

Do you have any other examples?

When I arrived at Silveira, specialists taught science twice a week, while the general education teachers were in the back of the room, sometimes doing other things. It bothered me, but I kept quiet until I heard teachers making comments like, "I've seen this lesson three times. I could do a better job." Eventually, I had heard enough and said, "Why don't you do it?" They asked how much the district was spending on the science specialists and whether we could put that money toward resources and other supplies. We found out that we could, and that the district was willing to let us pilot our own science program for a year.

We got $16,000 from the district, and joined the California Science Implementation Network (CSIN). One of our teachers took a summer workshop for facilitator/leaders and became our science lead teacher. CSIN provided a "coach" who taught in a neighboring school district. We asked high school teachers to help us understand content. And slowly we began to integrate science into other areas of the curriculum. Within a few years, the other schools in our district had followed our lead.

Our pond project began with a donation of two red-eared slider turtles that had outgrown their tank. The students wanted to create a more natural environment for the turtles. They generated a list of questions we needed to answer, including water depth, security, plant life, and so on. Students mapped the site and made a 3-D model of the pond. We worked with parents in the construction business, an engineer at the San Francisco Bay Model, and local businesses that offered donations and discounts on materials. Students worked with the Marin/Sonoma Mosquito Abatement District to learn about mosquito control and contacted the California Department of Fish and Game to determine what other kinds of wildlife they could introduce into the pond. Now the pond has a variety of plants and fish, including an albino channel catfish and ten turtles.

What responsibility does the principal have to be a model?

James Baldwin once said, "Children have never been very good at listening to their elders, but they have never failed to imitate them." We have only six hours a day with our students. The time is precious. We need to make sure that everything we do is important. The principal's behavior sets the tone for the school. I think that the principal is the head learner. I'm always putting articles or ideas in teachers' boxes, and sometimes my excitement is contagious. I talk to students about what they are learning. They teach me things all the time and they love it. Everyone knows I care deeply about the environment, because they see me taking care of the plants in the courtyard or trying to find a source for recycling bins for every classroom. They know I spend weekend time writing grants for specific projects.

Parents

How do you make parents feel that they are parts of this community?

Parents deserve patience, tolerance, and kindness. We sometimes see things differently, but I've learned to pay close attention to their requests, questions, and concerns. When they meet with teachers informally or in formal conferences, parents feel welcome and valued. We invite them to e-mail or drop off notes for teachers. Our Home & School Association invites teachers to present curriculum information. We survey parents every two years to find out how we are doing and what things we need to work on.

When parents are well informed and we have a shared vision, they become our best supporters. I send home or e-mail a parent newsletter every week, and teachers send home newsletters as well. Our Home & School Association publishes a monthly parents newsletter, and we have an outside bulletin board just for parents. Our parents are very present, active, and essential to the life of our school. A father who owns his own construction business assisted a classroom with the design for a greenhouse. Another father plays the guitar and regularly sings with us at Friday assemblies. Parents work on committees, help plan fundraising events, and donate their time to assist in classrooms or read to students in the library. At the end of the year we have a special assembly where each class does a presentation that lets parents know how much we appreciate them, but we try to tell them every day.

> Science Night gives the kids an opportunity to lead their parents through outdoor environments and teach us what we don't know.
> —BILL DONAHOE, Silveira parent

As part of integrating science into the curriculum and better involving parents, we dropped our old science fair and established Family Science Night, where parents not only see, but experience, what students are learning. Last year, the second-grade classes created a salmon "Jeopardy" game, where they asked parents and other students questions about the salmon's life cycle. Fifth-graders created hands-on interactive projects, such as a device that used gravity, a bowling ball, and a ramp to crush fifteen empty cans at a time. Third-graders created models of different environments and invited parents and other students to add the right animals, plants, and other objects to complete the ecosystems.

The Wider Community

What relationship does the school have to the neighborhood and the larger community around it?

We try to be good neighbors. We encourage community participation. One of our regular playground supervisors is an elderly neighbor; other neighbors help and take care of the garden in the summer. Our energy team joined the Affordable Communities Energy Education program, and devoted the 2003–

2004 year to working with local senior citizens in the Martinelli House, an affordable housing facility in downtown San Rafael.

> We go every so often to the Martinelli House and help them create their own energy team. We go around to the apartments checking that the lights are off or on, so that we can save them money on their energy bill. The money they save goes to the fun stuff they do.
> —SARA LEE, Silveira fifth-grader

The kids put up energy-reminder signs and doorknob bookmarks in English and Spanish, and helped the residents to replace traditional lightbulbs with energy-efficient compact fluorescent lightbulbs and to take other simple actions. They saved the seniors about 5 percent on their energy bills while learning about energy efficiency themselves. Kids feel good when they can actually help someone, when they have some expertise other people want.

How do you know if you're succeeding as a learning community?

Our vision statement says, "Mary E. Silveira is a place where students want to be." Teachers want to come to school. Parents want to spend time at the school. There's pride in the community. Students grow protective of the campus when they take an active role in developing and maintaining its outdoor learning areas. They go home and talk about the school, and parents become knowledgeable. People work hard and enjoy what they're doing. They feel motivated to try new things and see what happens. Teachers are more excited about teaching tomorrow than they were today. When I see students at a Science Night or some other event demonstrating that they really understand a concept like cycles or that they know enough to teach their parents about ecosystems, and I see their enthusiasm for sharing what they've learned, then I know that what we're doing works.

"It Changed Everything
We Thought We Could Do":
The STRAW Project

Michael K. Stone

The story of Students and Teachers Restoring a Watershed (STRAW) appears in the Relationship section of this book because of the crucial role played in STRAW's history and work by the extraordinary network it has developed. Ecosystems work by creating networks. STRAW's network includes students, teachers, administrators, schools, ranchers, for-profit businesses, philanthropic foundations and other nongovernmental organizations, and governmental agencies.

Not all of the members of that network are natural allies. An important piece of this story is the careful relationship-building required, for instance, to create mutual trust among ranchers, environmentalists, and schoolchildren. Another piece is the ongoing effort needed to nourish that network (for instance, through STRAW's yearly Watershed Week program).

The Shrimp Project that led to STRAW was possible because of a commitment that Brookside School in suburban Marin County, California, had already made to experiment with project-based learning, which some people prefer to call "environmental project-based learning" when the project entails getting kids into the natural world. While different people use the term differently (see, for instance, the preceding interview with Jeanne Casella and "Tapping the Well of Urban Youth Activism" in Part IV), the process usually involves some combination of the following features:

- Curriculum structured around the knowledge and skills necessary to complete a meaningful and often complex "real-world" project, often in service to the local social and environmental community;

- A high degree of student initiative, leadership, and participation in defining problems and in selecting and managing projects to address them;

- Learning in which results are not predetermined or fully predictable;

- Teachers as resources, fellow learners, and problem solvers rather than as dispensers of knowledge;

- Attention to skills such as setting goals and priorities, managing time, problem solving, and working with others.

Teachers and students are often very enthusiastic about the outcomes that project-based learning produces, but the drive for standardized examinations increases the difficulty of designing projects that both generate their own objectives and "cover" required subject matter.

Michael K. Stone is coeditor of this book. His other work as a senior editor and writer at the Center for Ecoliteracy has included interviews and writing for the Rethinking School Lunch project, guest-editing a special section on ecological literacy in the September—October 2004 issue of Resurgence magazine, and editing other Center publications. He and the Center became acquainted while he was working on this profile of the STRAW program, which appeared in a slightly different form in the spring 2001 Whole Earth magazine. Before joining the Center staff in 2004, Michael served as managing editor of the Millennium Whole Earth Catalog, as general manager of Point Foundation (Whole Earth's publisher), and for seven years as managing editor of Whole Earth magazine. Before that, he served for nineteen years—the last eight as academic vice president—on the faculty of World College West, a small innovative college in northern Marin County. He has also written for the Toronto Star and the New York Times, among other publications, and served on the staffs of the lieutenant governor of Illinois and the Illinois Arts Council.

ON A CRISP LATE-JANUARY MORNING in 2001, I'm on my way to Paul Martin's ranch in southern Sonoma County, California. The ten miles from Petaluma (a city of about fifty thousand) to Martin's ranch, and the ten from there to the coast, traverse rolling grassy hills, dotted with stands of oak, bay, and buckeye. Dairy and sheep-ranching country. I bicycle here sometimes, and the endless undulations are familiar. These hills know only two colors, golden brown and green. Since it's winter, the land is emerald.

Past Two Rock Presbyterian Church, large cardboard "STRAW" signs mark the ranch's driveway. I park by an open structure sheltering 10- or 12-foot-high stacks of hay bales. Laurette Rogers, director of STRAW (Students and Teachers Restoring a Watershed), greets me. "Listen to the meadowlarks!" she exclaims. "I don't recall ever seeing so many here."

From where we're standing, Stemple Creek's route through the pastureland is easy to trace by the lines of willows, interspersed with oaks, extending several feet on either side of the creek. The foliage is high and thick at the east end of the property, where STRAW did its first planting in 1993. Farther west, where the students will be planting today, it thins out considerably. "When we came for our first planting," Rogers says, "I didn't realize that that was the creek. It looked more like a drainage ditch."

The day's workers, fourth- and fifth-graders from Lagunitas and Wade Thomas Schools, arrive. I had envisioned big yellow school buses, but a line of sedans, station wagons, and SUVs, driven by parents, pulls in. About forty kids pile out and run to climb the hay bales. "Off, right now," yells Rogers. "We've been doing these projects for years without any injuries, and we're not going to have the first one today." Later she confides, "When I'm in the classroom, I'm very mellow. Out here, I get intense." Her carefulness is one reason Paul Martin trusts STRAW on his property.

Rogers directs the students' eyes to the lush growth in the original planting. "See those trees? The sprigs you're planting today will be that tall by the time you're in high school." The students pull calf-high rubber boots over their shoes and line up for work gloves. They're divided into groups of four, each group accompanied by a teacher or parent. Each team is issued a heavy digging bar, about six feet long and an inch in diameter, with one pointed end.

After a final reminder, "Last chance to use the portable toilet," students, parents, and teachers trek across a muddy field to the creek. They're led by Boone Vale, a staffer from Prunuske Chatham, Inc., a design and construction firm specializing in restoration that is overseeing today's restoration. Staff members from Prunuske Chatham and STRAW have already been out to the worksite, to lay temporary board bridges across the creek and double-check that Paul Martin's electric fences are turned off. On the other side of a barbed wire fence, a herd of Holsteins turns its full attention to the noisy newcomers.

The creek is three or four feet wide, a few inches deep, down two-foot embankments. The Prunuske Chatham workers have placed flags at the places they chose for planting the willows. Boone Vale shows the students how to use the digging bars, three or four people at a time, pounding them into the ground, wiggling them around, pounding again, until they've dug a narrow hole a couple of feet deep. He hands out three-foot-long willow sprigs, a half-inch in diameter, cut from trees on the property. He shows the students how to tell which end is "up," how to plant them and tamp down the earth. Recent rains have left the ground soft, making digging and planting easier. The children invent songs and chants to accompany themselves as they take turns with the digging bars. They work for about ninety minutes, break for lunch, then get back to work. By the time they leave, they've planted more than three hundred willow sprigs.

How It Started

STRAW originated in 1992 at Brookside School, about twenty-five miles north of San Francisco, where Laurette Rogers taught fourth grade.

She had showed her class a National Geographic film on rainforest destruction. "It was filled with haunting music and pictures of chainsaws," recalls Aaron Mihaly, a fourth-grader in 1992 and later a member of Harvard's class of 2005. A depressing discussion about endangered species followed, until one student raised his hand. "But what can we do?" "I looked into his eyes," says Rogers, "and somehow I just couldn't give him a pat answer about letter writing and making donations."

Because Brookside School had recently made a commitment to environmental project-based learning, Rogers had the flexibility to propose to her class
that they choose and design a project around which to organize lessons. She
turned to Meryl Sundove, a trainer for a now-defunct California State Adopt-
A-Species Program. Rogers gave her a couple of criteria: she wanted the species
to be local, and she wanted it to be obscure, to counter the bias toward beautiful and charismatic species being the most worth saving. Sundove suggested
a trout, a salmon, and the California freshwater shrimp, *Syncaris pacifica*
(about the size of a child's little finger), now found only in fifteen creeks in
Marin, Sonoma, and Napa Counties. The students voted for the shrimp, but
they weren't that enthusiastic. "We didn't expect to like it," Rogers says.

In retrospect, "the shrimp were perfect," says Aaron Mihaly. "We weren't
joining someone else's campaign to save a distant cuddly animal. No one had
ever heard of them, so we had to use our creativity to interest other people.
They fit our image of ourselves . . . we were just a little fourth-grade class. If
we didn't work on them, no one else was going to."

Meryl Sundove offered Rogers the key: "Pick any species. Go into depth
about its life. Find out all about it, and you'll fall in love with it." The class
did. They found that the shrimp are beautiful, almost transparent creatures.
The males are up to $1\frac{1}{2}$ inches along, the females up to $2\frac{1}{2}$ inches long, with
rust-colored spots. They've been in local creeks since the time of the dinosaurs
(a fact the fourth-graders loved). They are the creeks' garbage collectors, feeding on dead and decaying plant material. Because they are terrible swimmers,
they must cling to riparian roots in order not to be washed away.

Rogers learned an important lesson the first year. Most people think that
nine- and ten-year-olds need to see immediate payoffs. But her students worked
for six months on the shrimp before they ever saw one. (When they did,
"There was this big, 'Ahhh.' You'd think they had seen a movie star.") They
kept focused even after learning it would probably take fifty to a hundred
years for the restorations to have a significant impact on the shrimp's habitat.
They talked about taking their grandchildren to see their work, and telling
them, "We did that."

Rogers refused to predigest material for her students. She gave them original scientific papers on the shrimp; each fourth-grader was responsible for understanding and accurately reporting the most important information from one to two pages of a paper, including figuring out the scientific jargon. Students analyzed the data for each of the fifteen creeks where the shrimp live. They worked in class two hours a week, but frequently put in more time on weekends or after finishing other lessons. Other classroom lessons kept coming back to the shrimp—shrimp drawings during art lessons; shrimp poems, songs, and fairy tales during language arts sessions.

The students learned that the shrimp are threatened primarily because of habitat destruction around the streams where they live. Dairy, beef, and sheep ranches are the agricultural mainstays of west Marin and Sonoma Counties. In former years, agricultural agents used to advise dairy farmers to build their pastures near creeks to water their stock. Now, the students discovered, the shrimp habitats were pressured by the damming of creeks, petroleum and chemical runoff, manure in the water, and sedimentation from soil erosion caused by stock trampling the creek banks and grazing the foliage that could otherwise stabilize the soil. It wasn't just cows, though. It was also off-road vehicles, and dumping of trash, and damage by potato farmers. And it wasn't just shrimp that were affected. They turned out to be one strand of a web that includes trees, grasses, aquatic insects, songbirds, creeks, estuaries, and the entire San Francisco Bay. The students began to understand the "shrimp problem" as a watershed problem.

They learned that Native Americans used to eat the shrimp, which are now so rare that no one, including scientific researchers, can even touch one without a permit. They also saw how the story of "their" shrimp was repeated over and over again for other endangered species. (The only other known *Syncaris* species, *Syncaris pasadenae*, became extinct when the Rose Bowl was built over its entire habitat in the early 1920s.)

The class chose to focus on Stemple Creek, one of the most deteriorated, which flows from the hills of Petaluma, through about ten miles of cattle ranches, before passing into the Estero de San Antonio. They made presentations to meetings of the local Resource Conservation District and the Stemple Creek/Estero de San Antonio Watershed Program. Liza Prunuske, cofounder of Prunuske Chatham, introduced the class to Paul Martin. He was concerned about erosion, and wanted to improve his pasturage, but he also remembered the Valley quail he had grown up with and hoped to see them again on his land. However, he didn't know if he wanted a lot of fourth-graders running around on his property or environmentalists descending on him and dictating how he could run his business. As he tells the story, "I wasn't sure what they were up to. Then Laurette told me that she had told her students to imagine what it would be like if someone came into your bedroom and said, 'From now on, you can't get anything out of your closet—none of the toys, clothes, or anything.' You can imagine the kids saying, 'But that's our property, what do you mean?' Then Laurette told the kids that's how unfair it would be if they went to the rancher and started telling him what to do. After I heard that story I knew it would be all right, and we started working together."

Martin, now coordinator of environmental services for the Western United Dairymen, had another goal. He wanted "citified people" to know what his life was like. When the class came to his ranch, he brought out milk and ice cream, and reminded the students where they had come from. He helped them understand the economic pressures on family farmers, workdays that begin at 2:00 A.M., and why ranchers sometimes don't have the time or money for restoration work that they would like to do. "See that man?" he once asked a group of students who had come to a ranchers' meeting. "He'll be eating beans tonight. Five nights a week, that's all he can afford."

In March of 1993, the class did its first planting on the Martin ranch. Martin had already fenced off part of the creek, to keep the cattle from returning and undoing the work. The class planted willows and blackberries along the creek banks. "In our area, you get more bang for the buck with willows than anything else," says Rogers. "Students can see results. In four months, the sprigs they plant will have branches three to four feet long. In two years, they'll look like little trees. They stabilize the soil. They provide shade to cool the water and reduce evaporation. Birds nest in them, and bring in seeds of other trees like alders and oaks."

Students have returned to Stemple Creek every year since. The first plantings are now a tall, dense growth that blocks sight of the creek. Five years after the first plantings, the Valley quail, which Martin remembered from his childhood, came back. Songbirds are nesting in the trees. And, to everyone's surprise, California freshwater shrimp—which were not expected to reestablish themselves for decades—had migrated downstream by 1999 and begun clinging to the roots of willows planted by students six years earlier. It's many years too early to know whether the shrimp will establish long-term residence at the restored sites, multiply, and eventually be rescued from their endangered status, but the results from the first few years are encouraging.

"We Need to Go to Scale"

For the Brookside fourth-graders, the natural ecology of shrimp, cattle, willows, and streams overlapped with the social ecology of schools, agricultural economics, politics, and conflict resolution. Their "let's help a species" project eventually evolved into STRAW, a network of teachers (eighty to a hundred in three dozen schools), students, parents, ranchers, businesses, public agencies, nongovernmental organizations (NGOs), and foundations. About three thousand students participate yearly in rural and urban STRAW projects ranging from riparian restoration to insect and bird monitoring.

The first year's project didn't end with doing one planting. The fourth-graders wrote letters to government officials, testified at hearings before local government bodies and Congressional committees, addressed educational conferences, sold "Shrimp Club" T-shirts, arranged media coverage, painted a gigantic mural featuring a 6-foot-long shrimp at the local ferry terminal. They won Anheuser-Busch's "A Pledge and a Promise" award as the environmental project of the year for 1993, and increased the $32,500 they had won from the prize into a total of $100,000 for shrimp protection, all of it raised by the students.

The project gained an ally when the Center for Ecoliteracy, then a new foundation, became a sponsor. "The Shrimp Project was an ideal model of an integrated curriculum," says Fritjof Capra. "Lessons were organized around an issue kids were passionate about. They developed ecological values out of firsthand experience. They got excited about shrimp, which led them to learn about the problems caused by cows. They had to take into account the ranchers' ideas. To write letters to City Hall, they had to learn to spell well."

The Shrimp Project continued, on one or two ranches a year, until 1998. More ranchers were approaching Prunuske Chatham, requesting kids and projects. By then, Rogers had left Brookside. Ruth Hicks, who had taken over the Shrimp Project, told her, "We need to expand this thing. We need to go to scale."

At that point, Brookside students' networking paid off in an unexpected way. Grant Davis is executive director of The Bay Institute of San Francisco. TBI was founded in 1981 to promote work from the then novel perspective of seeing the entire bay-delta ecosystem (which covers 40 percent of California) as a single, independent watershed. TBI uses scientific research and advocacy on behalf of protecting that watershed. In 1998 TBI had just begun working with local schools. But five years earlier, when Davis was on Congresswoman Lynn Woolsey's staff, Shrimp Project students at Brookside School called to invite the Congresswoman and him to events. He remembered those calls—"How often do you get a call from a fourth-grader?"—and offered a base for expanding the Shrimp Project. The Center for Ecoliteracy stepped in with additional support. STRAW was born, initially as a joint project of The Bay Institute and the Center for Ecoliteracy. Laurette Rogers became its director.

Urban Restoration

In 1999, Liz Lewis, director of the Marin County Stormwater Pollution Prevention Program (MCSTOPPP) approached Laurette Rogers to suggest that STRAW add an urban component (which is possible since most of the county's urban streams are still above ground). Half of STRAW's projects are now urban.

MCSTOPPP—a joint effort of Marin County's cities, towns, and unincorporated areas to prevent stormwater pollution and enhance creek and wetlands quality—plays the same role that Prunuske Chatham does for rural restoration: it serves as liaison with property "owners" (e.g., parks, schools, and open space districts); plans projects; identifies and prepares sites; orients and oversees students; provides plant materials, equipment, and follow-up maintenance.

Urban projects have the added advantage of close proximity to students' neighborhoods and schools (students can walk to half of them from their classrooms). "It's important," Lewis says, "for students to see they're caring for their own neighborhoods. They'll think twice next time about throwing trash in the storm drain. It's also important that they learn where their water comes from, that water doesn't magically get treated on its way to them, how it must be filtered, that it's habitat for native animals, and that the health of the creeks affects the health of the people living near them."

The STRAW Network

STRAW follows the same basic format as the Shrimp Project—hands-on student projects related to watershed restoration, integrated into overall classroom work, intended to influence the culture of the whole school. The main difference is the extensive network that supports STRAW. The existence and maintenance of that network—a prime example of using ecological principles to promote sustainability—is as central to STRAW's story as is its restoration work. That network includes STRAW's main sponsor, its other funding partners, the participating schools, students and parents, the ranchers, restoration professionals, and NGOs.

Sponsor. The program, now formally known as "The Bay Institute's STRAW Project," is one of TBI's three major programs. TBI's strategies include advocacy of water policy reforms; scientific monitoring of government water projects; design, leadership, and evaluation of large-scale river and wetlands restoration projects; and annual assessments of the estuary's health. It works simultaneously at multiple levels, from projects on the Sacramento and San Joaquin Rivers costing billions of dollars to STRAW-directed restoration at a local community and school level, where impacts are more quickly visible to participants, while the next generation's citizens learn about the values and needs of their watersheds. Among its contributions, The Bay Institute

houses STRAW and takes responsibility for program administration, coordination, and outreach, and assists with some of its fund-raising.

Funding Partners. Besides The Bay Institute, STRAW's funding partners have included Autodesk, the California Department of Education, California State Coastal Conservancy, Center for Ecoliteracy, Dean Witter Foundation, Gabilan Foundation, Fred Gellert Family Foundation, Heller Charitable and Educational Fund, William and Flora Hewlett Foundation, Marin Community Foundation, Marin County Stormwater Pollution Prevention Program, Marin County Wildlife and Fisheries Committee, Marin Municipal Water District, JP Morgan Chase Foundation, the National Fish and Wildlife Foundation, National Oceanic and Atmospheric Administration, North Marin Water District, the Oracle Corporate Giving Program, Rainwater Charitable Funds, Rose Foundation, Salmon Creek Middle School, San Francisco Foundation, Sonoma County Fish and Wildlife Advisory Commission, Sonoma County Water Agency, the State Water Resources Control Board, and the Tides Foundation.

Schools. The day a typical class spends on a project site is "one of the last steps," says Prunuske Chatham ecologist Denise Fisher. Before that, representatives from STRAW and Prunuske Chatham or MCSTOPPP visit each class to describe the work the class will do and its importance to its watershed. They get the planting materials, tools, and portable toilets to the site, train the students, and supervise their use of equipment. "This was the easiest field trip I've ever done," fifth-grade teacher Molly Whiteley told me. STRAW handles the logistics, freeing teachers to concentrate on integrating the project into their teaching. For instance, Whiteley studies the life cycle of the coho salmon in a creek near her school, conducts laboratory simulations of erosion, and combines the study of native plants with study of Native American culture (including building and testing boats made of tules).

STRAW charges teachers nothing. It requires only a commitment to do a watershed project, and attendance at "Watershed Week" during the summer (on teachers' own time) and at two dinners and a culminating activity where participants present their projects. The Watershed Week and dinners are partly orientation and training, partly inspiration, partly chances for teachers to share

with each other. "When we started the Center for Ecoliteracy," says Fritjof Capra, "we thought we would be helping teachers design educational curricula. We didn't realize that so much of our work would be building personal relationships among teachers." Rogers tells program veterans, "Even if you already know how to do the program, we want you there to help the others."

The events are also a place to honor teachers for working above and beyond what their jobs require. Says Sandy Neumann, Laurette Rogers's old principal and inspiration and now a consultant to STRAW, "We find the most respectful place we can—like a beautiful site on the edge of the Bay—we get the best food we can, we give the teachers lots of time to walk by the water, we ask them what they want."

She says the program really works when it enters the culture of the school. Teachers come and go, but the principal provides continuity. It's very difficult for a teacher to take the risks that teaching in a different way requires unless she or he has a supportive principal. So STRAW also sponsors events to give its principals recognition and opportunities to share experiences.

Students and Parents. STRAW requires one parent or teacher for every four students on a project. The 4:1 ratio is partly a safety precaution, but it also draws parents intimately into their children's education and reaffirms the importance of the projects in students' eyes. "Parent involvement is key," said Bill Bryant, the father of a Wade Thomas fifth-grader participating in the restoration at Paul Martin's ranch. "We talk with the kids on the way out and back. We participate in field work with them. When it's time to fund-raise for the PTA, we're already committed."

Ranchers. Projects like this are rare on private land. They couldn't happen without cooperation by ranchers, who offer access to their property and contribute their own labor. Ranchers bear the cost, or must find funding, for installing and maintaining fences to keep their herds away after plantings.

"This is our land," Marin rancher Al Poncia reminds me. "We want to maintain it too." Says Rogers, "You can't help the shrimp without helping the ranchers." For many ranchers, the chance to give suburbanites a taste of their cultural heritage is an important bonus. At the time he and his wife married, says Al Poncia, "most of the parents or grandparents of everyone we knew

were farmers. Now most young people are two or three generations away from the farm."

The Professionals. The need for expertise and advice extended the project web to include private consultants such as Prunuske Chatham and governmental agencies such as MCSTOPPP. From the start, one of Rogers's watchwords has been, "Use good science."

"We discovered one time that we were actually pulling out native grasses in order to plant willows," says Rogers. It's not enough either just to repeat a "native good, nonnative bad" mantra. "Sometimes the nonnative blackberries are holding the bank together," says Jennifer Allen, Southern Sonoma County Resource Conservation District watershed coordinator. "Until you've stabilized the bank, you can't start pulling them out." The right action also needs the right timing. "We were going to pull out a bunch of nonnatives one year," says Rogers. "We called Melissa Pitkin, who was then the education coordinator at the Point Reyes Bird Observatory. She said, 'This is the wrong time. The birds are just starting to nest in them.'"

About half of STRAW's projects are on rural sites. STRAW hires Prunuske Chatham to work with these, seeing what ranchers want to do, figuring out what is doable, purchasing plants (or cutting shoots from plants already there), choosing and staking out the proper places to plant, overseeing students, and following up with maintenance.

Public agencies are also vitally linked to the network. The Marin County and Southern Sonoma County Resource Conservation Districts (RCDs) are special districts of the state. Because they have no regulatory authority, participation by landowners is voluntary. The RCDs offer technical assistance with soil, water, vegetation, and wildlife conservation. They sit down with ranchers, often around a kitchen table, to ask, "What do you see as problems?" A primary role is helping to secure funding from public and private sources for expenses such as fencing, water troughs, and cattle crossings. Grants often require matching funds and/or labor provided by the landowner; STRAW can sometimes count as part of the match.

NGOs. The Environmental Education Council of Marin (EECOM) brings together environmental, educational, community, and business organizations in the county, to make environmental education a lifelong learning process. "It helps us focus and highlight our work," says Rogers, who has served on EECOM's steering committee. "We can get above the day-to-day fray and think together about how to increase our influence."

EECOM helped STRAW expand its human network. Through EECOM, Rogers met Marin Conservation Corps (MCC) executive director Marilee Eckert. MCC is an NGO that combines environmental preservation with job training for eighteen- to thirty-year-old Corps members (ranging from high school dropouts working on GEDs to college graduates considering careers in teaching). With STRAW, Corps members help with classroom preparation and direct students on projects. "They're able-bodied, they don't mind getting dirty, and kids really look up to them," says Eckert. "They might have had trouble in school themselves, and it's empowering when the kids treat them as role models." They do heavy work with power tools, such as gas-powered brush cutters and chain saws, which are too dangerous to put into the hands of elementary school students.

In 1999, another NGO, the Point Reyes Bird Observatory (PRBO), joined the STRAW network. Birds are especially good for student programs, according to Melissa Pitkin. "They are easy to study, easy to see, and easy to quantify. And if birds are healthy, the ecosystem is healthy." STRAW now offers programs such as bird monitoring (partly to measure the success of restorations) and public education about bird conservation.

"The Shrimp Project was like a pebble thrown into the water," Laurette Rogers writes at the end of *The California Freshwater Shrimp Project*, her book on the project. "It did many things we did not know it would do. It touched many people we did not know it would touch." As for the students, then-fourth-grader Megan summed up her work on the project: "I think this project changed everything we thought we could do. I always thought kids meant nothing. I really enjoyed doing this, it was fun and I felt like our class just knew exactly what to do. I feel that it did show me that kids can make a difference in the world, and we are not just little dots."

Raising Whole Children
Is Like Raising Good Food:
Beyond Factory Farming
and Factory Schooling

Michael Ableman

Michael Ableman writes here of a "deep soulful nourishment" that is based on local, biological, interpersonal, and ecological relationships. That would be a good summary of the motivation behind much of the work described in this book. Among the other topics he addresses that recur throughout the book are educating and farming according to industrial models, the distinction between teaching and learning, the recognition that children don't all develop on the same schedule, and the vital importance of learning through observation. He presents them here in a deeply personal way—not as abstractions or prescriptions, but as reports from a life lived with open eyes and an open heart.

Ableman is a farmer, writer, photographer, organizer, and a remarkable educator. He founded and directs the Center for Urban Agriculture at Fairview Gardens in Santa Barbara, an urban working farm and nonprofit community education center that's one of the country's most important and successful models for urban agriculture and for farmland preservation. Over more than twenty years, it has inspired thousands of students to grow organic produce and to set up alternative methods of food buying.

Under Ableman's leadership the farm was saved from development and preserved under one of the earliest and most innovative active agricultural conservation easements of its type in the country. Ableman tells the story of that effort in On Good Land: The Autobiography of an Urban Farm *(1998), which the* Philadelphia

Inquirer *proclaimed was very much like the book that Henry David Thoreau would have written had he been a farmer. The book, graced with Ableman's lush photographs, argues articulately for farmland preservation and provides a blueprint for a farm that thrives in cooperation with its surrounding community.*

In 1984 Ableman traveled to China, where he observed the remnants of a traditional system of agriculture that had sustained people and the land for thousands of years. This experience inspired him to travel around the world to experience other cultures, culminating in From the Good Earth: A Celebration of Growing Food Around the World *(1993), one of the first books to visually document the dramatic changes taking place in food and agriculture worldwide. He is currently farming a small piece of land on an island in British Columbia and is working on a new book profiling innovative farmers across North America.*

Ableman's work is described in Beyond Organic, *an award-winning 2001 film directed by John de Graaf and narrated by Meryl Streep. This essay was edited from the transcript of his talk at that film's premiere, hosted by the Center for Ecoliteracy, which was a major funder of the film through one of our donor-advised funds.*

I'VE BEEN A FARMER for over twenty-five years, more than twenty years on the same plot of land. I've spent that much time and more in education—as a student and as a parent, teaching interns and leading groups of young people on visits and live-in programs on my farm. During that time, I've discovered some amazing parallels between agriculture and education, both in their industrialized versions and in the small-scale, personal alternatives that I've given my life to supporting.

A person who's not a farmer might assume that anyone who had worked on the same piece of land for over twenty years would have it all figured out. Perhaps I am unusually slow, but after all these years I've concluded that instead of having more answers, I actually have more questions. Each year is like starting over: the climate is different; the marketplace has changed; the condition of the soil may have improved, but in subtle and unpredictable ways.

Still, no matter how long a person has been farming, it is difficult to shake off the cultural programming that we carry with us: that farms or gardens should be made up of straight rows, filled only with what we put in them; that we are somehow in control; and that good farming is about technique. But as hard as we may try to mold and manipulate our farms and gardens into our own image, nature always has another idea.

I believe that whatever success I have had as a farmer has come when I have approached my farm with what Zen Buddhists call a beginner's mind: without presuppositions, open to seeing and learning from whatever I encounter.

Nobody ever told me about this way of learning when I started farming. Now I require apprentices to take a notebook and walk the farm several times a week, simply recording what they see. I want them to develop what I consider to be the most important agricultural skill—observation—and I want them to discover for themselves that biological systems never stay the same.

I've been hearing a lot of talk about education lately—from government officials, journalists, movie stars, political candidates. They all seem to be experts on the subject. But what does the word "education" really mean, and how much of their "expertise" comes from assumptions and how much from actually observing what goes on in our schools?

My own schooling took place in public schools in the state of Delaware. My junior high was much like a minimum-security prison, with block walls, cement floors, bars on the windows, and an atmosphere more like a well-guarded holding facility than a place for nurturing, education, and inspiration. I was attending junior high school when Martin Luther King was shot. We had armed National Guardsmen in the hallways, and we were required to have one of them accompany us to the bathroom. My education during those years had nothing to do with math or English or social studies. It was about survival.

I decided early on that if this was education, I didn't want to have anything to do with it. I quit before finishing high school, and I never went to college. Although I hold no degrees, I have written three books, and I lecture in many of the universities and institutions that my parents and grandparents prayed that I might attend. I farm, I teach, and I consider myself reasonably well educated—though not because of the schooling I endured.

When my first son was born I was determined that I was going to give him a different educational experience from my own. After Waldorf school and home schooling, and learning Spanish in Guatemala, and living at an orphanage in Nicaragua, and farming and cooking and taking care of animals, Aaron eventually ended up just like I had, in a public junior high school.

I remember visiting his school at lunchtime. There were no National Guard patrols in the hallways or bars on the windows, but the cafeteria had been shut down, and in its place were Pizza Hut and Snapple and Taco Bell burritos. The ladies with white aprons and hairnets and the trays with hot food that I remembered from my childhood were gone, replaced by vending machines and prepackaged corporate America.

Aaron told me about the crowd that would gather around when he unveiled the lunch that we had required him to harvest and prepare. He reluctantly disclosed that on most days he would sneak off to the restroom to eat his sandwich of homegrown tomatoes, basil, and cucumber, embarrassed to be so different.

Schools and farms have become a lot alike. They have both become factories, with assembly-line controls and engineered inputs, cranking out either grades and test scores or "food."

The industrialization of our food system and the industrialization of our education system treat us all as if we are just consumers, passively waiting to be fed disconnected information or prepackaged food. But we cannot insure the well-being of our children or the future this way. Raising whole young people is like raising good food. It is a sacred practice; it requires waking each day and seeing things anew, responding to the moment, listening, paying attention, observing.

Every time I plant a seed and see it emerge, it slows me down and allows me to experience one of the great mysteries of life, and each time I cannot help but be renewed. I can have this experience; I can plant and nurture and harvest and enjoy the bounty of the land right outside my back door.

But even as I am having this blessed experience, I often feel sadness. I am aware that most of our society no longer has this opportunity, no longer knows what it's like to pull a carrot from the ground, or eat the heart out of a water-melon still warm from the sun, or munch on beans that are so fresh that they explode in your mouth.

Being connected with the land provides another kind of nourishment less tangible than the carrots and the beans and the melons, a deeper soulful nour-ishment that I think our society desperately longs for. It cannot be had from food that travels an average of thirteen hundred miles from the field to the plate; it can't be absorbed from a package or from the shelves of the supermarket or from anonymous ingredients floating out of context. It cannot be enhanced or manufactured or engineered. Even the most complex preparations, the most sublime sauces, cannot bring back life to what is left after the essence has been processed away.

The kind of nourishment I am describing is based on relationships—local, biological, interpersonal, ecological. It is the result of understanding connec-tions, knowing the people who grew the food, knowing that their families were paid a living wage, knowing that the land has been well cared for and pro-tected from development, knowing that the food has not been assaulted with an array of chemistry and that its genetic makeup hasn't been messed with.

It seems to me that real education should be based on some of those same relationships, that what we have really lost in both our food system and our education system is context, a sense of how things relate to each other. Our children need to be fed knowledge and food in more than fragmented parts and pieces. They need to understand whole processes and the interconnec-tion of all things.

When the food system or the education system no longer fulfills the needs of people, then people take that responsibility into their own hands. The same community-driven changes we are seeing in the food system with the explo-sion of farmers' markets, community food programs, urban gardens, and small-scale regional farms is going on in education as well.

It's taking place in school gardens, in rebuilt cafeterias, and in a whole movement that is rethinking education from the roots up. This revolution is not originating in the halls of Congress or in school board meetings; it's happening in neighborhoods and towns, and it's being driven by everyday folks: parents, teachers, and thoughtful principals who see a need and respond to it.

Years ago, while thinking about this idea of gardens and fresh food in the context of a better way of educating, I realized I needed a young person's perspective, so I went straight to the source—my son Aaron. I thought I knew what he'd say—we'd taught him about the importance of good food (his first word was "peach," before "mom" or "dad"). He's the one who has always known, out of thousands of plants in a field, exactly where to find the first ripe strawberry or out in the orchards which part of the tree has the sweetest plums. But when I talked to him I found out he'd been paying more attention than I really knew and that somehow the concept of process—that food doesn't magically appear on the store shelf—helped him to understand other things as well.

Aaron really wanted me to talk about the bigger picture—he had heard about kids like Felipe Franco, who was born without arms and legs because his pregnant mother was working in the fields being sprayed with Captan. He remembered the children in Guatemala we had visited, seven and eight years old, carrying backpack sprayers that weighed more than they did, wearing no masks or protective clothing, spraying crops that would end up on Northern tables. I remember his puzzlement that with all the technology, cleverness, and scientific and technological prowess we have mustered to create a food system supposedly designed to feed and nourish people, twenty-five thousand children around the world still die each day as a result of malnutrition and related illnesses. My son understands, as he should, that we live in a world that is nutritionally divided: some of us are overfed and others are underfed.

Let's face it: Kids are worried—they worry about crime, global warming, hunger, war, a whole unsafe world that they feel is growing and consuming their future. Food is one of those areas where they can feel empowered to do something for themselves and for their families. Aaron told me that part of what knowing how to grow good food means to him is that some of the worries are set aside. It's something he can control.

The process of growing food is settling. It provides a clear and immediate sense of how one's actions affect the world. Gardens provide great metaphors for life, the circle of birth and death made palpable because it is seen firsthand, year after year. Working with the soil offers a sense of accomplishment and personal power. Talk and explanations become unnecessary as kids instinctively understand what they are learning when they grow things. I am always amazed at the response from young people when we offer a handful of living soil to examine and smell. Some are afraid to accept it, others squirm or hesitate, but when they learn that a single teaspoon can contain millions of different forms of life, when they realize that there is a whole world beneath their feet, they begin to see how much their lives depend on it and know viscerally that they shouldn't treat soil like dirt.

For many young folks, especially those living in the urban world, gardens may be their only connection to the natural world. Those gardens are not just places to plant a few vegetables or flowers; they are not just a little break from the endless, mindless stretch of pavement; they become gathering places, sanctuaries, cultural and social centers, and they are as important to the health of our civic life as are art museums, symphony halls, theaters, and great restaurants. They are part of a city's soul.

We all need to ask ourselves about the soul of those places where we send our children each day to be educated. What does education mean, who and what are the teachers, and can we rely solely on a few individuals housed in a cluster of buildings to adequately educate these young people, who are our future?

What do our kids really need anyway? I agree that they should probably learn to read and to write and know how to add and subtract. But do they all need to do it in the same way and at the same time? Some may be like my boy, who didn't read till the end of the third grade and wouldn't read a book until high school. Now I can't drag him out of his books; he loves literature, and by the time he was eighteen he was writing and performing his own plays and poetry. But he was given the space to develop naturally, not by some factory blueprint mass formula.

We can push our kids, and grade them, and judge them, and try to fit them into boxes, just as we design tomatoes more so that they will fit shipping boxes than for taste or nutrition. But real learning and education will only come, I believe, when they are allowed to develop at their own speed, given good nourishment, and provided with a sense of belonging and place and some connection to the natural world.

Imagine what kind of world we could create if every junior high school student in America learned about soil, about health and nutrition, about the physical environment in which they live. Shouldn't they learn to grow their own food, make their own clothing, build a structure, and cook, and shouldn't their education include community service?

These skills are not just about developing physical self-sufficiency. They provide young people with a sense of being rooted in the real world, not just hooked up to a computer screen. Most of all, their minds and imaginations and creative spirit will stay alive when we, each of us, whether or not we teach and whether or not we have kids, treat them with respect and give them love. Maybe we could start using the word "love" more in talking about education—and about growing food.

Now I have a second son. Every evening we wrap him in his favorite wool blanket and ever so slowly walk the length of the farm saying good night to the chickens, touching the leaves on the asparagus, rubbing our faces on various herbs and flowers, and quietly sneaking up on the thousands of frogs that inhabit our pond.

It's the same route each evening, but every walk reveals something new. Most nights just as we reach the farm-gate and turn to walk back home young Benjamin's eyes have started to close as he is lulled and calmed by the life on the farm, which is also drifting into sleep.

These walks include no talk, no explanations; there is no reading or study required to understand and learn from our experience. But I am sure that young Benjamin is absorbing it all, even when his eyes are closed and he is asleep.

It has never been my goal to raise my children to be farmers, although I would welcome that. Nor has it been to turn into farmers all of those thousands of people who come to us to have a different educational experience.

But just as I immerse my young son in the natural cycles of the farm, as I give him responsibilities to care for some of the animal and plant life that exists on it, and feed and nourish him from it, our society must find ways to offer similar experiences to all our families and to the communities in which we live.

As we bear witness to the disappearance of nature, and the disconnection of our society from it, we also see an increase in confusion, an extreme lack of compassion and understanding of how to care for each other and for our world, a loss of understanding with regard to cause and effect.

We have to deal with the world of worry in which so many of our young people live and the constant struggle between hope and despair, by focusing on the small successes: on local and incremental change; one handful of seeds, one child, one garden at a time.

Meditations on an Apple

Janet Brown

The apple we admire (or, for that matter, the apple we barely notice while mindlessly gulping down a snack on the run) reaches us through the efforts of myriad interconnected people, often unknown to each other, linked through millennia around the globe. Its growth depends on networks of pollinators and microscopic organisms, of orchardists and farmworkers, and on water and nutrient cycles and exchanges of captured sunlight. In Brown's beautifully wrought words, the story of a single apple becomes a whole curriculum in ecological literacy—and a reminder that taking the time to look closely at any part of the living world will almost always invoke wonder and gratitude.

Brown is the Center for Ecoliteracy's program officer for food systems. She is an organic farmer, known regionally for her 50 varieties of heirloom tomatoes and 250 varieties of heirloom roses and her peppers, sunflowers, and melons. A community food security activist, she is founder and president of the Marin Food Policy Council and vice president of Marin Organic.

Brown has connected the Center to a national network of food activists and brought the treasures of her eloquence, passion, commitment, and an astonishing knowledge of farming and land to her work at CEL, while helping to shape the Food Systems Project, direct Rethinking School Lunch, and guide Thinking outside the Lunchbox (see "Sustainability—A New Item on the Lunch Menu" in Part IV).

These meditations were first presented at a 2001 Bioneers Conference workshop on the Center for Ecoliteracy's food systems work. Workshop participants received freshly polished Red Rome Beauty apples, which they were invited to contemplate as Brown read the meditations. Brown wishes to thank Wendy Johnson, dharma teacher at Green Gulch Zen Center, Muir Beach, California.

HERE IN NORTHERN CALIFORNIA, in the early fall, while the leaves are still on the trees and no frost has yet touched the field, the apple harvesters are bringing in a treasure.

Hold this Red Rome Beauty apple in your hand.
Feel how its weight and coolness rest in your palm.

In a place in the world known as Ladakh, before each meal, members of the community take a moment to close their eyes. In the quiet moment, they give thanks for the meal by picturing the face of each person who contributed to bringing the meal to the table and remembering them.

In the same way, cradle the apple in your hand and close your eyes.

As you hold the apple, remember that the ancestor of all apple trees arose in southwestern Asia, in Turkmenistan, Uzbekistan, Tajikistan, Afghanistan, and all across the Caucasus mountains. Protected and nourished by observant stewards for thousands of years through their system of agriculture, their culture of the land, the apple contains their vision. In this moment, remember their contribution and offer your gratitude to these ancestors for their foresight, diligence, and skillful means.

Without them, you would not be holding this treasure in your hands.

The original apple, now called the Siberian crabapple, has traveled far and wide. Remains of apple trees have been unearthed near lake dwellings in Switzerland, evidence of the western migration of the apple thousands of years ago. The apple was carried, as all food crops have been carried into the world, by helping agents: blown by the wind, caught in the coat of the fox, dropped by the quail and the crow, wrapped safe in the pocket of an adventurer, sewn into the hems of garments by refugees running to safe ground. The apple contains their journeys. In this moment, remember their contribution and offer your gratitude to these many agents of dispersal who carry seed to the four directions.

Without them, you would not be holding this treasure in your hands.

In our garden at the Center for Ecoliteracy, we tend a small patch of Yugoslavian heirloom beans, a handful of which was brought out of Kosovo to England by refugees. The handful was divided two ways: one portion was left in England, and one portion was carried to America by a traveler. Once here, the half handful was again divided three ways, and twenty-seven beans came to be planted in our little garden. By the time the beans were sprouting, American troops were fighting in the place where the beans had grown for centuries. We plant them every year, save the seed, and give it away. "As many hands as possible" is the wisest practice for seed savers. We know that somehow the beans will be returned to their home ground when it is safe.

The apple is the oldest of the rose-family fruits, sharing a direct lineage with the pear, the quince, and many other Rosacea ancestors, among them the wild fruits of the woodlands and mountains, the alpine strawberry, and the thorny gooseberry. All apples have a true core. If sliced at the middle latitude, the cut reveals a five-pointed star at the heart of the fruit. In each protected oval chamber of the star rests a sable-colored seed. Apple trees of the past and the future are contained within the apple seed.

The parent of the Red Rome Beauty was known simply as "Rome." Settlers of the Ohio River Valley planted this hearty tree in the 1820s along the northern bank of the Ohio. During the spring, one tree happened to send up a shoot from below the graft—from a part of the tree that is not supposed to bear fruit. Orchardists lop these unwanted shoots off as routinely as they walk the rows. But by a fortunate oversight, this branch survived to bear splendidly colored, delicious fruit.

Neighbors recognized it for its beauty and flavor and began to take scions of the branch for propagation on their farms and fields. Over time, the apple became a regionally famous variety named for Rome Township, Ohio. In the great flood of 1884, the waters of the Ohio rose up and washed the parent tree downriver. But by then, the Rome Beauty was well established. It continued to be cultivated because of its size, handsome looks, and sweet flavor. Generations of skilled orchardists improved the apple's color, size, and luster. It became known as the Red Rome. The apple contains the diligence of these homesteaders. In this moment, remember the settlers of the Ohio Valley and the orchardist who allowed an errant branch to flourish. Remember too the careful and patient endeavors of seed savers, orchard tenders, and livestock breeders who work from a vision they know will not be realized in their lifetime.

Without them, you would not be holding this treasure in your hands.

Now, in the gathering fall, in the season known as "locking," the apple tree loosens her leaves. All summer long these leaves have been breathing, making sweetness from sunlight, breathing to form the apple in your hand. It takes the work of forty apple leaves to breathe an apple into life. As they breathe, the apple leaves exhale the moisture drawn up by their roots from deep beneath the soil horizon. A single apple tree, in full growth, returns fifteen tons of transpired water to the atmosphere in one growing season. The apple contains the breath of the apple tree. In this moment, remember to breathe deeply, inhaling and exhaling with the apple tree, air made sweet with apple making. Thank the apple tree that, through the process of life itself, renews the planet and fills our lives with sweetness.

Without these labors, you would not be holding this treasure in your hands.

Everywhere, apple leaves are releasing their hold, drifting back to earth to be broken down into richness by the winter rains and the living beings of the soil. In this world beneath our feet, filled with mystery and action, many creatures yet unnamed and uncounted contribute to our sustenance. We are all dependent on the living soil for our needs. In each crumb of living soil, billions of organisms are growing, reproducing, and dying. The apple contains their lives. In this moment remember the natural cycles of growth and decay and the unseen creators of the skin of the earth: the soil community of bacteria, protozoa, and nematodes; the molds, yeasts, and fungi; the mites, springtails, and earthworms; the spiders, beetles, and moles.

Without them, you would not be holding this treasure in your hands.

Lift the apple and breathe in its perfume. Rest the smooth burnished red skin of the fruit on your skin. Imagine the work of the bees, visiting the apple blossoms in spring, reaching into the apple flower to pollinate the fruit you hold. In her lifetime a honeybee produces a teaspoon of honey, each drop carefully stored in the waxy comb. The apple contains the artful bee. In this moment, remember her work in the sweetness of the fruit. Remember too the work of all pollinators: the butterflies, moths, and bats who, in their search for ethereal sweetness, feed us.

Without them, you would not be holding this treasure in your hands.

These apples were harvested from twenty-two acres of Red Rome Beauty and Gravenstein apple trees at Flatlands Flower Farm in Sebastopol, California. Situated seven miles from the ocean, the farm feels the marine influence in its air and soil. Step out onto the front porch of the farmhouse, looking north, and see Mt. St. Helena rising in the distance. Look west to the towering redwoods and ocean-tinted sky. Dan and Joanne moved to the orchard four years ago and set about transitioning it to organic in their first year. "We're bringing these trees back," says Dan, "through composting and cover cropping. We'll never go to grapes."

Sara, the orchard manager, tall, with long braided hair, picks and packs the nicest apples each week for the farmers' market and drives the heavy wooden boxes into town. She carefully sets up and tends the little farm stand, tipping the wooden boxes of red and green apples toward the hands of the people walking through the colorful, harvest-lined corridor of shade and sun.

Sara and all farmers, farmworkers, assistants, and interns, together with the interested customers and shoppers, are the market. According to ancient agreements between city folk and country folk, they make the market appear for moments in time and make it go away. During these moments, the fertility of the earth is exchanged. The apple contains these understandings in exchanges of captured sunlight. In this moment, remember the family farmer who recognizes the value of mature fruit trees and the need to protect and nurture them. Remember also the farmworker who carries the harvest in her arms and the young people who are drawn to farms, to labor and learn.

Without them, you would not be holding this treasure in your hands.

The apples were brought home from the market. Each one was hand polished, burnishing the natural wax to a fine gloss. Now the apple rests in your hands. Raise the apple to your lips and taste it. As you do, savor the millions of agreements and simple actions, held in a web of relationships, arrayed across time and space, connecting you to each other and to the land. The apple contains all these. They are its sweetness and beauty. In this moment, remember all that is given to you in the form of this apple and enjoy the fruit of these labors and intentions.

Without all this, you would not be holding this treasure in your hands.

Part IV

Action

Dancing with Systems

Donella Meadows

Donella (Dana) Meadows, who died in 2001, was one of the great minds and great hearts to grace the field of systems thinking and the movement for sustainability, which she anticipated and helped to inspire in 1972 when she coauthored The Limits to Growth. *A Harvard Ph.D. in biophysics, she was a professor at Dartmouth, a systems analyst, an organic farmer, an author, and a journalist. She helped found the Sustainability Institute and the Balaton Group on Sustainability.*

As "Dancing with Systems" shows, Meadows combined analytic depth and rigor with humility and an ability to explain complex matters in simple, straightforward prose. She practiced the qualities that she says here are required in order to live successfully in a world of systems: "our full humanity—our rationality, our ability to sort out truth from falsehood, our intuition, our compassion, our vision, and our morality."

This essay is derived from Meadows's draft for a chapter of a book on systems thinking that she was working on at the time of her death. (Her colleagues at the Sustainability Institute hope to edit and publish as much as possible of the unfinished project.) Even in its incomplete form, "Dancing with Systems" reveals the elegance of its author's thinking. It was first published in this form in Whole Earth *magazine, winter 2001.*

THE DANCE

1. Get the beat.
2. Listen to the wisdom of the system.
3. Expose your mental models to the open air.

4. Stay humble. Stay a learner.

5. Honor and protect information.

6. Locate responsibility in the system.

7. Make feedback policies for feedback systems.

8. Pay attention to what is important, not just what is quantifiable.

9. Go for the good of the whole.

10. Expand time horizons.

11. Expand thought horizons.

12. Expand the boundary of caring.

13. Celebrate complexity.

14. Hold fast to the goal of goodness.

People who are raised in the industrial world and who get enthused about systems thinking are likely to make a terrible mistake. They are likely to assume that here, in systems analysis, in interconnection and complication, in the power of the computer, here at last, is the key to prediction and control. This mistake is likely because the mindset of the industrial world assumes that there is a key to prediction and control.

I assumed that at first too. We all assumed it, as eager systems students at the great institution called MIT. More or less innocently, enchanted by what we could see through our new lens, we did what many discoverers do. We exaggerated our own ability to change the world. We did so not with any intent to deceive others, but in the expression of our own expectations and hopes. Systems thinking for us was more than subtle, complicated mindplay. It was going to Make Systems Work.

But self-organizing, nonlinear feedback systems are inherently unpredictable. They are not controllable. They are understandable only in the most general way. The goal of foreseeing the future exactly and preparing for it perfectly is unrealizable. The idea of making a complex system do just what you want it to do can be achieved only temporarily, at best. We can never fully understand our world, not in the way our reductionistic science has led us to expect. Our science itself, from quantum theory to the mathematics of chaos, leads us into irreducible uncertainty. For any objective other than the most trivial, we can't optimize; we don't even know what to optimize. We can't keep track of everything. We can't find a proper, sustainable relationship to nature, each other, or the institutions we create, if we try to do it from the role of omniscient conqueror.

For those who stake their identity on the role of omniscient conqueror, the uncertainty exposed by systems thinking is hard to take. If you can't understand, predict, and control, what is there to do?

Systems thinking leads to another conclusion, however—waiting, shining, obvious as soon as we stop being blinded by the illusion of control. It says that there is plenty to do, of a different sort of "doing." The future can't be predicted, but it can be envisioned and brought lovingly into being. Systems can't be controlled, but they can be designed and redesigned. We can't surge forward with certainty into a world of no surprises, but we can expect surprises and learn from them and even profit from them. We can't impose our will upon a system. We can listen to what the system tells us and discover how its properties and our values can work together to bring forth something much better than could ever be produced by our will alone.

We can't control systems or figure them out. But we can dance with them!

I already knew that, in a way, before I began to study systems. I had learned about dancing with great powers from whitewater kayaking, from gardening, from playing music, from skiing. All those endeavors require one to stay wide awake, pay close attention, participate flat out, and respond to feedback. It had never occurred to me that those same requirements might apply to intellectual work, to management, to government, to getting along with people.

But there it was, the message emerging from every computer model we made. Living successfully in a world of systems requires more of us than our ability to calculate. It requires our full humanity—our rationality, our ability to sort out truth from falsehood, our intuition, our compassion, our vision, and our morality.

I will summarize the most general "systems wisdom" I have absorbed from modeling complex systems and from hanging out with modelers. These are the take-home lessons, the concepts and practices that penetrate the discipline of systems so deeply that one begins, however imperfectly, to practice them not just in one's profession, but in all of life.

The list probably isn't complete, because I am still a student in the school of systems. And it isn't unique to systems thinking. There are many ways to learn to dance. But here, as a start-off dancing lesson, are the practices I see my colleagues adopting, consciously or unconsciously, as they encounter systems.

1. Get the beat.

Before you disturb the system in any way, watch how it behaves. If it's a piece of music or a whitewater rapid or a fluctuation in a commodity price, study its beat. If it's a social system, watch it work. Learn its history. Ask people who've been around a long time to tell you what has happened. If possible, find or make a time graph of actual data from the system. People's memories are not always reliable when it comes to timing.

Starting with the behavior of the system forces you to focus on facts, not theories. It keeps you from falling too quickly into your own beliefs or misconceptions, or those of others. It's amazing how many misconceptions there can be. People will swear that rainfall is decreasing, say, but when you look at the data, you find that what is really happening is that variability is increasing—the droughts are deeper, but the floods are greater too. I have been told with great authority that milk price was going up when it was going down, that real interest rates were falling when they were rising, that the deficit was a higher fraction of the GNP than ever before when it wasn't.

Starting with the behavior of the system directs one's thoughts to dynamic, not static, analysis—not only to "what's wrong?" but also to "how did we get there?" and "what behavior modes are possible?" and "if we don't change direction, where are we going to end up?"

And finally, starting with history discourages the common and distracting tendency we all have to define a problem not by the system's actual behavior, but by the lack of our favorite solution. (The problem is, we need to find more oil. The problem is, we need to ban abortion. The problem is, how can we attract more growth to this town?)

2. Listen to the wisdom of the system.

Aid and encourage the forces and structures that help the system run itself. Don't be an unthinking intervener and destroy the system's own self-maintenance capacities. Before you charge in to make things better, pay attention to the value of what's already there.

A friend of mine, Nathan Gray, was once an aid worker in Guatemala. He told me of his frustration with agencies that would arrive with the intention of "creating jobs" and "increasing entrepreneurial abilities" and "attracting outside investors." They would walk right past the thriving local market, where small-scale businesspeople of all kinds, from basket makers to vegetable growers to butchers to candy-sellers, were displaying their entrepreneurial abilities in jobs they had created for themselves. Nathan spent his time talking to the people in the market, asking about their lives and businesses, learning what was in the way of those businesses expanding and incomes rising. He concluded that what was needed was not outside investors, but inside ones. Small loans available at reasonable interest rates, and classes in literacy and accounting, would produce much more long-term good for the community than bringing in a factory or assembly plant from outside.

3. Expose your mental models to the open air.

Remember, always, that everything you know, and everything everyone knows, is only a model. Get your model out there where it can be shot at. Invite others to challenge your assumptions and add their own. Instead of becoming a champion for one possible explanation or hypothesis or model, collect as many as possible. Consider all of them plausible until you find some evidence that causes you to rule one out. That way you will be emotionally able to see the evidence that rules out an assumption with which you might have confused your own identity.

You don't have to put forth your mental model with diagrams and equations, though that's a good discipline. You can do it with words or lists or pictures or arrows showing what you think is connected to what. The more you do that, in any form, the clearer your thinking will become, the faster you will admit your uncertainties and correct your mistakes, and the more flexible you will learn to be. Mental flexibility—the willingness to redraw boundaries, to notice that a system has shifted into a new mode, to see how to redesign structure—is a necessity when you live in a world of flexible systems.

4. Stay humble. Stay a learner.

Systems thinking has taught me to trust my intuition more and my figuring-out rationality less, to lean on both as much as I can, but still to be prepared for surprises. Working with systems, on the computer, in nature, among people, in organizations, constantly reminds me of how incomplete my mental models are, how complex the world is, and how much I don't know.

The thing to do, when you don't know, is not to bluff and not to freeze, but to learn. The way you learn is by experiment—or, as Buckminster Fuller put it, by trial and error, error, error. In a world of complex systems it is not appropriate to charge forward with rigid, undeviating directives. "Stay the course" is only a good idea if you're sure you're on course. Pretending you're in control even when you aren't is a recipe not only for mistakes, but for not learning from mistakes. What's appropriate when you're learning is small steps, constant monitoring, and a willingness to change course as you find out more about where it's leading.

That's hard. It means making mistakes and, worse, admitting them. It means what psychologist Don Michael calls "error-embracing." It takes a lot of courage to embrace your errors.

5. Honor and protect information.

A decision maker can't respond to information he or she doesn't have, can't respond accurately to information that is inaccurate, can't respond in a timely way to information that is late. I would guess that 99 percent of what goes wrong in systems goes wrong because of faulty or missing information.

If I could, I would add an Eleventh Commandment: Thou shalt not distort, delay, or sequester information. You can drive a system crazy by muddying its information streams. You can make a system work better with surprising ease if you can give it more timely, more accurate, more complete information.

For example, in 1986 new federal legislation required U.S. companies to report all chemical emissions from each of their plants. Through the Freedom of Information Act (from a systems point of view one of the most important laws in the nation), that information became a matter of public record. In July 1988 the first data on chemical emissions became available. The reported emissions were not illegal, but they didn't look very good when they were published in local papers by enterprising reporters, who had a tendency to make lists of "the top ten local polluters." That's all that happened. There were no lawsuits, no required reductions, no fines, no penalties. But within two years chemical emissions nationwide (at least as reported, and presumably also in fact) had decreased by 40 percent. Some companies were launching policies to bring their emissions down by 90 percent, just because of the release of previously sequestered information.

6. Locate responsibility in the system.

Look for the ways the system creates its own behavior. Do pay attention to the triggering events, the outside influences that bring forth one kind of behavior from the system rather than another. Sometimes those outside events can be controlled (as in reducing the pathogens in drinking water to keep down incidences of infectious disease). But sometimes they can't. And sometimes blaming or trying to control the outside influence blinds one to the easier task of increasing responsibility within the system.

"Intrinsic responsibility" means that the system is designed to send feedback about the consequences of decision-making directly and quickly and compellingly to the decision-makers.

Dartmouth College reduced intrinsic responsibility when it took thermostats out of individual offices and classrooms and put temperature-control decisions under the guidance of a central computer. That was done as an energy-saving measure. My observation from a low level in the hierarchy is that the main consequence was greater oscillations in room temperature. When my office gets overheated now, instead of turning down the thermostat, I have to call an office across campus, which gets around to making corrections over a period of hours or days, and which often overcorrects, setting up the need for another phone call. One way of making that system more, rather than less, responsible might have been to let professors keep control of their own thermostats and charge them directly for the amount of energy they use. (Thereby privatizing a commons!)

Designing a system for intrinsic responsibility could mean, for example, requiring all towns or companies that emit wastewater into a stream to place their intake pipe *downstream* from their outflow pipe. It could mean that neither insurance companies nor public funds should pay for medical costs resulting from smoking or from accidents in which a motorcycle rider didn't wear a helmet or a car rider didn't fasten the seat belt. It could mean Congress would no longer be allowed to legislate rules from which it exempts itself.

7. Make feedback policies for feedback systems.

President Jimmy Carter had an unusual ability to think in feedback terms and to make feedback policies. Unfortunately he had a hard time explaining them to a press and public that didn't understand feedback.

He suggested, at a time when oil imports were soaring, that there be a tax on gasoline proportional to the fraction of U.S. oil consumption that had to be imported. If imports continued to rise, the tax would rise, until it suppressed demand and brought forth substitutes and reduced imports. If imports fell to zero, the tax would fall to zero.

The tax never got passed.

Carter was also trying to deal with a flood of illegal immigrants from Mexico. He suggested that nothing could be done about that immigration as long as there was a great gap in opportunity and living standards between the U.S. and Mexico. Rather than spending money on border guards and barriers, he said, we should spend money helping to build the Mexican economy, and we should continue to do so until the immigration stopped.

That never happened either.

You can imagine why a dynamic, self-adjusting system cannot be governed by a static, unbending policy. It's easier, more effective, and usually much cheaper to design policies that change depending on the state of the system. Especially where there are great uncertainties, the best policies not only contain feedback loops, but meta-feedback loops—loops that alter, correct, and expand loops. These are policies that design learning into the management process.

8. Pay attention to what is important, not just what is quantifiable.

Our culture, obsessed with numbers, has given us the idea that what we can measure is more important than what we can't measure. You can look around and make up your own mind about whether quantity or quality is the outstanding characteristic of the world in which you live.

If something is ugly, say so. If it is tacky, inappropriate, out of proportion, unsustainable, morally degrading, ecologically impoverishing, or humanly demeaning, don't let it pass. Don't be stopped by the "if you can't define it and measure it, I don't have to pay attention to it" ploy. No one can precisely define or measure justice, democracy, security, freedom, truth, or love. No one can precisely define or measure any value. But if no one speaks up for them, if systems aren't designed to produce them, if we don't speak about them and point toward their presence or absence, they will cease to exist.

9. Go for the good of the whole.

Don't maximize parts of systems or subsystems while ignoring the whole. As Kenneth Boulding once said, don't go to great trouble to optimize something that never should be done at all. Aim to enhance total systems properties, such as creativity, stability, diversity, resilience, and sustainability—whether they are easily measured or not.

As you think about a system, spend part of your time from a vantage point that lets you see the whole system, not just the problem that may have drawn you to focus on the system to begin with. And realize that, especially in the short term, changes for the good of the whole may sometimes seem to be counter to the interests of a part of the system. It helps to remember that the parts of a system cannot survive without the whole. The long-term interests of your liver require the long-term health of your body, and the long-term interests of sawmills require the long-term health of forests.

10. Expand time horizons.

The official time horizon of industrial society doesn't extend beyond what will happen after the next election or beyond the payback period of current investments. The time horizon of most families still extends farther than that—through the lifetimes of children or grandchildren. Many Native American cultures actively spoke of and considered in their decisions the effects upon the seventh generation to come. The longer the operant time horizon, the better the chances for survival.

In the strict systems sense there is no long-term/short-term distinction. Phenomena at different time scales are nested within each other. Actions taken now have some immediate effects and some that radiate out for decades to come. We experience now the consequences of actions set in motion yesterday and decades ago and centuries ago.

When you're walking along a tricky, curving, unknown, surprising, obstacle-strewn path, you'd be a fool to keep your head down and look just at the next step in front of you. You'd be equally a fool just to peer far ahead and never notice what's immediately under your feet. You need to be watching both the short and the long term—the whole system.

11. Expand thought horizons.

Defy the disciplines. In spite of what you majored in, or what the textbooks say, or what you think you're an expert at, follow a system wherever it leads.

It will be sure to lead across traditional disciplinary lines. To understand that system, you will have to be able to learn from—while not being limited by—economists and chemists and psychologists and theologians. You will have to penetrate their jargons, integrate what they tell you, recognize what they can honestly see through their particular lenses, and discard the distortions that come from the narrowness and incompleteness of their lenses. They won't make it easy for you.

Seeing systems whole requires more than being "interdisciplinary," if that word means, as it usually does, putting together people from different disciplines and letting them talk past each other. Interdisciplinary communication works only if there is a real problem to be solved and if the representatives from the various disciplines are more committed to solving the problem than to being academically correct. They will have to go into learning mode, to admit ignorance and be willing to be taught, by each other and by the system.

It can be done. It's very exciting when it happens.

12. Expand the boundary of caring.

Living successfully in a world of complex systems means expanding not only time horizons and thought horizons; above all it means expanding the horizons of caring. There are moral reasons for doing that, of course. And if moral arguments are not sufficient, then systems thinking provides the practical reasons to back up the moral ones. The real system is interconnected. No part of the human race is separate either from other human beings or from the global ecosystem. It will not be possible in this integrated world for your heart to succeed if your lungs fail, or for your company to succeed if your workers fail, or for the rich in Los Angeles to succeed if the poor in Los Angeles fail, or for Europe to succeed if Africa fails, or for the global economy to succeed if the global environment fails.

As with everything else about systems, most people already know about the interconnections that make moral and practical rules turn out to be the same rules. They just have to bring themselves to believe that which they know.

13. Celebrate complexity.

Let's face it, the universe is messy. It is nonlinear, turbulent, and chaotic. It is dynamic. It spends its time in transient behavior on its way to somewhere else, not in mathematically neat equilibria. It self-organizes and evolves. It creates diversity, not uniformity. That's what makes the world interesting, that's what makes it beautiful, and that's what makes it work.

There's something within the human mind that is attracted to straight lines and not curves, to whole numbers and not fractions, to uniformity and not diversity, and to certainties and not mystery. But there is something else within us that has the opposite set of tendencies, since we ourselves evolved out of and are shaped by and structured as complex feedback systems. Only a part of us, a part that has emerged recently, designs buildings as boxes with uncompromising straight lines and flat surfaces. Another part of us recognizes instinctively that nature designs in fractals, with intriguing detail on every scale from the microscopic to the macroscopic. That part of us makes Gothic cathedrals and Persian carpets, symphonies and novels, Mardi Gras costumes and artificial intelligence programs, all with embellishments almost as complex as the ones we find in the world around us.

14. Hold fast to the goal of goodness.

Examples of bad human behavior are held up, magnified by the media, affirmed by the culture, as typical. Just what you would expect. After all, we're only human. The far more numerous examples of human goodness are barely noticed. They are Not News. They are exceptions. Must have been a saint. Can't expect everyone to behave like that.

And so expectations are lowered. The gap between desired behavior and actual behavior narrows. Fewer actions are taken to affirm and instill ideals. The public discourse is full of cynicism. Public leaders are visibly, unrepentantly amoral or immoral and are not held to account. Idealism is ridiculed. Statements of moral belief are suspect. It is much easier to talk about hate in public than to talk about love.

We know what to do about eroding goals. Don't weigh the bad news more heavily than the good. And keep standards absolute.

This is quite a list. Systems thinking can only tell us to do these things. It can't do them for us.

And so we are brought to the gap between understanding and implementation. Systems thinking by itself cannot bridge that gap. But it can lead us to the edge of what analysis can do and then point beyond—to what can and must be done by the human spirit.

The Loupe's Secret:
Looking Closely, Changing Scale

Kerry Ruef

This selection from The Private Eye®—(5x) Looking/Thinking by Analogy: A Guide to Developing the Interdisciplinary Mind, Hands-on Thinking Skills, Creativity, Scientific Literacy, *by Kerry Ruef (2003), is included in the* River of Words Watershed Explorer™ Curriculum, *as one of the resources that* River of Words *(see "Helping Children Fall in Love with the Earth" in Part II) has found to be the best for helping students experience and connect deeply with the natural world in their home place.*

The Private Eye Project calls The Private Eye *a "K–16 through life" program. It's designed to build the habits of mind of looking closely, thinking by analogy, changing scale, and theorizing, which are all habits of scientists, writers, and artists— three primary ways of encountering the world that* River of Words *seeks to connect. Farmer, teacher, writer, and photographer Michael Ableman ("Raising Whole Children Is Like Raising Good Food" in Part III) argues that observation is one of the most important agricultural skills, and* The Private Eye *works in a way that Ableman finds essential—by making the observer slow down, look at objects one at a time, and then go back and look again and again. It reinforces observation by asking users to draw objects and to think in terms of analogies, which lead in one direction to hypotheses and theories and in another to poetry and art.*

The program uses a jeweler's loupe, natural objects, and increasingly sophisticated sets of questions and exercises to encourage creativity, higher-order thinking, and scientific literacy. It draws on ecological principles that recur throughout this book, such as recognizing patterns and tracking continuity and change at different levels of scale, and it facilitates the sense of wonder at nature that is almost a prerequisite to the emotional side of ecological literacy.

Kerry Ruef, the program's designer, is a poet, writer, amateur naturalist, and former classroom teacher. This project emerged from her efforts to identify habits of mind common to painters, poets, scientists, inventors, businesspersons, salespersons, great learners, and great teachers. After pilot testing in the Seattle public schools, the program spread to thousands of teachers and, by the Private Eye Project's count, to more than two million students.

The Private Eye Project (www.the-private-eye.com) also conducts workshops for educators across the country. In addition to The Private Eye *book, the project offers 5X loupes and a variety of individual and classroom kits with loupes and specimens.*

Why a Loupe?

A jeweler's loupe (a magnification tool) intensifies looking, intensifies wonder, intensifies concentration. It heightens hands-on experience of natural and manmade objects. Unlike a hand lens, it cuts out the rest of the world as you're looking (no diluting, peripheral information to distract the eye/mind!).

A loupe gives the ordinary person the heightened visual sensitivity of the artist, the writer, the scientist. Because the loupe isolates its subject as it magnifies, it makes the world slightly strange, increasing drama and wonder. Close observation—mixed with wonder—is essential for the development of artist, scientist, writer, as well as mathematician, humorist, inventor, and more.

How to Use a Loupe

Hold the loupe so that the wide end cups the eye, so it touches the bones around the eye. Cut out all peripheral light! (Close your other eye.) Then hold something two inches away from the lens-end of the loupe, until the object is sharp, focused. First try looking at your own hand. One loupe gives 5X magnification. If you nest two loupes, you will have 10X, so you will need to hold your object only ½" away. Note: If you wear glasses, first try without.

The Loupe Questions

The second tool of The Private Eye is a pair of questions to ask as you're looking through the loupe at an object (your hand, fingerprint, a seahorse, a leaf, a spider's tiny hooked toe, etc.):

What else *does it remind me of? What* else *does it look like?*

("What else does it remind me of?" evokes a larger range of patterns and analogies than just asking "What else does it look like?" So you need to put both questions to your mind simultaneously.)

This is thinking by analogy—the main tool of scientist, writer, visual artist, and mathematician.

Be sure to leave the word "else" in the above questions—you'll get better results! Ask the questions five to ten times for each object or part of an object. You can add on a phrase to specify a category: "What else does it remind me of—in mathematics? In literature? In music? In movement? In feelings?" If you write your answers down they become "bones-for-poems," bones for short stories, memoirs, naturalist essays, and more. Later they will serve as clues to theorize—"Why is it like that?"—as you observe some feature on your object.

Why Analogies?

Scientists would get rid of all their hardware, their fancy billion-dollar labs, before they could afford to get rid of this habit of mind, thinking by analogy, for it's the way that the majority of scientific breakthroughs have always come and will come.

Thinking by analogy is perhaps more obviously the tool of the *writer.* Analogies, listed, become the "bones-for-poems," the beginnings of short stories, naturalist essays, titles for articles, and more. (Metaphors and similes are compressed analogies; allegories and parables are extended analogies.) Thinking by analogy is perhaps more obviously, also, the tool of the *artist*, who works by equivalences. The artist's work, furthermore, has its effect on us by analogy, stirring layered associations.

The Analogy Magnifier

If you loupe-look but don't use the questions above, what happens? You'll go, "wow!" but you'll move on quickly to something else; you'll miss hundreds of details. You'll miss worlds. The analogy-provoking questions keep you looking. They build concentration. They help make sense out of the unfamiliar; they sort new patterns into your own familiar patterns. They make a barnacle, or a spider, or your fingerprint into "a friend." The analogy allows you to see more; it, too, is a magnifier.

On different days you have different associations, so it's wise to return again and again to even the same objects . . . to experience how much there is to see. Your analogies will, in this way, deepen.

Drawing as Close Observation

With The Private Eye you loupe-look, analogy-look, write, draw, and theorize as part of the ongoing, repeating process of becoming the scientist, artist, writer, thinker—all of whom begin with looking closely at the world.

Drawing with The Private Eye is both close observation and aesthetics. The loupe-plus-analogies give the ordinary person the heightened visual sensitivity of the artist, scientist, writer.

The magic of the loupe isn't really magic: it gives such intense visual feedback that even those who think they can't draw—can!

With loupe and the personalizing, magnifying help of analogies, students draw above their previous level. The loupe cuts out competing visual stimulation; its magnifying and isolating effect renders the subject a bit strange and wondrous. Clichés and stereotypes fall away . . . and real looking immediately begins. Even short, fifteen-minute drawing periods with the loupe can be deeply satisfying.

Remember: loupe drawing—to develop the feel and habit of close observation—is for every subject, from math to science, language arts to the social sciences. Did you know that in graduate school in science they say, "Draw! Draw! Draw!" Drawing is itself a form of close observation, a "magnifier." With the loupe's help, drawing becomes a dramatic learning tool.

Changing Scale

With The Private Eye you become more and more intimate with the world. You move from natural, everyday human-eye scale to *experiencing* the world 5X bigger with one loupe, 10X bigger (closer) with two loupes nested, then on to the world 50X bigger in a 50X microscope.

Later you can leap to an interest in 100X and 300X and on to worlds thousands of times bigger and closer or farther. You can become interested in meeting Mr. and Mrs. Protozoa, or Sinope, a tiny moon of Jupiter, if you first spend time becoming more intimate with the world at 5X and 10X.

It is usually difficult to teach the concept of "scale." Here you start with a physical experience and the concept comes easily. Scale is an issue in art, architecture, urban development, math, science, invention, humor, and, by analogy, in writing.

Change of scale (including a change of intensity) is almost always a necessary mental ingredient in invention. The ability to imagine a change of scale—to imagine something bigger or smaller, more or less intense, more or less crowded—is essential to understanding in many areas: demographics, overpopulation, issues of ecology, man's impact on the environment, the impact of toxins building and passing thresholds, and more.

The truism "a difference in degree is a difference in kind" gains meaning for us when we *physically* experience changing scale. Humorists typically work by changing scale. Graphic artists and fine artists work by changing scale. First they have to look closely at the world and have the habit of thinking by analogy, but close on the heels of those habits comes the ability to imagine things at a change of scale. As a habit of seeing—the ability to change scale is part of the ability to change paradigms.

The Second Set of Questions That Go with the Loupe

"Why is it like that . . . I wonder?" or *"What's going on here?"* (Your analogies serve as clues for theorizing.)

"If it reminds me of _____, *I wonder if it might function like that in some* way?"

Making analogies leads to . . . theorizing.

Loupe-look and record your analogies first. Then draw with the loupe. Before moving to theorizing, you may want to write and draw for *many, many days.* You can weave "theorizing" in *as* you work on the writing and drawing steps . . . or emphasize it in separate lessons. [An in-depth discussion of analogy-based theorizing appears in *The Private Eye,* from which this is excerpted. An even longer discussion, originally published in the *California Science Teachers Association Journal* with student examples K–12, can be requested from The Private Eye Project.—*Ed.*] Note: An hypothesis is a first-stage guess about what's true; if the guess holds up under lots of testing and deep scrutiny—which may take decades—but isn't yet fact, we call it a theory. But, for linguistic flow, we include "hypothesizing" with the term "theorizing" for most of this book.

To theorize: After becoming "friends" with your hand, a dragonfly wing, a piece of popcorn, a flower's center, or any of a million objects . . . go on to the second questions that go with the loupe, starting with: "Why is it like that . . . I wonder?" or "What's going on here?"

Your analogies will often help you answer the question. Here's why: 99 *percent of what's found in nature is functional. And, in nature, form is tightly linked to function.* Since your analogies are based on close observation of an object's *form* or *structure,* they often contain clues to the *function* of whatever feature you are observing—to why it is the way it is. In chemistry or physics, your analogy-based observations of a reaction, condition, or force may give clues to similar elements or mechanisms at work.

To theorize, use your analogy list for clues, asking, "If it reminds me of _____, I wonder if it might function like that, or work like that, in some way . . . that helps the plant or critter survive? Or that supports the reaction, condition, or force?" Start with the guesses that interest you most. If you have many analogies to choose from, some will bring you surprisingly close to truth (even if you're only eight or ten years old!), and you'll always be interested in "the answer" to the puzzle. (A vested interest!) Enough to design tests or check experts for current thinking or theory on the subject. You'll *always* get practice *theorizing* as scientists do . . . the first step to scientific literacy.

Tapping the Well
of Urban Youth Activism:
Literacy for Environmental Justice

Dana Lanza

This essay is based on a 2003 Bioneers Conference Ecoliteracy workshop presentation by Literacy for Environmental Justice (LEJ) founder and executive director Dana Lanza and LEJ youth. (Quotes from LEJ youth at the workshop have been interspersed throughout the essay by the editors.) Fritjof Capra introduced the workshop with these words:

> *The way to sustain life is to build and nurture community. If you translate this into the human realm, this means respect for cultural integrity and for the basic rights of communities to self-determination, self-organization, and access to space, resources, energy, and other fundamental needs. You see immediately that all this involves environmental justice, because that's precisely what so many communities around the world today do not have.*
>
> *And so sustainability and environmental justice are really deeply connected. Living sustainably means recognizing that we are an inseparable part of the entire web of life, of nonhuman and human communities, and that enhancing the dignity and sustainability of any one community will enhance all the others.*

Before coming to California in 1997, Dana Lanza lived and worked among the Samburu people of northern Kenya for several years. In addition to leading LEJ, she sits on several boards, including the San Francisco Citizens' Advisory Task-

*force on Power Plants, the Crissy Field Center, and Next Course. She has served
on the faculty of New College of California's Master's in Teaching Program in Critical Global Literacy, and is a fellow with the California Women's Foundation Policy Institute.*

*Her awards include the Bronze Addy Award for public education, the Vineyards
Award from the Association of Fundraising Professionals, the National Clearwa-
ter Award for Waterfront Development, KRON-TV's Golden Apple Award for
Service Learning, and SF Estuary's California Coastal Management Award.*

AS A TWENTY-SEVEN-YEAR-OLD low-income graduate student
in 1997, I moved into housing adjacent to the Hunters Point Shipyard, a federal Superfund site in San Francisco. Like many of my neighbors—whose children often climbed through holes in the fence in order to play in the shipyard—
I was not aware of the potential hazards of my new home. I was given no
disclaimer, and signed no waiver; there were no warning signs posted around
the site.

The Hunters Point Naval Shipyard, built in the late 1930s, covers 550
acres of ground, with another 1,400 acres underwater. (The Navy mostly
constructed submarines there.) During the Navy's tenure, toxic chemicals,
including lead, pesticides, PCBs, and asbestos, were often mishandled or
discarded into the surrounding bay and wetland ecosystems. Over time, they
spread throughout the site, contaminating the adjacent neighborhood. For
thirty years, the shipyard also secretly served as one of the country's largest
nuclear research labs, conducting radiological testing related to the creation of
the A-bomb and other weapons; many of its buildings are contaminated with
hazardous substances. After the Navy closed the shipyard in the 1970s, it
leased the premises to heavy industries that continued to pollute the area, despite Environmental Protection Agency fines. In 1986, the shipyard was added
to the National Priorities List (Superfund), meaning that it is one of the most
chemically poisonous places in the United States.

As an anthropology student I took a natural curiosity in Bayview Hunters
Point, my new community. I volunteered at the local recreation center and
joined nearby community-based environmental organizations. Through them,

I learned more about the environmental health risks near my home and the victorious grassroots struggle just two years earlier against a proposed new power plant in the district, which already had two. At the same time, I supported myself by teaching environmental education in San Francisco public schools.

As I learned more about environmental justice issues and became more sensitized to the concerns of Bayview Hunters Point, I began to see a disconnect between mainstream environmentalism and the environmental justice movement. When I sought an environmental group to speak to neighborhood kids about the Superfund site, or the other 325 toxic sites in our district, I found no one. Environmental justice advocates were focused on policy change or resistance; the mainstream environmental groups were promoting planting trees and getting kids into contact with the natural world. No one was ready or willing to explain to ten-year-olds the dangers on the other side of our fence.

I began volunteering with the summer latchkey program at the local recreation center, exploring the neighborhood with a small group of four- to nine-year-olds, while trying to steer them away from the shipyard and toward parks and safe natural places. One day a week, we picked up trash in front of the recreation center and talked about recycling and composting. I arranged for other environmental educators to lead activities. I developed the most popular children's program at the center. More important, I discovered how much these young people knew about their neighborhood. Their world was an amalgam of vacant lots, backyard shortcuts, routes to candy stores, and so on. The kids did not always understand the toxics issue, but I discovered their wealth of knowledge about their neighborhood, and how much they loved it.

I came to see young people—often the last to be included in community initiatives, but the first to be blamed for neighborhood problems—as an untapped community resource brimming with energy and indigenous knowledge. Touched by the children's curiosity, wit, and sense of place, I began to develop a vision for the program that later became Literacy for Environmental Justice (LEJ). I took photographs of the neighborhood and took a slide show into the schools to tell young people about the problems in our neighborhood. They listened.

The Roots of Environmental
Injustice in Southeast San Francisco

Those neighborhood problems had a long history. During the Gold Rush era, Mission and Islais Creeks and a rich wetland diverse in animal and marine life divided the area now called Hunters Point from the emerging city of San Francisco. As the city became more polluted following the influx of fortune seekers, the Hunter family, who homesteaded the Hunters Point peninsula, realized that they had the last pristine spring in the area and became wealthy by selling bottled water to outgoing ships.

San Francisco grew and spread southward, and the rich wetlands and waterways bounding this bucolic peninsula became a sink for industrial waste. Today, Bayview Hunters Point is one of the Bay Area's most polluted places, with heavy industry, 325 toxic sites, two Superfund sites, and two aging power plants. One of the city's most diverse communities, it is also one of the poorest. Ninety percent of area residents are people of color. More than 50 percent of area households are considered low- or very-low-income. Many of the thirty thousand Bayview residents, a third of whom are children, suffer from high rates of cancer and asthma—a possible consequence of the noxious air.

In Bayview Hunters Point, addressing human and environmental health means confronting environmental justice issues. Definitions of environmental justice abound; at LEJ, we say simply that environmental justice means the right of all people to have their basic needs met: clean water, healthy food, nontoxic communities, open space, safe energy, and equitable educational and job opportunities.

> I love to be in the water, but I have to spend at least an hour on the bus just to get to a beach, even though I live about ten minutes away from the Bay, because there are so many PCBs and other pollutants in the water.
>
> Most of my friends that live in Bayview Hunters Point cannot swim and have never been in a body of water much larger than your average community pool. They can't spend too much time outside the

community, because they have to take care of their families, and they can't go into the water near their homes, because it's too toxic.

—ERICA ANDREWS, LEJ Youth Research Assistant

A systemic look at communities like Bayview Hunters Point reveals the clear interrelationship between health, environmental degradation, racism, and economics. Bayview Hunters Point is home to 5 percent of San Francisco's population—and 30 percent of its hazardous waste sites. In the years before the civil rights movement, realtors' covenants and banks' redlining practices effectively created and maintained racial inequities. Segregation by class and income, and unjust zoning that permitted heavy industry in poor residential neighborhoods (but not in affluent white neighborhoods across town), kept poor people in places most susceptible to pollution.

This process is insidious. For example, the Pacific Gas and Electric power plant in Hunters Point, one of oldest, least efficient, and most polluting in the state, was built in the 1930s. Many people incorrectly think that the power plant was sited there as a kind of affront to the poor neighborhood. Actually, the power plant was already in place when the majority of the area's low-income housing tracts were built, starting in the 1940s; in effect, the largely African American community was relegated to the power plant's environs. The juxtaposition of odious industry and the homes of people of color was not the intention of a single polluting corporation, but required the combined participation of city planners, financiers, developers, and even the federal government through its public housing programs.

Building a Model for Environmental Justice Education

In 1998 I received seed money and office space from a neighborhood organization, the Southeast Alliance for Environmental Justice (SAEJ), and Literacy for Environmental Justice was born, as the first explicitly *environmental justice*—environmental education program in San Francisco's schools and one of the country's few environmental justice groups focused primarily on developing youth leadership. Our mission is to foster the principles of urban sustainability and environmental justice in order to promote the long-term health of the communities of southeast San Francisco.

LEJ's further vision is to engage urban youth of color in local environmental issues that affect their lives. By designing empowering, solution-based educational programs, we introduce them to careers in the environment and civic activism. LEJ has trained nearly two hundred community youth leaders and provided free educational programs to over ten thousand public school students. We annually employ as many as fifty high school—aged Bayview teens as organizers in the areas of food security, wetlands restoration, renewable energy advocacy, and youth-led program assessment. LEJ staff members are representative of the diverse communities that we serve; we value life experience, cultural competency, and academic training equally, as core values of the organization.

An Americorps volunteer working with LEJ told us, "People protect what they love." If we cannot recognize what we care about, and how much we care, we cannot access the well of energy we have to nurture change. Hence LEJ's work is designed to help young people recognize and articulate what they love and to find ways to advocate for and protect those things. Themes emerging over the years include community, land, children, health, and civil rights. Unsurprisingly, these are all necessary components of a sustainable society.

Social and environmental change does not spring from passion alone. Systemic change to long-standing social constructs usually requires proponents who are literate in science, civics, and history, and proficient in writing and speaking (hence our name, "Literacy for Environmental Justice"). They must learn to leverage strong communications skills with compassion, honesty, and conviction. Perhaps most important, they must develop strategic planning skills and the patience to find the way to change one step at a time.

I met Zenobia Barlow at the Center for Ecoliteracy at about the same time that I was developing the vision for LEJ. She offered me a short book by David Sobel, *Beyond Ecophobia*, that helped shape LEJ 's educational model by demonstrating the importance of allowing children—even urban children—to develop a positive relationship with nature before engaging them in the political sphere. This strategy protects young children from feeling overwhelmed and disempowered by complex social and environmental challenges created by adults. For these reasons, LEJ provides nature-based programming for children in kindergarten through sixth grade, while adding environmental health, history, and justice for grades seven and up. These programs utilize a project-based learning model incorporating actions (ideally designed with the participation of teachers and students) that demonstrate that youth have the ability to affect the problems that surround them. Each project follows these steps:

- A project-planning meeting with teachers and students

- In-class lesson(s) to contextualize the issue being addressed

- Field research / investigations

- An action project

- Evaluation / reflection

While presenting my environmental justice slideshow, I discovered that students, accustomed to studying the environment through staid textbook lessons about faraway places, were excited to see images from their own neighborhoods. As they shared their knowledge and stories, my sense of them as "community experts" was reinforced; even the most seemingly apathetic students found that they had something, and often much, to contribute. Teachers were often ecstatic to witness their students' sudden enthusiasm for the environment. After one of these visits, David Cohen, a teacher at the Urban School of San Francisco, wrote:

> I was unaware of the sheer number of toxic sites or of the effects these sites have on the people living around them. Your tour explained how multiple factors contribute to the health problems of Hunters Point

residents and at the same time revealed valuable information about different key sources of pollution.

Over the years an array of projects has emerged, unique to schools, times of year, and teachers' or school administrators' personalities. LEJ staff members help teachers connect the state-mandated curriculum to local environmental health and justice issues, and then work with the students to create projects that excite them. We have worked regularly with hundreds of public school teachers, helping foster their growth as effective environmental justice leaders despite social and economic barriers and the lack of resources.

Several of the projects have had immediate impacts. A program for Phoenix Academy, a dropout prevention program within the San Francisco school district, is one example. The teacher wanted to engage the students in writing exercises around environmental health concerns in the shipyard, but many of these extremely disenfranchised kids had given up on education. When presented the task of letter writing, they responded, "Nobody cares what we have to say. Who's going to pay attention to our letters? We can't even write a letter." A few did not even bother to raise their heads from their desks.

I was teaching the project with an LEJ-placed Americorps volunteer named Antonio Arenas, a respected young Latino activist. He was very frustrated with the students and saddened to see so many of them giving up so early in life. In our second or third session, he addressed the class: "Long ago people our age fought as warriors to defend their communities against all kinds of enemies. Sometimes they went into battle knowing that the odds were against them. But do you think they just sat down right there and gave up? No, they fought until the death for the honor and respect of their people and themselves. I know how you might feel, but you need to stand up and fight for your rights. You have a voice, learn to use it." It was a dare, which the Phoenix Academy students accepted.

They began to brainstorm around what they knew about the shipyard. Each of the students produced a compelling, well-reasoned argument to support their ideas for addressing the problems caused by the shipyard. They wrote the Navy officer in charge of the shipyard clean-up. They thought of asking the officer to hold a hearing in their classroom on the issues that they had raised. None of us thought that he would come (he was stationed in San Diego), but in the spirit of Antonio's dare we persisted. To our astonishment, he agreed to meet with the students. They prepared for the meeting and practiced their statements. They had decided that they wanted to convince the Navy to place hazardous warning signs in multiple languages on the shipyard fencing—a long-standing community request. The officer met with the students for two hours, responded to their questions, presented the Navy's position, and heard their demands. Within a month the signs requested by the students were posted.

We have also organized several projects combining students and teachers across grade levels and from different schools. The first of these, "Art Against Pollution," addressed the air pollution and epidemic asthma rates in Bayview Hunters Point. Classes studied the causes of poor air quality, related health effects, and alternative, less polluting energy production. LEJ staff members organized an asthma inhaler collection contest in five schools. An International Studies Academy High School art class used the inhalers to create two life-sized papier-mâché sculptures of youth with asthma. One was pulling its chest open to reveal wire lungs filled with inhalers. The second depicted an African American teen standing on a mound of inhalers, with neighborhood health statistics patterned across his clothing. Together, these pieces sent a powerful message.

Students worked with LEJ staff members to organize a press event at City Hall where they would present their work to then Mayor Willie Brown. They orchestrated the event to be part of another school event at City Hall that day, ensuring the attendance of some two hundred teachers, students, and parents. The young people really pressed the mayor, asking him tough questions and demonstrating their comprehension of air quality and health concerns. They were not at all intimidated by the fact that they were talking to the mayor of San Francisco. For them this was not a political event; they really wanted to present the truth about the causes of the conditions in their neighborhoods. A year later Mayor Brown's office created a $13 million environmental justice community grants program. I believe that the students' testimony influenced the decision to create this program.

Preparing the Next Generation:
Youth Leadership Development

Although LEJ built its foundation through working in schools, the organization is best known for its efforts in youth leadership development. Not long after the first season of school-based programs, I was invited to cofacilitate an embryonic environmental justice youth leadership program at the San Francisco League of Urban Gardeners (SLUG), where a ragtag team of youth from Bayview Hunters Point were being paid to work on tobacco control issues, an issue that didn't really excite them. We tried to connect this work to other community issues in order to engage the youth. Attempting to make the link between health and recreation, I asked, "Why do people go to parks?" I was answered by Juan Barragan, a thin, angry-looking fifteen-year-old. He responded passionately to my question about parks, "To bury guns!" Probably recognizing the surprise and horror on my face, he smirked without skipping a beat, "You ever need a gun, Dana, I got hella guns for you over at the park."

I recognized something special about this charismatic young man. Juan had dropped out of tenth grade; he explained that he was done with school because he felt that the teachers knew less about real life than he did. In hopes of persuading him to go back to school (something I never accomplished), I invited him to come into our office and help out during the day. He began by answering the phone and copying things, but I also invited him to "shadow" me in meetings with teachers and classroom lessons. He quickly offered ideas for making the presentations more engaging to the youth and started facilitating some of them with me.

Teachers were impressed with Juan's message: that everyone has something to offer the community. The students were fascinated by the youth-adult partnership that he and I embodied. Eventually, Juan moved on (he now manages an auto body shop in the South Bay and hopes to own a house before he turns thirty—a dream not realized by any of his family members), but the adult-youth partnership/teaching style we developed became the model for LEJ's youth leadership programs. Since then the programs have grown to focus in three distinct areas: food security, renewable energy, and open space restoration.

> Not only do we provide jobs for the youth to keep them off the streets and doing god knows what, but we work on restoring this wetland. Our goal is to restore all the wetlands in Bayview Hunters Point, but we started with Yosemite Slough. We do much research on birds, because they tell whether an ecosystem is healthful or not.
> —ERICA ANDREWS

LEJ puts youth interns through a fairly rigorous selection and training process. We ask that they be willing to extend themselves into the community through public speaking, writing, and workshop facilitation. We look to foster other talents as well, such as art and graphic design. Many of the projects are scientifically technical in nature, so interns must be prepared to focus on what can feel to young minds like minutiae, yet for the most part we find that they become extremely dedicated to the environmental justice cause, demonstrating heartfelt advocacy and a precocious sensitivity to threats to the environment or their community.

As our expectations for our interns have risen, so has their performance. In the past two years, over 90 percent of our high school graduates have gone on to college—including some of the best universities in the country: Cornell, UC Davis, Fisk, and UC Berkeley—and this from a community in which more than 30 percent of entering freshmen do not even complete high school. To many people, Bayview youth are disposable members of society, but at LEJ and hundreds of similar organizations around the country, we are demonstrating that with belief, "tough love," and compassion these young people will succeed and share their lives with others in inspiring ways. There is a tremendous sense of community, personal strength, and integrity in places like Bayview Hunters Point; if we can connect with this energy we can tap a deep source for social and environmental change.

LEJ youth interns work with our partners in government, business, and

other nonprofit agencies. They become accustomed to sitting as equals to adults
at the planning table and are encouraged to take leadership roles in public settings. Our highly successful Youth Envision program, for example, annually
trains and employs seven to ten young people as community food security advocates. Given the dense prevalence of toxic sites, environmental health, particularly nutrition, is a top neighborhood concern; if people living in this toxic
environment have a nutritious diet, their bodies can fight better against cancer and other debilitating environmental illnesses.

> It takes an average of an hour to get to a grocery store that has fresh
> meat or fresh produce. And it takes an average of three buses to get
> to any grocery store, period.
> —JESSICA MARSHALL, LEJ Intern, Youth Envision

The San Francisco Department of Public Health has found that 15 to 20
percent of African American and Latino constituents suffer from diabetes,
while another 40 to 50 percent suffer from obesity, and 20 to 25 percent
smoke. The high rates of these diet-related illnesses may be connected to the
very limited access to nutritious and fresh food; what fresh food local stores
do carry is of extremely poor quality. Studies conducted by LEJ Youth Envision have documented that less than 5 percent of the products sold in the
community are fresh produce or meat items, while 26 percent are alcohol and
cigarette products. The top three products not related to alcohol or tobacco
that are sold along Third Street, the main thoroughfare, are cookies, crackers,
and cereal.

> When you walk into one of the corner stores on Third Street, you'll
> see plenty of tobacco and alcohol advertisements everywhere, in front
> of the door, inside the store, behind the counter, in your face, on back
> of some chips, you never know. There's no produce, nothing healthy.
> A tear would drop from your eye if you've ever seen a real store in
> a nice community. But when they were thinking about stores in
> Bayview Hunters Point, I guess they just said, Give them all tobacco.

That's all they need. Some smokes and some drink . . . and some
crackers and some chips, maybe. But we need healthy food. We need
fruits and vegetables just like anybody else.
    —JASMINE MARSHALL, LEJ Youth Leader, Youth Envision Program

Through merchant interviews, LEJ Youth Envision determined that one
of the biggest obstacles to improving food access and nutrition in Bayview
Hunters Point is large corporations' advertising and incentives to merchants.
With the input of Karen Pierce from the Bayview Hunters Point Advocates
and the San Francisco Department of Public Health, they devised the "Good
Neighbor Project." Participating businesses receive city and privately sponsored economic incentives in exchange for a 20 percent increase in healthy
food stock, the elimination of tobacco and alcohol advertising from their stores,
and for abiding by city health codes. The first participating store reports that,
since it joined the program, produce has come to represent 30 percent of its
sales. Meanwhile, volunteer chefs from the Jardinière and Acme Chop House
restaurants are teaching the kids to teach other people how to select and prepare fresh vegetables and cook nutritious, gourmet meals—skills that can be
lost when people have not had access to fresh food.

Diversifying the Environmental
Movement for the Twenty-First Century

As I discovered when I started looking for environmental organizations who
could teach Bayview Hunters Point children about the toxics in their community, there is a divide, and sometimes hostility, between the traditional environmental movement and the environmental justice movement. The basic
principles of ecology include balance through diversity, but this concept is frequently absent from the "sustainability" discourse. For too long people of color,
low-income people, and youth have been forgotten or intentionally marginalized from efforts to heal ecological systems, revitalize cities, and conserve precious resources. Outreach efforts are often culturally inappropriate because
target populations are minimally represented in environmental fields. The un-

derrepresentation of low-income people and people of color enables environmental inequity to continue because these populations have no forum to share their voices and talents.

A popular slogan during the formative years of the environmental justice movement was "We ain't about saving the whales," a statement made by social and environmental leaders of color who felt unseen by the existing conservation movement. People living at or near a subsistence level are obviously challenged to devote attention to far-off causes, and environmental justice leaders felt that significant environmental concerns in their communities, such as pesticide drift, toxic siting, and mining, were not being adequately addressed by the environmental movement.

This stance should not be misunderstood to imply that traditionally marginalized populations do not care about or understand environmental issues. These communities may in some cases have a hyperawareness of such concerns because they must daily confront the consequences of poor environmental management. For instance, a seventy-six-year-old African American community elder who had lived in Bayview Hunters Point nearly her whole life once told me, "My dream is to see all the houses in Hunters Point remodeled to have a little steeple on the roof with a windmill inside it. That way we can have green energy in this community, close the awful power plant, and end the asthma problems." She has volunteered her time for decades to plan the redevelopment of the shipyard and make this vision a reality.

The youth at LEJ see themselves as environmental activists whose environment happens to be urban. They really spend a lot of time listening and trying to understand people's needs, which are in fact the same needs as those of the natural environment. People of color and low-income people are suffering from habitat loss in the same way that endangered species are. They've lost access to a healthy habitat that they need in order to survive. These urban environmentalists do care, and they want to help, and they need support.

Sustainability—A New Item
on the Lunch Menu

Michael K. Stone

Janet Brown, the Center for Ecoliteracy's program officer for food systems, has called eating "an ecological act of unparalleled significance." "We want children to identify eating as a fundamental part of life," she says. "Since all life forms 'eat,' this act accounts for the greatest impact of the earth's resources of any of the life processes."

This brief history of the Center for Ecoliteracy's food programs—from supporting The Edible Schoolyard to working with the Berkeley Unified School District to the Fertile Crescent Network to the Rethinking School Lunch project—illustrates how the Center itself applies the ecological principles it has learned from examining ecosystems.

As this report notes, working with food and schools illustrates clearly the wisdom of Wendell Berry's "Solving for Pattern" (in Part I). Fragmented attempts to address individual "problems" can lead to larger, even less tractable problems, while identifying the pattern that connects problems offers the opportunity to seek solutions that reinforce each other.

This history also illustrates the flexibility required to work effectively with dynamic systems. CEL was not intending to get involved in school lunches, but it recognized an opportunity when one presented itself. At several points the programs faced the prospect of bogging down, and CEL had to shift direction by invoking some of the systems principles enunciated by Fritjof Capra in "Speaking Nature's Language" (in Part I): moving between different levels in nested systems, creating and supporting networks, revisioning strategies in response to feedback from partner organizations.

The Berkeley Unified School District Food Policy, which concludes this piece, garnered the school district international attention. Predictably, the media found an "only in Berkeley" hook in the policy's goals of ensuring to the extent possible that food served in Berkeley schools be organic and free of additives and irradiated or genetically modified ingredients. Its more far-reaching goals, beginning with the sweeping commitment to ensure that no Berkeley student goes hungry, received less attention. The policy has served at least one function well, providing a clear and consistent vision in spite of turnover in the superintendent's office, the food service department, and elsewhere in the district, and through daunting financial challenges.

This article is based on a longer report from an earlier point in CEL's food systems history, published in Whole Earth *magazine, spring 2002.*

LUNCH IS AN ACTIVITY shared by most students. Health, nutrition, and food are undeniably linked. Food is as basic as sustainability gets. Learning how food gets from seed to table requires some understanding of fundamental natural processes—energy flows, nutrient cycles, how one organism's waste becomes another's food. It also requires an understanding of the relationship of educational, agricultural, economic, social, and political systems.

As the Center for Ecoliteracy learned during a ten-year engagement with school food systems, efforts to improve school food can reveal some of the deep mental and social disconnections that frustrate attempts to think and act sustainably: actions disconnected from consequences, farms from communities, health from environment, schools' explicit curriculum from their "hidden curriculum."

The Center didn't start by looking to be involved in school lunch. One of its early strategies consisted of identifying and supporting exemplary schools with holistic curricula organized around place-based projects. These schools had discovered that cooperation and learning often increased, and grades and retention improved, when learning was integrated with hands-on natural-world projects such as watershed restoration and school gardens. They recognized that these experiences were instrumental in forming children's values and sense of responsibility for themselves, their communities, and the environment.

In 1995, one of these schools, Martin Luther King Middle School in Berkeley, provided a chance to address food in a whole-systems way. King principal Neil Smith had met Alice Waters, the charismatic chef, founder of world-famed Chez Panisse restaurant, and tireless promoter of fresh ingredients from local sources (what was later dubbed "California Cuisine"). "There are gardens in lots of schools," she told him. "There are kitchens. There are cafeterias. But there aren't gardens and kitchens and cafeterias that are of a piece. I started to get the idea for an ecological curriculum run as a school lunch program that could transform education." She presented a bold vision, given that King didn't even have a cafeteria at the time.

Eventually, The Edible Schoolyard (ESY) blossomed at King, garnering national attention. ESY combined garden work and cooking classes for every student. A mutual friend introduced Waters to Center for Ecoliteracy executive director Zenobia Barlow, and the Center became one of ESY's first financial supporters, including funding a team of King's teachers to work on integrating curriculum with garden and kitchen experiences. Even teachers who had initially viewed the kitchen and garden sessions as time away from the curriculum began to look for ways to make ESY lessons part of the curriculum. A Spanish class spoke Spanish while cooking Venezuelan food. A mathematics class costed out a meal's ingredients. Children experienced the natural cycles, learned to compost, discovered the satisfaction of sitting down to eat together. ESY and other garden and cooking programs exploded one widespread assumption: that children are irretrievably addicted to junk food. In fact, they will eat—and love—nutritious fruits and vegetables, even unfamiliar ones, that they've grown and cooked themselves.

A Harvard Medical School—based study commissioned by CEL concluded that ESY students showed greater gains in ecological understanding, and greater overall academic progress, than did students in a comparable non-ESY school. Teachers reported better behavior in class. Students who gained most in ecological literacy were also shown to be eating more fruits and vegetables.

As impressive as ESY is, CEL took seriously what systemic school reformers had discovered in the late 1980s: systems don't exist in isolation. Classrooms are nested within schools, which are embedded in school districts, which reside within communities that are parts of bioregions and foodsheds inside nations within a global economy. Long-lasting change requires addressing multiple levels simultaneously.

An opportunity to work at the district as well as the school level arose in 1998. As the result of a process begun in response to parents discontented with the quality and choice of food available in the Berkeley schools, the school district's board unanimously adopted the first districtwide school food policy in the United States (see below). Among its goals: "ensure that no student in Berkeley is hungry; . . . provide nutritious, fresh, tasty, locally grown food that reflects Berkeley's cultural diversity; . . . ensure that the food served shall be organic to the maximum extent possible; . . . maximize the reduction of waste by recycling, reusing, composting, and purchasing recycled products."

The superintendent of schools had asked Tom Bates, a former California legislator (and later mayor of Berkeley), to help coordinate the process that led to formulating the policy. Twenty years in the legislature had taught Bates that policies without enforcement mechanisms are hollow. Therefore, the policy required the food service to report annually to the board of education. It also established a Child Nutrition Advisory Committee (CNAC) to oversee progress on the policy's goals.

Meanwhile, Barlow met Janet Brown, a Marin County farmer, community food security activist, and founder of the Marin Food Policy Council. Brown became a consultant to the Center for Ecoliteracy and later its program officer for food systems. They discovered a U.S. Department of Agriculture Community Food Security program that drew on the same place-based, systems-based premises as the Center's work. As the lead agency for a network of seventeen community organizations and individuals, CEL received a three-year Community Food Security grant to create a "Food Systems Project." Tom Bates became its first director. Many of the project's goals corresponded to those of the district food policies.

The Food Systems Project network and the school district recorded several notable accomplishments (gardens in every district school, kitchen and cooking classes in eleven schools, Farm-to-School Field Studies programs that took urban students to farms and brought farmers to classrooms, a city food policy, a successful bond measure including funds for school cafeterias and kitchens). At the conclusion of the grant, CEL was reminded that dramatic systems change can be slow, long-term work. Three years was long enough to lay some important groundwork, but change of this magnitude may take more like ten years. CEL continues to work with the Berkeley schools. This collaboration reached another milestone in 2004, when the school district and the Chez Panisse Foundation, in partnership with the Center for Ecoliteracy and the Children's Hospital Oakland Research Institute, signed a memorandum of understanding to implement a district School Lunch Curriculum Initiative.

The Center also acted on its commitment to building networks and seeking bioregional solutions by convening a "Fertile Crescent Network" of CEL grantees and their allies (including food service directors, educators, farmers, and community-based organizations) from five counties on the urban/rural frontier of the San Francisco Bay Area. Building on their own efforts and CEL's, this network has worked both together and in county subgroups to "migrate" the work initiated in Berkeley—from developing district food policies to sharing experiences with farm-to-school projects.

In assessing its work in Berkeley and determining where to move next, CEL was reminded of the ecological principles that govern systems change: trying to change a district's food service alone isn't enough. School food services and local food systems are hard to change partly because they are embedded in larger educational, economic, and political systems that in turn reflect much bigger trends—among them centralization, industrialization, standardization, and globalization. Marilyn Briggs, the author of the next essay, gives an example: apricot orchards in California are being plowed under to build housing complexes. The apricot farmers can't make a living as a result of an apricot surplus caused partly by world trade agreements that make Turkish apricots cheaper to food distributors (including those that supply schools). Meanwhile, the schools don't have mechanisms to buy from local farmers.

In "Solving for Pattern" (in Part I), Wendell Berry distinguishes among "solutions" that worsen the problem they're supposed to solve, those that initiate cascades of other problems, and those that "cause a ramifying series of solutions." A bad solution is designed for a single purpose. It acts destructively on the patterns that contain it. A good solution addresses the interlocking pattern in which it is embedded.

School food systems, at least in the United States, are rife with single-purpose solutions that generate new problems. School districts "solve" chronic underfunding by demanding that food services break even, or even generate surpluses, on minimal government subsidies for feeding poor children. The USDA "solves" farmer income problems by buying surplus commodities (often high-fat cheese or meat) and offering them to schools. To save money, schools abandon the labor-intensive preparation of fresh food and "solve" the problem of undernourished children by serving preprocessed and frozen food that's been shipped thousands of miles, burning fossil fuel and discharging air pollutants along the way. Processing leaches nutrients, and usually appearance and taste, from food, a problem that students "solve" by dumping it into the trash, where it rejoins the same packaging (50 percent of food costs, some say) that it arrived in.

Schools "solve" poor academic performance by mandating more standardized testing and more hours in class (sometimes by shortening lunch and exercise periods, though educators know that undernourished students perform poorly). The crisis of obesity and nutrition-related illness inspires classroom nutrition lectures and slick, colorful teaching materials, while cash-strapped schools install soft-drink machines in the hallways and PTAs sell pizza and candy to subsidize art and music programs and purchase computer equipment. Small farms, which could grow the fruits and vegetables that children need, struggle to survive, while school food dollars support mass agribusiness operations that are driving small farmers out of business. Farmland sold to developers when farms close is lost to agriculture, compromising communities' future sustainability.

Bad solutions lead to cascading waves of additional problems, but Berry also says that solving for pattern can set in motion a ramifying series of solutions. CEL has joined with other organizations to support a "farm-to-school" movement that links schools and farms, bringing local farmers income and giving children the chance to learn to love good food. The Center is also supporting efforts to create whole-school curricula that begin with serving meals that complement rather than contradict classroom lessons on nutrition and health. These curricula use gardens and kitchens as laboratories for teaching science, math, art, social studies, and many other subjects.

Sustainability issues must be approached from many directions and at many levels. CEL's years of working with food systems culminated in 2004 in a project called Rethinking School Lunch. This project addresses ten interlocking areas, including nutrition, facilities, procurement, finances, waste management, and curriculum integration. It offers the wisdom and experience of experts and practitioners, and provides districts and schools with usable tools, beginning with a guide available on its website (www.rethinkingschoollunch .org). For instance, in a recent poll school officials listed "money" as the greatest obstacle to improving school food, but food service directors often lack the planning tools to assess their operations or evaluate options for affordably offering better food. So the website offers an interactive spreadsheet for testing different scenarios. Other tools on the website include menus, architectural drawings, curricular plans, and extensive pointers to other resources. The Rethinking School Lunch project also includes a series of experts' viewpoints ("Thinking outside the Lunchbox") and outreach programs.

The Center hopes that these resources will inspire and serve the nascent movement to redefine the role of food in schools and to reconnect farms with communities, food with public health, and school curricula with student experiences. Schools have the opportunity to improve students' health while helping them both understand concepts of nutrition and health and experience the pleasure of good food, in order to build lifelong habits of good eating. At the same time, schools can educate for sustainability by what they teach in class *and* by how they serve as models of sustainability—redirecting the drift toward centralization, industrialization, standardization, and globalization and moving consciously toward diversification, human-scale systems, biological and cultural diversity, and community-based economics.

Berkeley Unified School District Food Policy, Adopted August 1, 1999

Responsibilities

The Board of Education recognizes the important connection between a healthy diet and a student's ability to learn effectively and achieve high standards in school. The Board also recognizes the school's role, as part of the larger community, to promote family health, sustainable agriculture, and environmental restoration.

The Board of Education recognizes that the sharing of food is a fundamental experience for all peoples; a primary way to nurture and celebrate our cultural diversity; and an excellent bridge for building friendships, and intergenerational bonds.

Mission

The educational mission is to improve the health of the entire community by teaching students and families ways to establish and maintain life-long healthy eating habits. The mission shall be accomplished through nutrition education, garden experiences, the food served in schools, and core academic content in the classroom.

Goals

1. Ensure that no student in Berkeley is hungry.

2. Ensure that a healthy and nutritious breakfast, lunch, and after-school snack is available to every student at every school so that students are prepared to learn to their fullest potential.

3. Eliminate the reduced-price category for school lunch, breakfast,

and snacks, so that all low-income children have healthy food available at no cost.

4. Ensure that all qualified children become eligible for free meals by frequently checking with Alameda County Social Services.

5. Ensure maximum participation in the school meal program by developing a coordinated, comprehensive outreach and promotion plan for the school meal programs.

6. Shift from food-based menu planning to nutrient-based planning (as set forth under USDA guidelines) to allow for more flexible food selection.

7. Ensure that the nutritional value of the food served significantly improves upon USDA Dietary Guidelines by providing nutritious, fresh, tasty, locally grown food that reflects Berkeley's cultural diversity.

8. Ensure that the food served shall be organic to the maximum extent possible, as defined by the California Certified Organic Farmers.

9. Eliminate potential harmful food additives and processes, such as bovine growth hormones, irradiation, and genetically modified foods.

10. Serve meals in a pleasant environment with sufficient time for eating, while fostering good manners and respect for fellow students.

11. Maximize the reduction of waste by recycling, reusing, composting, and purchasing recycled products. Each school site shall have a recycling program.

12. Ensure that a full service kitchen will be installed at school sites where public bond money is expended to repair or remodel a school.

Strategies

A. Integration into the Curriculum
   1. Integrate eating experiences, gardens, and nutrition education into the curriculum for math, science, social studies, and language arts at all grade levels.
   2. Establish a school garden in every school. Give students the opportunity to plant, harvest, prepare, cook, and eat food they have grown.
   3. Establish relationships with local farms. Encourage farmers and farm workers to come to the school classroom and arrange for students to visit farms.

B. Student Participation
   1. Solicit student preferences in planning menus and snacks through annual focus groups, surveys, and taste tests of new foods and recipes.
   2. Ensure that 5 students are represented on the Child Nutrition Advisory Committee.

C. Waste Reduction
   1. Ensure that cafeterias are part of the environmental education of students and staff through reducing waste, composting, recycling, and purchasing recycled material.

D. Sustainable Agriculture
   1. Purchase food from school gardens and local farmers as a first priority, based on availability and acceptability. Child Nutrition Services will coordinate its menus with school garden production and provide to garden coordinators a list of the produce it wishes to purchase.

2. Work with the Alameda County Cooperative Bid (13 school districts) to increase the amount of products purchased from local farms and organic food suppliers.

E. Nutrition Education and Professional Development
   1. Provide regular professional development to enable the Food Services Staff to become full partners in providing excellent food for our students.
   2. Provide regular training, at least annually, to teachers and the Food Service Staff on basic nutrition, nutrition education, and benefits of organic and sustainable agriculture.
   3. Provide Child Nutrition Services with USDA-approved computer software, training, and support to implement nutrient-based menu planning.

F. Business Plan
   1. The Board of Education shall do a comprehensive cost/benefit analysis and business plan. The plan shall include an examination of different development models of increased fresh food preparation at the central and satellite kitchens.

G. Public Information
   1. Each year in March, Child Nutrition Services shall prepare The Director's Annual Report for the Board of Education, which will include:
      a.) Description of the level of service for each site and level of participation;
      b.) Profit and Loss Statement for the past fiscal year;
      c.) Outreach and Promotion Marketing Plan (with assistance from Advisory Committee);
      d.) Budget for the future year;
      e.) Report on the progress in meeting the food policy goals;
      f.) Nutritional quality of the food being served;

g.) Inventory of equipment;

h.) Budget for maintenance and replacement equipment;

i.) Accounting of Child Nutrition Services' financial reserve and a budget allocating the reserve.

2. The Berkeley Unified School District's Food Policy, Director's Annual Report, Monthly Menus, and food policy information shall be available at District Office and on the Board of Education's website.

3. A summary of the Director's Annual Report shall be distributed as part of the April and May menus.

H. Public Policy

1. Advocate for label disclosure:

a.) Request State and Federal representatives support legislation that will clearly label food products that have been irradiated, genetically modified, or have been exposed to bovine growth hormones.

b.) Send a Board of Education resolution requesting support for labeling legislation to:

1.) Every School Board in the State of California

2.) The State School Boards Association

3.) The National School Boards Association.

I. Establishment of a Child Nutrition Advisory Committee

1. Child Nutrition Advisory Committee shall be established to discuss food-related topics of concern to the school community and help make policy recommendations to the Board of Education.

2. The 24-member Child Nutrition Advisory Committee shall be as follows:

a.) 10 Community/Parent representatives appointed by the Board of Education.

b.) The Superintendent.

c.) The Director of Child Nutrition Services.

d.) 3 Classified employees appointed by their employee organization.

e.) 3 Teachers (elementary, middle, and high school) appointed by their employee organization.

f.) 1 Principal appointed by their employee organization.

g.) 5 Students (3 middle school and 2 high school) appointed by student government.

3. The Advisory Committee shall meet at least six times a year at hours convenient for public participation.

4. The Duties and Responsibilities shall be as follows:

a.) Present to the Board of Education an Annual Report in April of each year on the status of meeting the food policy goals. The report shall contain:

1.) Review and comment on the Director's Annual Report, Profit and Loss Statement, Marketing Plan and Business Plan.

2.) Recommendations for improving the delivery and cost effectiveness of food services.

b.) Assist the Director of Child Nutrition Services in the development and implementation of the Outreach and Promotion Marketing Plan.

c.) Review and report by February 1 to the Board of Education on recommendations to eliminate potentially harmful food additives and processes.

d.) Make periodic reports, as the Advisory Committee deems necessary.

e.) Establish rules for decision-making.

J. Maintenance and Repair of Equipment

1. The Board of Education instructs the Maintenance Committee to include kitchen facilities, food preparation, and storage of equipment as high priority in its comprehensive maintenance policy.

2. Modernize computer equipment and programs, and institute an automated accounting system.

K. Community Use of School District Property
   District facilities, including school kitchens shall be available to community based groups for their use and enjoyment under terms established by the Board of Education.

Rethinking School Lunch

Marilyn Briggs

One outcome of the Center for Ecoliteracy's years of work at the intersection of food systems and schools, described in the previous chapter, is the Rethinking School Lunch project. The project includes a Web guide, for which this essay is the introduction, an ongoing series of "Outside the Lunchbox" perspectives written by experts in the field, and seminars and workshops for practitioners (see www.rethinkingschoollunch.org).

The Web guide was designed with the recognition that solving for pattern with respect to school food requires attention to all the facets of a school district's operations. Accordingly, the guide includes essays, interviews, resources, and practical tools in ten areas: food policy; curriculum integration; food and health; finances; facilities design; the dining experience; professional development; procurement; waste management; and marketing and communications. As the introduction demonstrates, the nutrition-related health crisis of the past few years can be traced partly to schools' attempts to educate whole children through fragmented programs, policies, and practices.

Farm-to-school programs, which Marilyn Briggs invokes here, provide school lunch programs with fresh food from local sustainable family farms, connect students to their food sources through meals and field trips, improve the nutritional content and quality of food in schools, and help local farms remain economically viable.

Briggs served with the California Department of Education for sixteen years, most recently as Assistant Superintendent of Public Instruction and director of the Nutrition Services Division, after service as administrator and acting director of the Child Nutrition and Food Distribution Division. She was a nutrition education specialist and assistant food service director of the San Juan Unified School District, a public health nutritionist for the Hawaii State Department of Health, an in-

structor at the University of Hawaii, and assistant director of the Dietetics Department at American River College. She was the first recipient of the Award for
Outstanding Contributions from the California Conference of Local Health Department Nutritionists. She has served as an officer in many nutrition organizations,
including the editorial board of the Journal of Nutrition Education, and was president of the Society for Nutrition Education. She is completing a doctorate in nutrition sciences at the University of California, Davis.

wow

ACCORDING TO THE U.S. DEPARTMENT of Health and Human
Services, poor diet and physical inactivity are responsible for as many pre-
mature deaths in the United States as is tobacco—more than twelve hundred
a day. The Centers for Disease Control (CDC) identifies diet as a "known risk"
for the development of the nation's three leading causes of death—coronary
heart disease, cancer, and stroke—as well as for diabetes, high blood pressure,
and osteoporosis, among others.

If one of the primary goals of educators is to help students prepare for healthy
and productive lives, then nutrition and health education are central to that goal.
The most systematic and efficient means for improving the health of America's
youth is to establish healthy dietary and physical activity behaviors in childhood. The CDC reports that "young persons having unhealthy eating habits
tend to maintain these as they age. . . . Behaviors and physiological risk factors
are difficult to change once they are established during youth." Yet fewer than
one-third of schools provide thorough coverage of nutrition education related
to influencing students' motivation, attitudes, and eating behaviors.

Connecting Nutrition and Curriculum

Most school administrators already connect nutrition with health. Going one
step further and connecting health with educational goals effectively connects
nutrition education with both academic performance and academic content.

There is so much concern over test scores these days. But if kids aren't in
a position to learn because they're hungry or they don't get enough nutritious
food at home, then schools that don't make the nutrition/performance con-

nection end up undermining what they're trying to do in the classroom. They know this, too. When schools administer the standardized tests, they will often tell kids to eat breakfast the morning of the test or they may offer a breakfast on campus.

Studies repeatedly link good nutrition to learning readiness, academic achievement, and decreased discipline and emotional problems. A hungry child can't learn. Any teacher knows that if children are hungry, they're not thinking about their lessons, but educational theorists and administrators sometimes forget that.

In 2003 I served as one of the writers for a joint position statement of the American Dietetic Association, the Society for Nutrition Education, and the American School Food Service Association. Part of our statement read:

> Comprehensive nutrition services must be provided to all of the na-
> tion's preschool through grade twelve students. These . . . shall be in-
> tegrated with a coordinated, comprehensive school health program and
> implemented through a school nutrition policy. The policy shall link
> comprehensive, sequential nutrition education; access to and promo-
> tion of child nutrition programs providing nutritious meals and snacks
> in the school environment; and family, community, and health serv-
> ices' partnership supporting positive health outcomes for all children.

To me, that means connecting health/nutrition education with the whole curriculum—not just as one of the components in the curriculum, but as something that's embedded in all aspects. It means making school meals part of the nutrition program. That connection feels self-evident, but schools and districts have been slow to make it. The lunch period has more often been regarded as time stolen away from the curriculum, rather than as part of the curriculum.

Connecting Operations throughout the School District

Implementing a program that addresses nutrition, health, and school lunches through an integrated curriculum requires many steps. Ultimately it requires coordinating decisions about virtually every facet of the district's operations: facilities, budgets, personnel, procurement, waste management, public relations, curriculum. It's a circle that can be entered through many points, as the Rethinking School Lunch guide shows. But it all starts with the food on children's plates.

Menus are the heart of the whole system. Districts should design their kitchen facilities to prepare the kind of food they want to serve, not choose menus to suit the kitchens. Menus also provide the basis for reviewing food service staffing needs and staff development, along with all the other district functions that a change in food priorities will affect.

School meal programs can provide students with better nutrition for one or two meals every day, which would be a great health improvement for many students. Even the average lunch brought from home provides less than one-third the recommended dietary allowance of food energy, vitamin A, vitamin B-6, calcium, iron, and zinc.

But it's not enough that school food be nutritious. It doesn't matter how healthy the meal is if the students reject it or throw it out. The food also needs to be delicious and attractive. Fortunately for nutrition educators, good fresh food usually does taste better. When children taste freshly picked or prepared foods—sometimes for the first time—they often discover that they like them. And when school gardens or cooking classes are also integrated into the curriculum, so that children grow or prepare the foods they eat, the food almost always becomes more attractive.

I much prefer this approach to the negative approach of "Do not eat this, and do not have that." It's a more positive, much more educational way when students learn how delightful and wonderful and fun it can be to add fruits and vegetables and whole grains to their diet. Rather than calling attention to a banned food, which then becomes *more* attractive, using fresh food's natural tastiness helps to establish new lifelong eating habits (which lead automatically to a healthier diet with reduced fat intake).

However, offering nutritious food by itself, even if it tastes good, may still not be enough. The pervasive availability of high-fat foods, non-nutritious foods served in the influential environment of restaurants geared to young children, and children's predisposition to these foods all contribute to unhealthy diets. The media have the capacity to persuade children to make poor food choices; studies have shown that even brief exposures to televised food commercials can influence preschool children's food preferences. A successful program may also need to use the tools of marketers to reach both children and parents.

Connecting Schools and Farms

Buying food locally, and preparing and serving it fresh, helps local farmers, who are often struggling to compete with agribusiness. It gives local farmers a chance to diversify their markets, and that in turn helps the local economy.

Healthy farms provide jobs, pay taxes, and keep working agricultural land from going to development. The benefits from undeveloped farmland include lower costs of community services, more open space, valuable flood control, diversified wildlife habitat, and greater community food security.

Schools represent a reliable and steady demand that farmers can plan for, allowing farms to establish better controls on planting, harvesting, and marketing. Buying locally also reduces the transportation costs, packaging, fossil fuel use, and exhaust emissions caused by shipping food over long distances. In many cases, food bought locally costs schools less. Having local food sources also enables schools to create curricula that put human faces on the food, by bringing farmers to the classroom or by meeting farmers on field trips to farms and at farmers' markets.

Connecting How Food Is Served
and the Lessons Students Learn

The lifelong nutrition habits and lessons that children acquire from school food programs don't end with eating better food. A food systems curriculum promotes understanding about where food comes from and the natural cycles that produce it. The way that meals are served and eaten is part of the hidden curriculum that tells students what the school really believes about food. Does the school model a belief that mealtime is part of living a healthy life? Industrial cafeteria lines, allotting too little time for lunch, and combining lunch with recess teach kids that meals are something to rush through on the way to somewhere else.

Recent research shows that children eat better when they also have a quiet time after they eat. The ideal seems to be to have physical activity in the morning, have a quiet study time of some type before lunch, have lunch, and then a reading or quiet time after that, with physical activity delayed until later in the day. It's pretty obvious when kids go right from lunch to P.E., as is the case in many schools, then kids are anxious to get out on the playground and short-cut their meals.

I advocate serving meals family style, around a table, as an alternative to "grab and go" through a cafeteria line. When the social experience of sitting together with other students and calmly eating the food is a positive experience, children want to make time to have that experience with their friends and families. In order for this to happen, the cafeteria needs to be a positive environment in all respects. Some people argue that cafeteria lines are faster and more efficient, but family style can actually be faster. It's all set up in advance. The kids come in, and the food's there on the table. They actually have the full lunch period to eat without having to stand in line.

Connecting Schools, Parents, Communities, and Cultures

Serving family style successfully requires an adult in the role of "table host" at each table. It quickly becomes too costly if the school relies on paid staff, but I've been involved in very successful programs in which senior citizens served as the table hosts. Those programs worked very well. The kids ate in a better atmosphere; the senior citizens were able to make a valuable contribution and enjoy a nutritious lunch. The table hosts received stimulation from interacting with the kids; the kids were exposed to new role models. A program like that also helps connect schools and their communities, which can create more advocates for the schools when bond issues and other funding measures come before the community.

We think of today's kids as having grown up within a junk food generation, but it's often their *parents* who grew up surrounded by junk food and passed on those habits to their children.

We've lost a lot of parent role modeling. Parents often lack the ability to make wise food choices or lack the skills to prepare fresh food. We've lost our home economics courses. Even so, time and time again, I have seen children take food knowledge home and really make a difference with their parents. They often help teach their parents about healthy, fresh food. Sometimes they take their parents to the farmers' market. Sometimes they bring home food preparation skills that their parents forgot or never had.

When we connect schools and parents, we find that many parents have skills that they can bring into the classroom. This is especially true of parents who know traditional cooking from different cultures. I've seen it happen in school so many times, where a parent who might not be participating at all in school is asked to come in and share ethnic recipes—often a traditional recipe that incorporates local seasonal foods. They come, they meet people, they see the values of their culture being recognized and honored

That reminds me of a study among Laotian Hmong people living in Berkeley. Their kids were taking home processed food like pizza, and the parents felt, "Okay, this is the culture, and I want to learn this culture. So, we'd better serve this at home." Meanwhile, the study was highlighting the wonderful, delicious, high-nutrient fruit-and-vegetable recipes that the parents knew. Seeing their culture valued and themselves perceived as having something to contribute can be the door that leads those parents to become much more involved in the school and in the community. I've seen that happen repeatedly.

Connecting Food System Changes and Staff Development

Food service is often the last district operation to be brought into the change process, but it is the one upon which all others rely for success. School districts, especially those undergoing food policy changes, should plan on implementing a program of professional development for their food service staff. Professional development is a direct and critical investment in the individuals the district is counting on to make the change.

New menus based on cooking from scratch may require food service workers to learn new skills, especially if the current service is thaw-and-serve. It is also true that food service workers' jobs become more rewarding and satisfying when the work is less routine and requires skillful execution. Through professional development, food service staff members acquire valuable and transferable skills that might qualify them for higher pay. When food service staffs find the work more satisfying and receive the respect they deserve, enthusiasm will build for the new program.

Though many food service directors provide professional development, it's not a requirement. The California Department of Education offers training through community colleges and colleges that will bring the courses to the schools. An entire infrastructure is set up, but it's hard to fill the classes if no specific requirement exists.

At a policy level, I would advocate for better pay for food service workers and development of some professional requirements and expectations for anyone who is involved in the preparation of food for children. These would include cooking skills and basic sanitation and safety training. We're not there yet. For instance, a state requirement for basic sanitation and safety training only emerged in California in the last five years, and it requires only one person in the district to be certified in sanitation and safety.

Connecting Good Ideas and Meaningful Change

Moving from good ideas to action is never easy. School systems are among the most entrenched in our culture, often for good reasons. We see programs succeed most often when a key administrator, especially a superintendent, supports them. But if administrators aren't ready, or if school lunch and nutrition education programs are too far down their priority lists, the change process can be done from the ground up. It can begin with a food service director, or a parent, or a school nurse. I've seen it begin with a school board member who became very interested, inspired the rest of the board, and dragged the principal into it. I've even seen students take it on as a project.

Change can move from the top down or from the ground up, but it's ideal if it comes from both directions. The most important thing is to start somewhere and stay with it. Probably more than anything else, people promoting change need an advocate, someone who will spend the time and energy to stay with this process, which often moves slowly and can generate frustration. The desired change is so positive that many people will be drawn toward it. But they still need an advocate to bring the different groups together.

Effecting change begins by building partnerships, among administrators and parents, or teachers and nurses, or between schools and the agricultural community. I've used food as a way to involve new partners in the effort. For instance, I did that with school bus drivers, who look skeptically at programs that require changes in the bus schedule—one of the big obstacles to successful breakfast programs. Food talks. I invited the bus drivers to dinner. We talked about goals and imagined working together to make the program happen for the kids. The next thing I knew, the drivers were adjusting their schedules to encourage breakfasts for children.

It is possible to break into the implementation circle at many points. The most important thing is to start somewhere, and stick with it.

Changing Schools:
A Systems View

Ann Evans

Working to bring institutional change of the magnitude envisioned by many of the authors in this book can be hard, challenging work. Understanding the difficulties as systemic can suggest ways of facing them. A longtime food and education activist who has worked both inside and outside state education bureaucracies, Ann Evans uses systems thinking here to explain the obstacles inherent in education systems and some of the strategies for overcoming them.

Evans is a nutrition education consultant with the California Department of Education. She assists school districts in developing hands-on programs, modeled on The Edible Schoolyard in Berkeley, that integrate school gardens, cafeterias, and classrooms. She serves on a team that oversees nine school districts piloting the development of a healthy nutrition and physical education environment through a project funded by the California Department of Food and Agriculture and administered by the Department of Education.

A former mayor of Davis, California, Evans cofounded the Davis Food Co-op and the Davis Farmers Market, on whose board she serves. While with the state's Department of Consumer Affairs, she helped establish the legal framework for California's system of certified farmers' markets and food cooperatives. She is a partner in a small specialty food company, Evans & Main, which makes and markets products from the fruits of Yolo County farms practicing sustainable agriculture. She has served as a columnist on food and agriculture for the Davis Enterprise and was a Bioregional Writer in Residence with the University of California at Davis. In 2004, she cofounded Slow Food Yolo.

This article is based on a talk Evans gave at a 2003 Bioneers Conference sem-

inar on farm-to-school programs, presented by the Center for Ecoliteracy. As a farm-to-school advocate, she offers practical advice here to fellow activists.

IMPLEMENTING LASTING CHANGE IN SCHOOLS can feel like turning around an ocean liner. Stopping the ship takes a long, long time. Then you need more time to turn it around and yet more time to develop momentum to go in the new direction. And then, if you don't remember to turn off the autopilot, the ship will return to its old course. In the case of new ideas and complex ideas (such as integrated farm-to-school programs), that effort takes place on a stormy sea—within a culture that does not place high value on the promised results of the changes we are seeking. (In the case of farm-to-school, such results as increasing fresh and organic food in school lunches, sustaining family farmers, and nourishing rural community traditions are not yet high on most educators' agendas.)

I take great joy in this work, and I don't want to dwell on its difficulties. I hope that I can provide some reassurance for people feeling frustrated by the pace of change, but I also want to look realistically at public education as a system, to understand why change can take so long. At the same time, I want to maintain a sense of respect for the institution of public education, for its age-old processes, and for the people who've given their lives to working in it.

When we talk about introducing change as comprehensive as a farm-to-school lunch program, we're talking about a lot more than adding an organic or sustainably grown apple to the lunch tray, as hard as *that* can be to do. Systemic change in schools means changing the educational environment, structure, patterns of communication, values, and priorities. It means reconnecting broken parts of our educational system. That reconnection will nurture us, our young, the practice of education, and our place on earth. But it will take time, and it will require persistence.

I believe that schools are among the more conservative of our society's democratic institutions, and therefore among the slowest to change. Perhaps that's for good reason: they are designed to resist experimentation on our most precious natural resource, our children.

Those of us wanting to make changes in this system must partner with professional educators. It is in part *their* system that we enter. As bright-eyed and bushy-tailed as we may be with our ideas and as passionate as we are about the need for change, it's important to retain a sense of humility when we approach systems that good people have created, with the best of intentions, over a long period of time.

A Program for Nine Students or for 750,000?

School districts vary enormously, and that greatly impacts the introduction of new programs. California, where I work, is made up of fifty-eight counties, with a total of some one thousand school districts. Some counties, such as San Francisco, comprise a single school district. Marin County, with a population a third the size of San Francisco's, has nineteen districts. Other California counties contain anywhere from five to fifty districts. Most counties have an elected superintendent of education, but within the county, the school districts are autonomous, and range in size from nine students each in three rural districts to nearly 750,000 in Los Angeles. The majority of the state's districts are medium in size, between 5,000 and 15,000 students; the state's twenty-five largest school districts range from 34,000 to 750,000.

Because of this variety, no one has devised, or could devise, a blueprint for change appropriate to every district. However, systems theory tells us that the same systems principles apply at different levels of scale, and all districts share a number of characteristics. School district policy is set by a democratically elected board of trustees, which hires a professional superintendent to be responsible for the district's day-to-day operations. Board members are responsive to what they perceive as the needs and desires of the voters who elect them, but especially attentive to their political colleagues and supporters. School districts and their administrators are chronically short on money and long on demands placed on them by all kinds of interested parties (not the least of them, unions and the legislature) with important competing priorities.

Competing Priorities and the Snicker Factor

Though education administrators have the concerns and education of the children at heart, and though I do not believe that they would intentionally ignore us, their minds are occupied with widely shared community concerns such as funding, class size, and student achievement. Society is just beginning to recognize new concerns such as the linkages between health, food, farms, and schools. The toughest part of this business, in my view—the business we're really in—is adult education. The kids often immediately understand the connections we're talking about—and are quick to perceive the disconnections when, for instance, they're taught about conservation in the classroom, then see their lunch arrive on throwaway Styrofoam trays in the cafeteria. Adults often need more time to develop a whole-systems perspective, beginning with having to unlearn a lot of what they think they know.

We may be convinced that a program like farm-to-school "solves for pattern," to use Wendell Berry's phrase (see "Solving for Pattern" in Part I), and that by changing the apple on the tray we begin a process that leads to the healing of the school community and all those within it, but that's a very difficult concept to put across in an office with a school superintendent or a school board member. In fact, one of the problems confronting food reformers has been the "snicker factor," the "you can't be serious" reaction to efforts to make school food a priority for educators faced with high dropout rates, low academic achievement, violence on campus, and other pressing issues.

By fortuitous timing, public attention is sometimes grabbed by the symptoms of the systems issues we are trying to address. When that happens, we need to be ready to take advantage before that attention shifts, as it always will. We've recently seen widespread attention directed at obesity and other nutrition-related health issues, and a change in public perception about what kinds of products are appropriate for schools or student stores to sell on campus. Such concerns, which the public and elected officials share, can be an entrée for demonstrating how seemingly separate problems are connected and how food, nutrition, and health affect students' ability to pay attention, learn, and succeed in school.

Standards

Even when we can connect our solutions to publicly recognized problems, we still need to link better food and waste reduction and recycling and farm tours to curriculum as it's understood in today's educational climate. And that means as it relates to the standards, by subject and by grade, on which kids will be tested and schools will be funded, under both state legislation and federal legislation such as No Child Left Behind. Think what we will about standardized testing and our proclivity to measure educational success by test scores, the tests aren't going away soon, and proposals for curricular reform that ignore the mandated standards will face rough going. We need instead to make the case that the programs we are advocating will make the material required by the standards come alive, and will increase the likelihood that children will learn it.

Cash Flows

The state expenditures for the K–12 public school system represent over half the California state budget, and yet very little of that goes toward food. School food service operations are an "enterprise fund"—they must generate enough revenue to pay for their expenses, less reimbursement from the National School Lunch Program. Despite the paltry amount of this reimbursement ($2.17 per student per lunch in 2003–2004), food services are often expected to generate *surpluses* to help meet shortfalls in other parts of districts' budgets. In that situation, the promise of additional income from selling junk food in vending machines and student stores becomes increasingly seductive.

To be reimbursable by the state and federal government, the meals must meet standards for nutrition and calories as determined by the United States Department of Agriculture. Once the meal program reaches its financial objectives—often a significant accomplishment—and meets the mandated nutrition standards, then most district administrators, if they think about school lunch at all, assume that the goals of the program are met. End of discussion. Mission accomplished. On to the other district goals that haven't been met. Introducing additional nutritional and purchasing and educational goals for a program such as farm-to-school, on top of a program where the goals have been met, is a non sequitur for many school district administrators and food service directors. It's incumbent on reformers to demonstrate that their proposals provide opportunities for saving money or generating more income—or that they so effectively help the district meet its other goals, particularly advancing students' academic achievement, that they deserve to be a higher priority than the current uses of the same money.

Communications Disconnects

School district operations are generally divided into two "sides of the house"— the business side, where school food service, maintenance and operations, personnel, and budget functions reside, and the educational (or curriculum and instruction) side, where everything that goes on inside the classroom resides. The two sides of the house don't have much communications circuitry established between them, as they usually need very little communication to get their jobs done. So when we start talking systemically (about food as curriculum or waste reduction as curriculum, for instance), we're reconnecting parts to the whole, and we will need to establish new communications circuitry as well as credibility. That's one reason to consider working to establish districtwide policies, such as a food policy, that function at a higher level of organization (the school board or the superintendent's office) to which both sides of the house report. This is another potentially time-consuming process, but it might be a necessary one.

Sometimes the higher-level structure that could make efforts at change easier doesn't exist, at least not yet. For instance, the state of California mandates that cities and counties reduce waste. But there are no waste reduction goals for school districts, and therefore few comprehensive recycling programs connected with the preparation and consumption of school meals, classroom activities, and landscape maintenance. Changing schools' practices could require either working for legislation to establish waste reduction requirements for schools or demonstrating the fiscal rewards that can accrue from voluntarily changing the system. That's fairly easy to achieve with waste reduction (in Davis, we reduced solid waste by half), and so will probably be accepted and understood more quickly—as in three to four years—than other food system changes.

Leaders Needed

There are no funding streams for garden-based learning, such as there are for curriculum and instruction. Nevertheless, there are over three thousand school gardens in California alone. This raises the issue of educational leadership. This remarkable blossoming of school gardens can be attributed to the efforts of innumerable hard-working teachers, parents, and volunteers, as well as the Center for Ecoliteracy, chef-restaurateur Alice Waters, and others, and—in no small part—to Delaine Eastin, California's Superintendent of Public Instruction from 1995 to 2002. In 1995 she called for a garden in every school. Her proposal met with a large "snicker factor." Superintendent Eastin took a risk in expending her political capital to advocate a garden in every school. However, many, many teachers thanked her, with tears in their eyes, for validating to educational leaders the importance of the work that the teachers had been engaged in.

Leaders take calculated risks. There are still too few in the education system who are willing to say that food is important. For an education administrator to talk seriously about food, or about other innovations that would require fundamental changes in school systems, is a huge risk. And yet several are beginning to take that risk in California and across the nation. We need to treasure, support, and cultivate these leaders.

It is in the nature of systems to resist change. The challenges facing anyone wanting to change the education system are formidable. Achieving the changes we seek will take time. Fortunately, altering one part of a system, like disturbing a thread of a spider web, creates movement everywhere in the system. Change can begin anywhere. For school food systems, change can start with meals, waste, gardens, cooking in the classroom, anywhere. What's important is to move beyond where we began, to persist when change comes slowly, to identify and cultivate leaders, to build networks of support, and to make use of everything we know about the dynamics of systems.

Our reward can be the creation of learning environments where curriculum and practice are connected, where process and content are one, and where learning is part of real life, natural cycles reflect cycles of knowledge, and we experience again the pleasure of being grounded in place.

I can think of no more important work.

Resources

General

Center for Ecoliteracy
at the David Brower Center
2150 Allston Way, Suite 270, Berkeley,
CA 94704-1377
510-845-4595
www.ecoliteracy.org

Foreword

Organizations and Websites

Bioneers
1607 Paseo de Peralta, Suite 3, Santa Fe,
NM 87501
877-BIONEER
www.bioneers.org

The Jane Goodall Institute
8700 Georgia Ave., Ste. 500, Silver Spring,
MD 20910
240-645-4000
www.janegoodall.org

Ocean Arks International
176 Battery St., Ste. 1, Burlington, VT 05401
802-860-0011
www.oceanarks.org

Rocky Mountain Institute
1739 Snowmass Creek Rd., Snowmass,
CO 81654
970-927-3851
www.rmi.org

Schumacher College
The Old Postern
Dartington, Devon TQ9 6EA, United
Kingdom
www.schumachercollege.org.uk

Books

Orr, David W. *Ecological Literacy: Education and the Transition to a Postmodern World.* Albany, NY: State University of New York Press, 1992.

Stone, Michael K., and the Center for Ecoliteracy. *Smart by Nature: Schooling for Sustainability.* Healdsburg, CA: Watershed Media, 2009.

Part I. Vision

Organizations and Websites

Adam Joseph Lewis Center for Environmental
Studies
Oberlin College
122 Elm St., Oberlin, OH 44074
www.oberlin.edu/ajlc
*A primary example of ecodesign; conceptualized
and designed under David W. Orr's leadership in
a cooperative effort of students, staff, and
professionals.*

Association for Supervision and Curriculum
Development
1703 No. Beauregard St., Alexandria,
VA 22311-1714
800-933-2723 (toll free, U.S. and Canada)
1-703-578-9600 (all other countries)

Chez Panisse Foundation
1517 Shattuck Ave., Berkeley, CA 94709
510-843-3811
www.chezpanisse.com

En'owkin Centre
RR2, S50, C8, Lot 45
Green Mountain Rd., Penticton BC, V2A 6J7,
Canada
250-493-7181
www.enowkincentre.ca

Fritjof Capra's website
www.FritjofCapra.net

The New Farm
www.newfarm.org
A Web-based successor to The New Farm
*magazine, in which Wendell Berry published
frequently.*

The Orion Society
187 Main St., Great Barrington, MA 01230
413-528-4422, 888-909-6568 (toll free)
www.orionsociety.org
*Regularly publishes the writings of Wendell Berry,
David W. Orr, and other important thinkers.*

Slow Food
Via Mendicità Istruita, 8, 12042 Bra (CN), Italy
39-0172-419-611
www.slowfood.com

Slow Food U.S.A.
434 Broadway, 7th floor, New York, NY 10013
212-965-5640
www.slowfoodusa.org

Books

Armstrong, Jeannette, Delphine Derickson, Lee
Maracle, and Greg Young-Ing, eds. *We Get
Our Living Like Milk from the Land.* Penticton,
BC: Theytus Books Ltd., 1994.

Berry, Wendell. *The Gift of Good Land: Further
Essays Cultural and Agricultural.* New York:
North Point Press, 1982.

Berry, Wendell. *The Unsettling of America:
Culture and Agriculture.* San Francisco, CA:
Sierra Club Books, 1996.

Callenbach, Ernest. *Ecology: A Pocket Guide.*
Berkeley, CA: University of California Press,
1998.

Capra, Fritjof. *The Hidden Connections:
Integrating the Biological, Cognitive, and Social
Dimensions of Life into a Science of Sustainability.*
New York: Doubleday, 2002.

Capra, Fritjof. *The Tao of Physics: An
Exploration of the Parallels between Modern
Physics and Eastern Mysticism.* Boston:
Shambhala Publications, Inc., 1975.

Capra, Fritjof. *The Turning Point: Science, Society, and the Rising Culture.* New York: Simon & Schuster, 1982.

Capra, Fritjof. *Uncommon Wisdom.* New York: Simon & Schuster, 1988.

Capra, Fritjof. *The Web of Life: A New Scientific Understanding of Living Systems.* New York: Anchor Books, 1996.

Cardinal, Douglas J., and Jeannette Armstrong. *The Native Creative Process: A Collaborative Discourse between Douglas Cardinal and Jeannette Armstrong.* Penticton, BC: Theytus Books Ltd., 1994.

Center for Ecoliteracy. *Ecoliteracy: Mapping the Terrain.* Berkeley, CA: Learning in the Real World®, 2000.

Collins, James C., and Jerry I. Porras. *Built to Last: Successful Habits of Visionary Companies.* New York: HarperBusiness, 1994.

Honoré, Carl. *In Praise of Slowness: How a Worldwide Movement Is Challenging the Cult of Speed.* New York: HarperCollins, 2004.

Lappé, Frances Moore, and Anna Lappé. *Hope's Edge: The Next Diet for a Small Planet.* New York: Jeremy P. Tarcher/Putnam, 2002.

Macy, Joanna R. *World as Lover, World as Self.* Berkeley, CA: Parallax Press, 1997.

Schwab, Joseph J. *The Practical: A Language for Curriculum.* Washington, DC: National Education Association, 1969.

Todd, Nancy Jack, and John Todd. *From Eco-Cities to Living Machines: Principles of Ecological Design.* Berkeley, CA: North Atlantic Books, 1994.

Waters, Alice. *Chez Panisse Fruit.* New York: HarperCollins, 2002.

Articles and Periodicals

Gray, Francine du Plessix. "Starving Children." *The New Yorker.* October 16, 1995: 51.

Holt, Maurice. "Slowing Down Our Fast-Food Schools." *Education Digest.* February 2003: 4–12.

Jensen, Derrick. "Thinking Outside the Classroom: An Interview with Zenobia Barlow." *Sun Magazine.* March 2002: 4–7.

Gatherings: The En'owkin Journal of First North American Peoples
RR2, S50, C8, Lot 45
Green Mountain Rd., Penticton, BC V2A 6J7, Canada
250-493-7181
www.theytusbooks.ca

Part II. Tradition/Place

Organizations and Websites

International Rivers Network
1847 Berkeley Way, Berkeley, CA 94703
510-848-1155
www.irn.org

River of Words®
2547 Eighth St., 13B, Berkeley, CA 94710
510-548-7636
www.riverofwords.org

The Center for the Book
Library of Congress
101 Independence Ave., SE, Washington,
DC 20540-4920
202-707-5221
www.loc.gov/loc/cfbook/
*Cosponsors River of Words Annual Art and
Poetry Contest.*

Books

Anderson, Eugene N. *Ecologies of the Heart:
Emotion, Belief, and the Environment.* New York:
Oxford University Press, 1996.
*Explores human interactions with the environment
from the viewpoint of native peoples.*

Barzun, Jacques. *The American University: How
It Runs, Where It Is Going.* Chicago: University of Chicago Press, 1968.

Berg, Peter. *Discovering Your Life-Place: A First
Bioregional Workbook.* 1995. Available for $10
($13 postpaid) from Planet Drum Foundation,
P. O. Box 31251, San Francisco, CA 94131,
Shasta Bioregion, USA.
www.planetdrum.org/energy_xchange.htm.

Carson, Rachel. *The Sense of Wonder.* New
York: Harper & Row, 1965.

Dale, Edgar. *Audio-Visual Methods in Teaching.*
New York: Holt, Rinehart, and Winston, 1969.

Freire, Paolo. *Pedagogy of the Oppressed.* New
York: Continuum, 1970, 1993, 2004.

Gardner, Howard. *Frames of Mind: The Theory
of Multiple Intelligences.* New York: Basic Books,
1983.

Hutchison, David, and David W. Orr. *A
Natural History of Place in Education.* New
York: Teachers College Press, 2004.

Leopold, Aldo. *A Sand County Almanac, and
Sketches Here and There.* New York: Oxford
University Press, 1949.

Margolin, Malcolm. *The Ohlone Way: Indian
Life in the San Francisco—Monterey Bay Area.*
Berkeley, CA: Heyday Books, 1978.

Michael, Pamela, ed. *River of Words: Images and
Poetry in Praise of Water.* Berkeley, CA:
Heyday Books, 2003.

Merton, Thomas. *Love and Living.* San Diego,
CA: Harcourt Brace Jovanovich, 1979.

Midgley, Mary. *Utopias, Dolphins, and
Computers: Problems of Philosophical Plumbing.*
London: Routledge, 1996.

Momaday, N. Scott. *The Way to Rainy
Mountain.* Albuquerque: University of New
Mexico Press, 1969.

Nabhan, Gary Paul. *Coming Home to Eat: The
Pleasures and Politics of Local Foods.* New York:
W. W. Norton & Company, 2001.

Nabhan, Gary Paul. *Gathering the Desert.*
Tucson: University of Arizona Press, 1985.

Nabhan, Gary Paul, and Stephen Trimble. *The
Geography of Childhood.* Boston: Beacon Press,
1994

Orr, David W. *Earth in Mind: On Education,
Environment, and the Human Prospect.*
Washington, DC: Island Press, 1994.

River of Words Watershed Explorer™
Curriculum Educator's Guide. Available from
www.riverofwords.org.

Snyder, Gary. *A Place in Space: Ethics, Aesthetics, and Watersheds.* Washington, DC: Counterpoint, 1995.

Sobel, David. *Beyond Ecophobia: Reclaiming the Heart in Nature Education.* Great Barrington, MA: Orion Society, 1996.

Sobel, David. *Place-Based Education: Connecting Classrooms and Communities* (Nature Literacy Series Vol. 4). Great Barrington, MA: Orion Society, 2004.

Articles and Periodicals

News from Native California
P.O. Box 9145, Berkeley, CA 94709
510-549-2802
www.heydaybooks.com/news/

Part III. Relationship

Organizations and Websites

The Bay Institute of San Francisco
500 Palm Dr., Ste. 200, Novato, CA 94949
415-506-0150
www.bay.org

Communities for a Better Environment
1611 Telegraph Ave., Ste. 450, Oakland, CA 94612
510-302-0430
www.cbecal.org

Kids Gardening
National Gardening Association
1100 Dorset St., South Burlington, VT 05403
800-538-7476 (800-LETSGRO)
www.kidsgardening.com

Life Lab Science Program
1156 High St., Santa Cruz, CA 95064
831-459-2001
www.lifelab.org
One of the first hands-on garden-based science programs for K–5 students.

Mary E. Silveira School
375 Blackstone Dr., San Rafael, CA 94903
415-492-3741
http://dixiesd.marin.k12.ca.us/
marysilveira/index.html

North Coast Rural Challenge Network
P.O. Box 1154, Mendocino, CA 95460
707-937-5164
www.ncrcn.org

Students and Teachers Restoring a Watershed (STRAW)
The Bay Institute
500 Palm Dr., Ste. 200, Novato, CA 94949
415-506-0150
www.bay.org/watershed_education.htm

Books

Ableman, Michael. *From the Good Earth: A Celebration of Growing Food around the World.* New York: Abrams, 1993.

Ableman, Michael. *On Good Land: The Autobiography of an Urban Farm.* San Francisco, CA: Chronicle Books, 1998.

Goleman, Daniel. *Emotional Intelligence: Why It Can Matter More Than IQ.* New York: Bantam Books, 1995.

Lickona, Thomas. *Character Matters: How to Help Our Children Develop Good Judgment, Integrity, and Other Essential Virtues.* New York: Touchstone Books, 2004. *Recommended by Jeanne Casella.*

Rogers, Laurette. *The California Freshwater Shrimp Project.* Berkeley, CA: Heyday Books, 1996.

Articles and Periodicals

Ableman, Michael. "The Quiet Revolution." *Earth Island Journal.* Autumn 2000: 41–44.

Stone, Michael K. "Solving for Pattern." *Whole Earth* magazine. Spring 2001: 77–83.

Film

Beyond Organic: The Vision of Fairview Gardens, produced by John de Graaf, narrated by Meryl Streep, and distributed by Bullfrog Films at www.bullfrogfilms.com or 800-543-3764.

Part IV. Action

Organizations and Websites

Caine Learning
P.O. Box 1847, Idyllwild, CA 92549
909-659-0152, 888-452-2803 (toll free)
www.cainelearning.com
The website of Renate and Geoffrey Caine, leaders in application of brain/mind research to teaching and learning.

Center for Food and Justice
Urban & Environmental Policy Institute
Mail Stop M-1, Occidental College
1600 Campus Rd., Los Angeles, CA 90041
323-259-2991
http://departments.oxy.edu/uepi
Coordinators of the National Farm-to-School program.

Commercial Alert
4110 SE Hawthorne Blvd., #123, Portland,
OR 97214-5426
503-235-8012
www.commercialalert.org

Community Alliance with Family Farmers
P.O. Box 363, Davis, CA 95617
530-756-8518
www.caff.org

Community Food Security Coalition
P.O. Box 209, Venice, CA 90294
310-822-5410
www.foodsecurity.org

The Edible Schoolyard
Martin Luther King Middle School
1781 Rose St., Berkeley, CA 94703
510-558-1335
www.edibleschoolyard.org

Fairview Gardens
P.O. Box 396, Goleta, CA 93116
598 North Fairview Ave., Goleta, CA 93117
805-967-7369
Founded by Michael Ableman.

Food and Society Initiative.
W. K. Kellogg Foundation
One Michigan Ave. East, Battle Creek,
MI 49017-4012
269-968-1611
www.wkkf.org

Food Routes
P.O. Box 443, Millheim, PA 16854
814-349-6000
www.foodroutes.org

Funders for Sustainable Food Systems
423 Washington St., 4th Floor, San Francisco,
CA 94111
415-421-4213 X14
www.foodfunders.org

Greenaction for Health & Environmental
Justice
One Hallidie Plaza, Ste. 760, San Francisco,
CA 94102
415-248-5010
www.greenaction.org
Recommended by Dana Lanza.

Literacy for Environmental Justice
800 Innes Ave., Unit 11, San Francisco,
CA 94124
415-282-6840
www.lejyouth.org

National Campaign for Sustainable Agriculture
P.O. Box 396, Pine Bush, NY 12566
845-361-5201
www.sustainableagriculture.net

The Private Eye Project®
P.O. Box 646, Lyle, WA 98635
509-365-3007
www.the-private-eye.com

Rethinking School Lunch
A project of the Center for Ecoliteracy
2528 San Pablo Ave., Berkeley, CA 94702
510-845-4595
www.rethinkingschoollunch.org

Sustainable Agriculture and Food Systems
Funders
Environmental Grantmakers Association
11 W. Pedregosa St., Santa Barbara, CA 93101
805-867-0551
www.safsf.org

Sustainability Institute
3 Linden Rd., Hartland, VT 05048
802-436-1277
http://sustainer.org/
*Founded by the late Donella Meadows to apply
systems thinking and organization to economic,
social, and environmental challenges.*

Youth United for Community Action
(YUCA)
1848 Bay Rd., East Palo Alto, CA 94303
650-322-9165
www.youthunited.net
Recommended by Dana Lanza.

Books

Association for Supervision and Curriculum Development (ASCD). *ASCD Topic Pack, 2001–2002: Brain-Based Learning.* Arlington, VA: ASCD, 2002.

Caine, Geoffrey, and Renate Nummela Caine. *The Brain, Education, and the Competitive Edge.* Lanham, MD: Rowman & Littlefield, 2001.

Caine, Renate Nummela, Geoffrey Caine, Carol McClintic, and Karl Klimek. *12 Brain/Mind Learning Principles in Action: The Fieldbook for Making Connections, Teaching, and the Human Brain.* Thousand Oaks, CA: Corwin Press, 2004.

Center for Ecoliteracy. *The Edible Schoolyard.* Berkeley, CA: Learning in the Real World®, 1999.

Fullan, Michael. *Leadership and Sustainability: System Thinkers in Action.* Thousand Oaks, CA: Corwin Press, 2004.

Gottlieb, Robert. *Environmentalism Unbound: Exploring New Pathways for Change.* Cambridge, MA: MIT Press, 2001.

Hardiman, Mariale M. *Connecting Brain Research with Effective Teaching: The Brain-Targeted Teaching Model.* Lanham, MD: ScarecrowEducation, 2003.

Hart, Roger. *Children's Participation: The Theory and Practice of Involving Young Citizens in Community Development and Environmental Care.* New York: UNICEF; and London: Earthscan, 1997.

Literacy for Environmental Justice. *Calling Nature Home: Restoring Environmental Justice to a Wetland Habitat.* Available from www.lejyouth.org.
This K–12 curriculum focuses on themes of watershed studies, animals and habitats, plants, birds, water quality, marine biology, urbanization and habitat destruction, environmental justice, and environmental health.

Meadows, Donella H. *The Global Citizen.* Washington, DC: Island Press, 1991.

Meadows, Donella H., Jorgen Randers, and Dennis L. Meadows. *Limits to Growth: The 30-Year Update.* White River Junction, VT: Chelsea Green Publishing, 2004.

Orr, David W. *The Nature of Design: Ecology, Culture, and Human Intention.* New York: Oxford University Press, 2002.

Ruef, Kerry. *The Private Eye®—(5x) Looking/Thinking by Analogy: A Guide to Developing the Interdisciplinary Mind, Hands-on Thinking Skills, Creativity, Scientific Literacy.* Lyle, WA: The Private Eye Project, 2003.

Wheatley, Margaret J. *Turning to One Another: Simple Conversations to Restore Hope to the Future.* San Francisco, CA: Berrett-Koehler Publishers, Inc., 2002.

Wheatley, Margaret J. *Leadership and the New Science: Discovering Order in a Chaotic World.* San Francisco, CA: Berrett-Koehler Publishers, Inc., 1999.

Articles and Periodicals

Fullan, Michael, Al Bertani, and Joanne Quinn. "New Lessons for Districtwide Reform." *Educational Leadership.* April 2004: 42–46.

Stone, Michael K. "A Food Revolution in Berkeley." *Whole Earth* magazine. Spring 2002: 38–52.

Wheatley, Margaret J. "Bringing Schools Back to Life: Schools as Living Systems." In *Creating Successful School Systems: Voices from the University, the Field, and the Community,* edited by Francis M. Duffy and Jack D. Dale. Norwood, MA: Christopher-Gordon Publishers, 2001.

Wheatley, Margaret J. "Stressed-out Kids." *Shambhala Sun,* September 2002.

Wild Duck Review 4, no. 2., n.d., special issue on education.
This volume includes interviews with Joseph Chilton Pearce, Jane Healy, and Fritjof Capra and essays by David W. Orr, Chet Bowers, and others, as well as letters from Wendell Berry and Joanna Macy.

Shambhala Sun
1660 Hollis Street, Suite 603, Halifax, Nova Scotia, B3J 1V7, Canada.
www.shambhalasun.com

Wild Duck Review
P.O. Box 388, Nevada City, CA 95959
www.wildduckreview.com

Publication Credits

We gratefully acknowledge permission to reprint the following copyrighted material.

"Dancing with Systems," from *Whole Earth* magazine, Winter 2001. Copyright © 2001 Point. Reprinted with permission.

"Finding Your Own Bioregion," from *Discovering Your Life-Place: A First Bioregional Workbook*, by Peter Berg. Planet Drum Books, 1995. Reprinted with permission.

"'It Changed Everything We Thought We Could Do,'" adapted from "Solving for Pattern: The STRAW Project," *Whole Earth* magazine, Spring 2001. Copyright © 2001 Point. Reprinted with permission.

"The Loupe's Secret," adapted from *The Private Eye*. © 2003, 1998, 1992 by Kerry Ruef. The Private Eye Project. Reprinted with permission.

"On Watershed Education," from *River of Words*, Pamela Michael, ed. © 2003 Robert Hass. Heyday Books. Reprinted with permission.

"Place and Pedagogy," reprinted by permission from *Ecological Literacy: Education and the Transition to a Postmodern World*, by David W. Orr, the State University of New York Press. © 1999 State University of New York. All rights reserved.

About the Editors

Michael K. Stone is senior editor at the Center for Ecoliteracy and the primary author of the Center's book, *Smart by Nature: Schooling for Sustainability.* He was previously managing editor of *Whole Earth* magazine and the *Millennium Whole Earth Catalog.* He has written for numerous publications, including *The New York Times* and the *Toronto Star,* and he served on the staffs of the Lt. Governor of Illinois and the Illinois Arts Council. He was a founding faculty member at World College West in Northern California, where he directed the program in Meaning, Culture, and Change and served as academic vice president.

Zenobia Barlow, a cofounder of the Center for Ecoliteracy, has been the Center's executive director since its founding, providing leadership in applying theory to practice in philanthropy committed to education for sustainability. She has designed strategies for fostering ecological and indigenous understanding in K–12 eduction, including The Ford Systems Project, Rethinking School Lunch, and Smart by Nature. She previously served as executive director of The Elmwood Institute, an ecological think tank and international network of independent scholars and activists, as executive editor of an international publishing company, and as an academic administrator at Sonoma State University. A Fellow of the Post Carbon Institute, Barlow is also an accomplished still photographer.

About Bioneers

Since 1990, Kenny Ausubel and Nina Simons have been assembling bioneers for an annual conference, a gathering of scientific and social innovators who have demonstrated visionary and practical models for restoring the earth and people.

Bioneers are biological pioneers who are working with nature to help heal nature and to heal ourselves. They have peered deep into the heart of living systems to devise strategies for restoration based on nature's own operating instructions. They come from many diverse cultures and perspectives and from all walks of life.

Bioneers are scientists and artists, gardeners and economists, activists and public servants, architects and ecologists, farmers and journalists, priests and shamans, policymakers and everyday people committed to preserving and supporting the future of life on earth. They herald a dawning Age of Restoration founded in natural principles of kinship, interdependence, cooperation, reciprocity, and community.

Uniting nature, culture, and spirit, bioneers embody a change of heart, a spiritual connection with the living world that is also grounded in social justice. Their pragmatic strategies effectively address many of our most pressing ecological and societal challenges.

Above all, bioneers represent a culture of solutions. Their stories demonstrate that just as people have created the environmental and social problems we face, people can also solve them, through a reciprocal partnership with nature. Over and over, they show how great a difference the actions of one individual can make.

The Bioneers Conference is a "big tent" where people from many disparate yet related fields come together. The gathering cross-pollinates both issues and networks and serves as a fulcrum for cutting-edge ideas, resources, and connections. The conference has spawned several other projects that convey the inspiring bioneer culture to the greater public:

- *Beaming Bioneers* broadcasts live portions of the Bioneers Conference to partner sites as a focal point around which they organize their own conferences that address local issues and enhance community organizing efforts.

- The radio series *Bioneers: Revolution from the Heart of Nature* features personal interviews and dynamic presentations from the Bioneers Conferences. Each year, Bioneers provides thirteen half-hour programs free to public radio stations across the country and around the world. In 2003, the series won a prestigious Silver WorldMedal for excellence in environmental programming from the New York Festivals International Radio Programming Competition. In 2002, the series received a Bronze WorldMedal and was a finalist for the United Nations Department of Public Information Award. Each series is available for purchase in CD format from Bioneers.

- The Bioneers website (www.bioneers.org) offers a rich source of accessible information and connections to numerous other key groups and individuals working for ecological restoration and social justice.

- *Bioneers Buzz* is a monthly electronic newsletter that features news and updates on the activities of the Bioneers network. It is available by subscription through the website.

- *Bioneers Letter*, a biannual newsletter for members of Bioneers, features articles, program updates, and a calendar and networking section.

- The Bioneers Youth Initiative integrates young people into the Bioneers network and helps build connectivity among young activists year-round. Bioneers actively fosters the development of a vibrant network that supports and expands opportunities for young people who are seeking to create a restorative future.

- Bioneers presents "Wisdom at the End of a Hoe" training workshops led by top practitioners of sustainable agriculture and ecological restoration to equip farmers and gardeners with state-of-the-art knowledge on advanced ecological growing methods.

For more information about Bioneers, or to become a member, please contact www.bioneers.org or call toll-free 1-877-BIONEER.